Jewish Poland

LEGENDS OF ORIGIN

Raphael Patai Series in Jewish Folklore and Anthropology

A complete listing of the books in this series can be found at the back of this volume.

Jewish Poland

LEGENDS OF ORIGIN

ETHNOPOETICS
AND
LEGENDARY CHRONICLES

Haya Bar-Itzhak

WAYNE STATE UNIVERSITY PRESS
DETROIT

Library of Congress Cataloging-in-Publication Data
Bar-Yitshak, Hayah.
Jewish Poland—legends of origin : ethnopoetics
and legendary chronicles / Haya Bar-Itzhak.
p. cm. – (Raphael Patai series in Jewish folklore and anthropology)
Includes bibliographical references and indexes.
ISBN 0-8143-2789-3
1. Legends, Jewish—Poland—History and criticism.   2. Jews—Poland—Folklore.   3.
Legends, Jewish—Poland.   4. Jews—Poland—Origin—Folklore.   I. Title.   II. Series.
BM530 .B3115 2001
398.2'089'9240438—dc21   00-011672

Translation by Lenn Schramm

In memory of
my father,
Yoseph Goldman
and to
my mother,
Menuha Goldman

Contents

Illustrations

Preface

The first appearance of Jews in Poland and their adventures during their early years of settlement in the country are concealed in the undocumented shadows of history. The written record indicates that, beginning in the thirteenth century and particularly in the fourteenth century, Poland was a destination for Jewish refugees from Germany and from the areas along the southeastern borders of Kievan Rus (Cygielman 1991, 26). Going back further, late-twelfth-century documents refer to the existence of Jewish communities in Poland (Feldman 1934; Weinryb 1973, vii). Some historians, however, believe that Jews reached Poland as early as the tenth and eleventh centuries–and perhaps even the ninth century (Sternberg 1878, 6–15; Lelewel 1851–56, 18; Kraushar 1865, 40, 57, 65; Bałaban 1948, 1–5; Schipper 1926, 15). According to Cygielman, the tendency to represent the Jews as Polish autochthons was prominent mainly in Jewish intellectual circles, in support of their sociopolitical thesis that the Jews, as original inhabitants of Poland, merited full civil rights (Cygielman 1991, 27–28). This teaches us something about the nature of historiography; as Weinryb puts it, the historians of Eastern European Jewry created their own myths (1962, 10–12).

Nineteenth-century historiography was influenced by the struggle for liberalism and progress; for minority groups like the Jews, this struggle was focused in their campaign for emancipation. The writing of history became part of the political contest. Historians who wanted to present the Jews as Polish autochthons but lacked written sources to ground their claim sometimes built on the legends of origin of Polish Jewry. These

11

scholars transcribed the legends and contributed to their preservation—as did their opponents, who cited the same legends while seeking to refute their historical reliability.

Even if we accept the hypothesis that Jews did not settle in Poland until the thirteenth and fourteenth centuries, historians agree that in Poland they enjoyed rights and privileges denied them elsewhere in Europe. In this context mention must be made to the privileges granted to the Jews by King Bolesław of Kalisz in the thirteenth century and expanded in the next century by Casimir the Great of the House of Piast. These privileges brought prosperity for the Jews, accompanied by a spiritual flowering reflected in the theological production of the rabbis and sages who arose in Poland.

By "Polish Jewry" I mean the historical community that first coalesced in the kingdom of Poland, without reference to the vicissitudes of political geography. This kingdom, large and powerful until the mid-eighteenth century, ceased to exist as an independent political entity in 1795, when it was partitioned among Russia, Prussia, and Austria. The independent Polish republic was not reconstituted until after World War I. Communist Poland, after World War II, was assigned different boundaries. Hence, although it is difficult to speak of Polish Jewry in geopolitical terms, we may accept Rosman's contention about the Jews of post-partition Poland:

> The Jews who lived in areas that were formerly Polish territory and had become parts of the kingdom of Prussia and the Austrian and Russian empires did not undergo any radical and immediate religious, economic, or social changes. Rather, they remained steadfast to the way of life that had characterized Polish Jewry. . . . Even when the changes caused by partition intensified, Jewish society and its religious, social, and economic institutions endured and displayed an impressive capacity for survival. The descendants of the Jews of Poland preserved the unique features that were immediately evident to them, to other Jews, and to the non-Jewish world. (Rosman 1991, 19)

Polish Jewry was annihilated during World War II. Although there were still Jews in post-Holocaust Poland, one can no longer speak of Jewish communities. Hence, according to the legendary chronicles, we are dealing with a millennium of Jewish life and creativity in Poland.

The history of Polish Jewry and the output of its rabbis have been studied extensively. By contrast, their folk art has received precious little attention. The present study deals with the literary manifestations of the folk art of Polish Jewry, with a particular focus on their legends of origin. What are "legends of origin"? Before answering this question I would like to offer a few words about folk literature in general and legend in particular. The development of folklore studies has altered the definitions of folklore and

Arthur Szyk, "The Kalisz Statutes." An illustrated text of the first privileges Bolesław of Kalisz granted the Jews in 1264. With kind permission of the Jewish Historical Institute, Warsaw.

folk literature. Whereas the emphasis used to be on the circumstance of oral transmission and the element of tradition–that is, the fact that the work is passed from generation to generation (Noy 1982, 7–9), contemporary folklore studies emphasize the element of communication and defines the folk tale as one type of communication process (Brunvand 1968, 5; Georges 1983, 135). Ben-Amos, in his article "Toward a Definition of Folklore in Context," sees the folklore in general and the folk tale in particular as a process of small-group communications by means of an artistic medium (Ben-Amos 1971).

Changes of definition entail modifications of research approaches. Modern folklore studies responded to the concept first advanced by Parry and Lord (1953–54), which emphasizes the dynamic nature of the composition and the personality of the individual performer. Research turned to examine the cultural context, the narrative situation, the interaction between teller and audience, and the modes of performance; it focused on *parole* rather than on *langue*.

Nevertheless, all research methodologies agree that folk narrative expresses both the individual artist and the entire ethnic group–or, as Noy put it, the literary work recited by the narrator-transmitter embodies the heritage of the generations and attests to the nature of the ethnocultural *I* (1982, 9). The folk narratives of Polish Jewry illuminate the multifaceted picture of their life as it was preserved in the collective memory: both among themselves and in their interaction with their non-Jewish surroundings, the privileges and hostile edicts, the joys and the persecutions.

This book deals only with legends of origin. The legend is a genre with historical pretensions. The Brothers Grimm were the first to insist that it be differentiated from the fairy tale: A legend is anchored in historical time; fairy tales are not. Legends are associated with a particular historical incident or personality and take place in the geographical space inhabited by the narrator. Later definitions are not far removed from this pioneering one. Bascom (1965) and Dorson (1972, 159–162) hold that legends rest on the real world, fairy tales on a fantasy universe. Many scholars have emphasized that legends seek to convey a sense of credibility concerning what they relate, whereas fairy tales consciously highlight their fictional nature (Georges 1971, 1–13; Dégh and Vazsonyi 1976). According to Dorson, legends deal with real persons, places, and events; their touchstone, and the secret of their endurance, is that they are known to a group of people who live in a particular region and share an ethnic identity or common destiny. This group preserves and transmits the legends. Local chronicles and related written sources, including literature, reinforce the oral traditions.

The treatment of legends of origin focuses on only part of the legendary history of Polish Jewry: the myths that relate the first arrival of Jews in Poland and their reception there; how a Jew became king of Poland and paved the way for establishing the magnificent Piast dynasty; how Jews received privileges; the Jewess who became queen of Poland; and the construction of synagogues in various localities. These are etiological stories that endeavor to explain and justify life in the present through a story that anchors it in a sanctified past. Alternatively, stories that describe an idyllic life in the past are used as ammunition in the struggle to alleviate the distress of the present.

Every student of folklore is aware of the problems involved with the terms "legend" and "myth."[1] These terms, which have been in vogue since the earliest days of folklore studies, are analytical categories imposed on the ensemble of stories from various cultures, stories that have similar lineaments. The classification ignores the existence of ethnic categories as well as the distortion that occurs when one applies terms implying fictiveness and contradiction of the "truth" to stories that the narrating society considers to be part and parcel of existential reality (Ben-Amos 1976).[2] According to the traditional definitions used in folklore studies, myth differs from legend chiefly on the time axis. Whereas a "myth" is a sacred tale that explains the creation of the world, humanity, and the condition of both, a "legend" takes place in the post-creation era, that is, in historical time (Dundes 1996). The term "myth" does not simply designate a genre. In its broader signification, it indicates a particular aspect of human consciousness. There is a mythical quality, of course, in myth as a genre; but the same quality can be found in other genres as well, as was shown by Hill (1988, 8).

According to Raphael Patai, a legend is a story based on fact; accordingly, it is recounted as a true story. This feature is shared by legend and myth and the line of demarcation between them is not clear-cut (Patai 1979, lii; Finnegan 1970, 361). Every society relates to its "myths" as stories that are part of real and authentic life.[3] Hence one can understand the intense emotional opposition aroused when an attempt is made to reject or refute these myths, from the outside or from the inside. This opposition is the consequence of a sense that the existential truth and the sanctified normative world are in danger. Our use of the term "legends of origin" is not meant to deny the veracity of the stories; on the contrary, it emphasizes the importance and sanctity that the narrating society ascribes to them. The story is true as long as its narrators believe it to be true, and it becomes an element of the definition of the genre.

The legends of origin of Diaspora Jewry, including those of Poland, constitute a genre that combines and emphasizes the dimensions of time and space. These legends tell of the initial settlement in a new territory, with all that this involves; they are about "making a place"—in our case, the Judaization of this region. Because this is the first settlement, however, the legends deal with time as primeval time and describe this epoch as it was perceived by the narrating society in the various periods when the legends circulated. The birth of settlement in a strange place involves various and sometimes conflicting qualities. On the one hand, it is accompanied by anxiety in the face of the unknown and unfamiliar; the community's relative success or failure in coping with this anxiety will have a major impact on its chances for survival or liquidation. On the other hand, it is also a time of renewal and hope, of an eruption of creative force and activity aimed at getting to know, understand, dominate, and assimilate the new reality. As stated, legends of origin are not recounted only by the generation that actually lives the encounter with a new place, although we may assume that this is the period when they begin to take shape. These legends were told throughout the centuries of the Jews' residence in Poland, metamorphosing from time to time into new shapes. In this sense they manifest the collective memory of the primeval time. Because there is a difference between time experienced and time remembered, every period gives a different quality to the primeval time as the age when everything began, a sort of creation in miniature—the creation of a community.

In this respect legends of origin are similar to myth. The age of initial settlement occupies a central place in the mind of the community as a time that stands out from the normal course of the centuries and is perceived not quantitatively but qualitatively. It is a period that, as in myth, determines the nature of the days that follow (Gerber-Talmon 1952). It is the age when the very identity of the society is molded and defined. The importance of legends of origin in every generation throughout the life of the community then follows. The primeval era is reshaped in order to mold the present and future while deriving legitimacy from the distant and hallowed past. A society is always molding its first days in a way that can be used to justify how it lives in the present—or alternatively, if it wishes to change this life, that can justify change or even revolution. Tracing the legends of origin of Polish Jewry, as they crystallized and were told in various periods, allows us to expose the narrative of the Jewish community in Poland and the changing cultural awareness of the narrating society.

As we have noted, in the absence of written chronicles about the first arrival of Jews in Poland, the oral tradition has great influence, consecrated by the memories of the generations; even chroniclers derive their information from it. Although these legends are only a side dish for historical research, they are the main course of the present volume. Their study will disclose how the community creates its own chronicle, how it structures and consolidates its identity through the medium of stories about its founding, and how this identity varies from age to age. A fascinating question in its own right is what happened to these legends after the Holocaust of Polish

Jewry, when the human space they describe no longer exists except as an imaginary realm preserved in memory.

Another significant difference between our discussion here and historical research is that when historians approach legends of origin they focus on dissecting out the core of truth from the fictional accretions. For us, however, a historical legend does not reflect the time and place where its plot is set or the historical figures who appear in it; hence the question of truth is of only marginal interest to us. What concerns us, rather, is how historical legends reflect the world of the society that tells or retells the story—its problems, distresses, and aspirations (Noy 1967, 106–131; Bar-Itzhak 1984, 311–313; Zefatman 1983, 14).

My first task was to find and document the stories. As will be seen later, because a significant proportion of the legends of origin of Polish Jewry are no longer being related orally, it was necessary to refer to written sources. This posed the first difficulty. As Yisrael Zinberg notes, even though every cultural historian is aware of the major role played by the Jews as intermediaries in the field of European folklore and as artists who wove their hopes into legends and wonder tales from the heritage of folklore they received from previous generations, "almost all of this has remained an oral tradition, and only by chance have a few elements of this folklore material been preserved" (Zinberg 1958–71, 4:89). When students of folk culture wish to uncover these sources, they must rely on written material that was transcribed and preserved "by accident." I have related to the place where a story was transcribed as to a context that is involved in the shaping of the text itself, a context to which one must relate just as one relates to the circumstances in which an oral text is performed. The folk literature of Polish Jews exists in many languages—Hebrew and Yiddish, of course, but also Polish, German, and Russian (An-Ski 1925, 257–262; Noy 1962, 49–56)—as is reflected in the sources on which the present volume draws. All translations of the stories included in this volume are my own.

The first sources are tales found in chronicles and historical studies, starting with *Sefer Zemaḥ David,* by the sixteenth-century astronomer and historian David Ganz. The second group of sources on which I have relied is comprised of the stories preserved at YIVO, the Institute for Jewish Studies, especially those gathered by the famous An-Ski expedition of 1912–14. Some of these have been published in Yiddish periodicals and anthologies; as Noy notes, however, they have not yet been the subject of a comprehensive study (1982b). A third source includes stories that were published in German and Polish, that is, outside the narrating culture itself. Some of these have been published in periodicals such as *Am Ur Quell–Monatsschrift für Volkskunde, Der Orient, Wisła, Lud, Izraelita,* and *Jutrzenka*; others were published in anthologies assembled by non-Jews, such as Klemens Junosza's *The Miracle in the Cemetery* (Junosza 1905). The

17

An-Ski in 1916. YIVO.

transcription and publication of Jewish material in non-Jewish languages was the result of the heightened interest in ethnographical studies in Germany and Poland before World War I and during the interwar period, spurred by Romanticism and especially the rise of nationalism in Europe (Goldberg-Mulkiewicz 1989). The drive for emancipation, too, led to the publication of legends of origin in the Gentile vernacular, allowing their use in that struggle.

A project seeking to transcribe the folk tales of Polish Jews in Israel began in the 1950s. Initiated by Dov Noy, its files, in Hebrew and Yiddish, are

18

located in the Israel Folktales Archives (IFA), at the University of Haifa. Polish Jewry is the ethnic group represented by the largest number of stories in the archive, numbering around 2,600. This material, along with the stories in Hebrew, Yiddish, and Polish that I transcribed during my field work with Polish-born Jews, served as my fourth source. These reflect the stories as they are told today by Jews of Polish origin.

Another important source, one that has not yet been exploited by students of folklore, are the memorial volumes ("Yizkor Books") of the Polish Jewish communities destroyed in the Holocaust, both the collective works and the memoirs of individuals (see Goldberg-Mulkiewicz 1991, 187–199). Most of these volumes were printed in limited editions and intended chiefly for survivors of a particular town. The readers were generally personally acquainted with the author; this created an immediate bond between narrator and audience, with the roles of readers and writers switching back and forth in the course of the book. This is a species of small-group communications typical of the modern definition of folk literature (Ben-Amos 1971; Kugelmass and Boyarin 1983). These books are a treasure trove of narrative material, including older stories that have been reprinted as well as those told in the post-Holocaust context and perspective.

The use of all these sources added historical depth to my study. As folklore, legends are dynamic creations that are always being modified in accordance with the problems that preoccupy a society at a particular time and which reflect these problems. The origins of a community are depicted in a way that best suits the community at the time the tale is recounted. Hence legends are always an expression of the period when they are consolidated and recounted. It follows that narratives that were shaped, recounted, and transcribed in different periods reflect the changing cultural awareness of Polish Jewry. By drawing on different sources, I was also able to examine the important theoretical issue of the transcription of folklore outside its natural context–that is, extracultural transcription.

The legendary annals are an inseparable component of a people's culture; their power lies in their great charm, which wins over hearts and inspires imaginations. Legendary annals provide the basis for great artistic creations in literature, music, and the plastic arts. Folk legends have provided the basis for written literature (compare Shenhar-Alroy 1984, 11–14; Shenhar-Alroy 1989). With regard to the legends of origin of Polish Jewry, the most prominent writer was S. Y. Agnon, in the German-language anthology on Polish Jews he published in collaboration with Aharon Eliasberg (Agnon and Eliasberg 1916)[4] and in his Hebrew volume *Poland: Legendary Tales,* first published in 1925. "If you want to get to know the common thread running through S. Y. Agnon's work," writes Yitzhak Lamdan, "read his legends." According to Lamdan, legends are a central

The inside cover pages in German (above) and Hebrew (right) of the
anthology by S. Y. Agnon and Ahron Eliasberg, *Das Buch von der polnischen
Juden* (Berlin: Jüdischer Verlag, 1916).

כנסת ישראל בפולין

פּוֹלִין

הַמְּדִינָה הַקְּדוּמָה

לְתוֹרָה

וְלִתְעוּדָה

לְמִיּוֹם סוּר אֶפְרַיִם מֵעַל

יְהוּדָה:

element in all of Agnon's writing, the element that endows it with its special light: "But this light is preserved and endures particularly in the legends that he expounds, which may seem to be ephemera but are in fact the leavening in his work" (Lamdan 1938, 59). Nevertheless, the folk legends assume a new guise in Agnon's retelling. As P. Lahover puts it: "S. Y. Agnon relates these things with the reticence of the folk narrative and his own unmistakable imprint. He did not copy this world of living tradition, the world of legend, but created it with its own form and image" (Lahover 1938).

In this way, the folk legend becomes the work of a specific author (*kunst sage*) as part of the transition from the oral to the written medium. Thus an examination of the legends of origin of Polish Jewry leads to a consideration of the interrelations between the folk narratives of Polish Jews and written literature, including cross-fertilization and the changes wrought to a folk legend when it is shaped by an author who adds his own voice to the cultural discourse of legends. In my discussion of Agnon I will show that he uses the legends of origin of Polish Jews while inverting and subverting them by creating a covert plot that runs beneath the overt plot. The overt plot of Agnon's legend sticks close to the folk version; but the covert plot, fashioned by Agnon's use of language, builds an opposing and subversive message. The Jews of Poland recounted their legends of origin as etiological tales meant to legitimize their residence in that country, both to the outside world and to themselves, and to provide a basis for their right to live there. Agnon undermines this message and uses his subtext to convey the antithetical message, namely, that any hopes for a life of security and a true alliance between the two peoples during the period when the Jews lived in Poland were foredoomed to failure. In this way Agnon uses the legends of origin of the Jews of Poland to express his historiographical inclination, which was also expressed by his personal decision to settle in Palestine[5]– namely, that Jews can have a secure life only if they establish a national entity in the land of Israel, in accordance with the Zionist vision.[6]

The five chapters that comprise this book constitute a single ethnopoetic study of legends of origin. Chapter 1 deals with the legend of the arrival of Jews in Poland and the way this legend–*Po-lin* ("Poland"; in Hebrew "lodge here")–as well as local origin legends turn Poland into a Jewish country. In this chapter the legends are considered first of all thematically, with reference to the themes that historians have identified in them. To these I add a new thread that escaped their notice–the attempt to provide, for internal consumption, a spiritual and theological justification for the very fact of Jewish residence in Poland. This theme has been overlooked because earlier scholars examined the legends of origin as directed to the outside, Gentile world, when the legends were also intended for the narrating society itself.

22

We shall also examine the use of archetypes from ancient Jewish literature and how the story of the Jews' wandering across Europe to Poland
and their settlement there draws on the story of the original wandering
and settlement in the Land of Canaan—thereby making Poland into a
Jewish country. The Judaization of the alien territory was accomplished
in part by means of the literary device of the name-midrash, familiar from
the Bible and traditional Jewish literature over the ages. The homiletical
interpretation of Slavic toponyms, which constructs a meaning for these
place names in a Jewish language (Hebrew or Yiddish), and the application
of archetypes from the sanctified Jewish world turned the landscapes of
Poland into those of the Jewish Study. Within the legends themselves, the
Judaization and adoption of the alien space raise questions about the role
of the Land of Israel and of the myth of redemption in the collective mind
of the community. This question, too, will be addressed in Chapter 1.

Chapter 2 deals with the legends of the Jews' initial reception and
focuses on two issues, thematically and formally: relations between Jews
and Gentiles, and the links between the reception legends of Polish and
Spanish Jews. The thematic linchpin of the acceptance legends is the
relations between Jews and Poles. I have examined these stories using the
concepts developed by Lévi-Strauss for studying myth: binary oppositions
and mediating elements. These concepts, as well as those about the hero-
donor formulated by Propp (1968), are applied to construct a paradigm
of Jewish-Polish relations in the various legends and juxtapose a model of
segregation and isolation against those of cooperation based on compassion and cooperation based on equality. These models reflect the change
that took place in the actual situation of the Polish Jews and their changing
cultural awareness.

Chapter 3 examines the legends about Abraham Prochownik, the Jew
who became a king of Poland and was instrumental in the coronation of
Piast, the ancestor of the medieval Polish dynasty. As this chapter reveals,
one version of the story was transcribed in an extracultural setting. In
this chapter, the thematic discussion and literary critique will be supplemented by a consideration of monarchy as a central theme that expresses
the problems that preoccupied the Jews of Poland with regard to their
status in the country. I will show that the rejection of the Polish crown
by Abraham(!), the primordial ancestor of the Jews of Poland, makes
possible a dialogue with Polish society that can calm its anxiety about
Jewish ambitions while at the same time treating the problem of Jews'
preserving their national and religious identity from within the Polish
Diaspora.

Chapter 4 deals with stories about Esther and Casimir, the Great King of
Poland; the problematic nature of relations between a Jewess and a Gentile;
and the fact that these relations are not condemned only when they are

interpreted as being decisive for the survival of the entire community—in this case, the grant of the right of settlement and expansion of the privileges of the Jews of Poland because of Esther. We also shall examine various local legends that give a special twist to the legend. In each of these four chapters I also consider the reciprocal relations between folk legends and authorial legends and examine the poetics of each type.

Chapter 5 deals exclusively with local legends. Although the earlier chapters cite variations of several local legends, these stories are in fact legends of origin of Polish Jewry as a whole. Here I deal only with local legends about the synagogues of the narrating community. Because these stories are still being recounted today and can be found in the memorial books, whereas the general legends of origin are hardly told anymore, this chapter, more than any of the others, permits an examination of the process experienced by Polish Jewish legends of origin in the post-Holocaust context. Following the destruction of the Polish communities, the places referred to by the legends survive only in memory. For the Jews of Poland after the Holocaust, the legends of origin undergo a fascinating transformation into legends of destruction.

Thus this book as a whole, with the legends it recounts and their analysis and interpretation, constructs the narrative of the Jewish community of Poland, a narrative that begins within the first settlement and concludes with destruction.

The study of the legends of origin of the Jews of Poland is only one aspect of the legendary chronicle of a glorious community that flourished for so many centuries. I see this study as only a beginning: In the future I hope to be able to trace other facets of these legends, such as the image of women, stories of cemeteries and tombstones, tales about Polish rabbis, and narratives about the immigration of Polish Jews to Israel and their absorption there.

Given the vast scope of this topic, I knew at the outset that I was embarking on a long journey whose conclusion could not be foreseen. Still, my work on the legends of origin of Polish Jews has fulfilled my expectations of a fascinating voyage, filled with curiosity and new discoveries, speculation and adventures, all of which I hope to impart in this volume.

I would like to thank the various foundations that supported my studies of the legends of origin of Polish Jewry: the Memorial Foundation for Jewish Culture, the Lucius N. Littauer Foundation, and the Research Authority Fund at the University of Haifa. A generous grant from the Lucius N. Littauer Foundation underwrote the translation of my text into English.

I owe a special debt of gratitude to the late Professor Raphael Patai, who encouraged me at various stages of the composition of this book and invited me to publish it in the series he edited. I regret that the book was not published during his lifetime and take consolation from the fact that the series of which it is part bears his name.

I wish to thank from the bottom of my heart Professor Dov Noy, who encouraged me to study the folk tales of Polish Jewry, as well as Professor Dan Ben-Amos, Professor Barbara Kirschenblatt-Gimblett, and Professor Aliza Shenhar, who read the entire manuscript and offered excellent suggestions for improving it.

I have delivered lectures on the topics covered in the book at various academic conferences and taught them to my students at the University of Haifa, the University of Pennsylvania, and the University of California at Berkeley. These colleagues' and students' questions and comments have proved invaluable at various stages of the work. My thanks to all of them.

I have had the great fortune of working with a translator of the caliber of Lenn Schramm. His comments in the margins of his draft made a contribution to the manuscript, and I thank him for his superb work. I would also like to thank Wayne State University Press—the director of the Press, Arthur B. Evans, the editor of the series, Professor Dan Ben-Amos, the managing editor, Kathryn Wildfong, and copy editor, Mindy M. Brown. Finally, a special "thank you" to my husband, Zeev Bar-Itzhak; without his help and encouragement this book could not have been written.

1

The Geography of the Jewish Imagination

PO-LIN AMONG TREES
WITH LEAVES FROM THE GEMARA

Bernard Weinryb, the historian of Polish Jewry, examined legends of origin from a historical perspective and found a striking resemblance among the legends of the various Jewish diasporas. He ascribed this similarity to the common lot of all such communities–the parlous situation that confront a minority that settles in the midst of another people (Weinryb 1962). After comparing legends of origin from various countries, he identified five themes typical of these legends; every such legend incorporates one or more of them:

1. Jews first settled in the region in the distant past, usually at the dawn of history of the country and its people.
2. The Jews were invited to settle there by the people or by the rulers, because of the benefits they would bring with them.
3. The Jews saved the land from drought, plague, or some other catastrophe, or made a significant contribution to the general welfare.
4. In the distant past, the Jews enjoyed fair treatment and equal rights. The deterioration in their circumstances came later, usually quite recently.
5. The first settlers brought with them the traditions of an established Jewish community, which confers a certain prestige on them.

Weinryb's scheme, based on thematic comparisons, permits the classification of many legends of origin. It does not cover all legends of origin, however, nor all of the themes that appear in them. This shortcoming may stem from the fact that Weinryb considered the legends as oriented chiefly toward the outside—as a means whereby a minority group sought to justify its residence in the land of the autochthonous majority *to* that majority. Indeed, his dating of some of the Polish Jewish legends of origin rests on the concept that the legends were devised in a later period to serve the polemic or apologetic needs of that period.[1] There is no doubt that the legends of origin did play this role; like all oral legends, they were adapted to address contemporary needs and problems. Nevertheless, one must not deny their antiquity in other guises and versions that have not survived.[2] Modern folklore studies dealing with immigrant groups have found that folk creations flourish precisely at the time of the first contact with the new locale, fertilized by culture shock and the need to deal with it (Kirschenblatt-Gimblett 1978; Bar-Itzhak 1998).[3]

Yet we must also acknowledge the ways in which legends of origin were told not only for the outside world but also for internal reasons. The refugees who arrived in a new place had to deal with the unknown and unfamiliar, with strange landscapes, names, inhabitants, customs, and more. This encounter and the emotional processes it engenders stimulate creative activity to convert the alien to the known, the distant to the intimate, as well as to find a spiritual—and, in our case, theological—justification for the very act of settlement. Such creativity is an expression of the need and attempt to adopt a new country.

Settling in an unfamiliar place, asserts Mircea Eliade, is "equivalent to a new act of Creation." The alien regions are assimilated to the primordial chaos. Settling a new territory turns the chaos into cosmos by means of a ritual that makes it real and valid (Eliade 1991, 9–10). The legend of origin about the migration and settlement is an expression of the ritual act as well as part of it. How is this reflected in the legends of origin of Polish Jewry? What rhetorical and poetic devices are used to implement the various strategies?

Human beings create on the basis of archetypes, following the models for artistic creation that are sanctified in their culture (Eliade 1991, 10). Myth, according to Northrop Fry, is the realization of a cosmic system that is also a literary model. This model represents a process that is embedded in some fixed regularity, which is revealed in the myth or ritual connected with the fundamental processes of human existence (Frye 1957, 112–114). The legends of Polish Jewry recreate Poland according to a Jewish archetype whose most conspicuous expressions involve the Judaization of place names by means of homiletical explanations (*midrashim*) of the alien-sounding names.

28

The homiletical exposition of names, including place names, goes back to the Bible, which attaches great importance to explaining names and to exploiting their phonetic and semantic components. This practice is a direct consequence of the role allotted to names in the Biblical world view and also, perhaps, of the dominant view in related coeval literatures (Garsiel 1987). The preoccupation with expounding names and the creation of "name-midrashim" continued in the post-Biblical period. The Apocrypha preserves and expands name-midrashim, and many are preserved in the ancient translations. The liturgical poetry of the first millennium frequently incorporates name-midrashim. There is an abundance of midrashim on Biblical and post-Biblical names in the rabbinic literature of the Talmudic era, and thereafter in the traditional commentaries over the generations (ibid., 20–21). Thus we are dealing with an ancient tradition; name-midrashim can be considered to be part of the broader phenomenon of paranomasia, including alliteration, puns, and plays on words, or as etiological stories.

At the same time, there is a difference between the name-midrashim and etymologies[4] found in the ancient Jewish sources and those in the folk literature and traditions of Polish Jewry. In the former, name-midrashim rely on mellifluous, rhythmic, and phonetic wordplay—puns, metatheses of letters, and inversion—all of it in Hebrew. The name-midrashim of Polish Jewry, by contrast, are multilingual.[5] In this respect they resemble the midrashic etymologies of the Talmudic sages. Sometimes a Biblical word being expounded by the sages is understood according to the meaning expressed by its phonemes in some other language—often Greek or Arabic. (Rabbi Akiva even inferred a legal prescription from an etymology based on two foreign languages that are quite unknown to us [Frenkel 1991, 117].) All these Talmudic midrashim, however, involve a Hebrew word explained by recourse to another language. In the case of the midrashic exposition of Polish place names, by contrast, we are dealing with a Slavic name explained on the basis of Jewish languages. The Slavic name is understood not as a random and arbitrary set of phonemes, but as a concatenation that conveys a meaning in a Jewish language—Hebrew and/or Yiddish. The name-midrash unveils this meaning, which allows the newcomers to identify with the place by Judaizing it. The name-midrash or explanation is incorporated into a literary work and creates a legend of origin.

Let us consider a few examples:

> What is the source of the name Shebershin? Tradition has it that the town of Shebershin was first of the nine communities where Jews settled after the expulsion from Spain. So they called it Shebershin, meaning "settle first" (Hebrew *shev rishon*).[6]

The Judaization of the place-name begins with its pronunciation, as Mahler notes in his article on the Jewish names of places in Old Poland (1953, 146–161).[7] The Jews pronounced the name "Shebershin," whereas the Poles pronounced it "Sczebrzeszyń."

The name is expounded in Hebrew. According to Dov Sadan, the hallmark of Yiddish folk etymologies is that names are interpreted on the basis of their Hebrew forms (1954, 142). The sounds that make up the Slavic name, as it was pronounced by the Jews, make possible a midrash that can be incorporated into the tale of the Jews' flight from Spain and their arrival in Poland. Sczebrzeszyń is turned into a Jewish city by means of an internal Jewish code–the Jew's own language–and is consecrated by the power of the Holy Tongue. In terms of Weinryb's scheme, we can identify two themes here: the first, dealing with the antiquity of the community, and the fifth, associating the community with an older center of Jewish settlement.

Stories like this keep cropping up in various forms and various eras, motivated by the desire to express significant events in the life of the community. Consider another Hebrew name-midrash on Shebershin, this one referring to a later period, the nineteenth-century Polish insurrection against the czar.

> What is the origin of the name Shebershin? The old people recounted that the town of Shebershin in Poland used to have a totally different name. But after much of the kingdom of Poland was occupied by the Russian czar, two hundred years ago, the Poles revolted against the Russians.
>
> Once–it was on the Sabbath–the Polish insurgents came to the town. On the way encountered a very observant Jew, so pious that on the Sabbath he would not utter a single syllable of profane talk and spoke only in the Holy Tongue. They asked him the name of the town, but he did not answer, because he did not want to desecrate the Sabbath. They asked him once, twice, the same question: "What's the name of this town?" But since he would by no means answer them, they flew into a rage and beat him and slapped him on the face. The Jew, confused and frightened, began to cry out: *"Shever shin! Shever shin!"* [Hebrew: "broken tooth"]. Ever since then the town has been called Shebershin.[8]

Not only does this story expound the name of the town in Hebrew, it credits the Jews with the change of name: "The old people recounted that the town of Shebershin in Poland used to have a totally different name." The story, with the irony at one's own expense that is typical of Jewish humor (Noy 1982a; Oring 1992, 118–121), expounds the name in the context of well-known events and incidentally reflects the relations between Jews and non-Jews.

In these two stories, only Hebrew is called on to explain the Polish name. The next example adds Yiddish to the mix[9]:

30

What is the source of the name Ostre? Hundreds of years ago, when Talmudic scholars, *geonim*, and rabbis like the great Maharshal Luria, the holy Maharsha, and others lived there, the city earned the name Ostre—that is, *Ois Torah* [Ashkenazi Hebrew: "mark of Torah"]. Today, by contrast, when the Jews no longer devote themselves to learning and the houses of study stand empty, the city is still *Ois Torah* [Yiddish: "without Torah"].[10]

Here, too, the explanation is based on the Jewish pronunciation, "Ostre," rather than the Polish Ostróg. The midrash exploits the homonymity of the Yiddish *ois* 'out' and the Ashkenazi Hebrew *ois* 'mark', 'sign'. It is no coincidence that Hebrew is used to express the holiness of the city in bygone days, whereas Yiddish, the profane vernacular, denotes its deterioration in the later era. The story employs the double midrash on the name of the town to convey a facet of internal Jewish history—Torah study and its place in the Jewish world. In this way, geography is Judaized and placed at the disposal of Jewish history.

In the story "The Annals of Our House," S. Y. Agnon relates humorously to the name-midrashim of Polish Jews.

> Where did our great-great-grandfather go after he emerged from the forest? Our ancestors didn't tell us that. As for what the people of Dubinka, putting on airs, say—that that righteous man came to them first and that their city is called Dubinka after the bear [Hebrew: *dov*] he was riding on—we can't agree with them. For if you are going to expound names, you'll find a number of cities whose names allude to a bear, such as Dubno and Dubromil. (1967, *Ha'Esh ve'Ha'Etzim*, 30–31)

Name-midrashim and explanations are intended to provide a theological imprimatur for Jewish residence in these places. Conferring such approval on residents of the Polish diaspora is a central theme of the legends of origin, meant exclusively for Jewish consumption; as such it is not covered by Weinryb's scheme. The same applies to Ostre when its name is linked to Torah study, or to Kolomyja when it is described as "*kol m-ya*" (Hebrew: voice of God).[11]

This brings us to the legend of origin that deals with the first arrival of Jews in Poland, which will be the focus of this chapter: the *Po-lin* legend that expounds the Hebrew name for Poland and translates it as "lodge here."[12] The oldest written source in which I have found a midrash on a Hebrew name for Poland is the "Elegy on the Massacres in Polonia,"[13] an elegy on the pogroms of 1648–49 by the seventeenth-century Jacob b. Moshe Halevy, first printed in Venice in 1670–71. According to H. I. Gurland, in his introduction to the elegy:

> This elegy was recited by the holy communities of Venice for their fellow Jews who perished by the sword in Poland and its appanages, and for the death of numberless great scholars and wise men on account of sins, who

died unnatural deaths. In the scroll of lamentations, the elegist wrote, "why forever, in great distress, will these cities be desolate, full of the blood of the slaughtered, and his blood flowed like wine [after Deut. 32:14] on the land beneath them. In the year "may He save you from the *fowler's* trap" [Ps. 91:2] [i.e., 5416 = 1655–56] they read it with an aching heart, solemnly and in a low voice, "when the plague was over." [Num. 26:19]

The name-midrash appears in the third stanza of the elegy:

The glory of the earth has now become
the shame of all towns, a disgrace among cities.
A place of Torah learning–here God lodges [Hebrew: *po lan Yah*][14]–
is now full of sadness and great mourning,
instead of the poetry and song that used to be
in them. Just as by the waters of Babylon,
the joy of my heart has been exiled, and all my prosperity.
Behold, is there any anguish like my anguish?

Here Poland is described as "the glory of the earth. . . . A place of Torah learning–here God lodges." The devastation wreaked by the pogroms of 1648–49 creates a contrasting analogy to the former greatness and glory. (We shall return to this theme later in this chapter.)

Stories that incorporated or were based on the name-midrash *Po-lin* were first transcribed at a much later date. Louis Lewin cites the legend from an oral tradition of the late nineteenth or early twentieth century (1907, 147).[15] He merely summarizes the story, which refers to the exiles from Spain: When the Jews were expelled from Spain and their wanderings had brought them to the east, they said, "po lin," or "lodge here"; this is the source of the name *Polin*, or "Poland." The legend attempts to explain the name of the country, associate it with the exiles from Spain, and incorporate it into the history of the Jews and the role that Poland played as the place where they found a safe haven and refuge (see also An-Ski 1920).

Berl Marek cites another version of the story which refers to refugees from Germany (1957, 190). According to his summary of the legend, a Jewish survivor of the massacres in Germany arrived in Poland, where he heard a heavenly voice say, "Po lin," or "lodge here." The two legends differ both with regard to the origin of the newcomers and the type of hero– the group versus an individual. The second version adds the element of divine intervention in the form of the heavenly voice that declares that the survivor should stay in Poland. This turns the story into a sacred legend and gives a theological imprimatur to the act of settling in Poland.

The difference between the traditions may be why Agnon, in his version of the *Po-lin* legend, "Antecedents" (*Qedumot*), which opens the anthology *Poland: Legendary Tales,* does not specify the country from which the Jewish refugees were fleeing:

32

Antecedents

This is a traditional legend we received from our ancestors who migrated to Poland.[16] The Jews saw that the persecutions continued and continued and the troubles were always renewed afresh and their bondage kept getting worse and the evil kingdom issued decree after decree, until their was no chance of recovery for the enemies of Israel.[17] They stood by the roads and considered, inquiring about ancient paths: Which is the road to travel and find tranquillity for themselves? A slip of paper fell from the skies: "Go to Poland." They went to the land of Poland and gave the king a mountain of gold. The king received them with great honor. The Lord had mercy on them and caused the king and ministers to show mercy to them. The king allowed them to settle in all the lands of his kingdom, to trade throughout the length and breadth of the country, and to worship the lord according to the tenets of their religion. The king protected them against every foe and adversary. So Israel dwelled in safety in Poland for many days. They engaged in commerce and in every craft and trade. And the Lord ordained blessings for them and blessed them in the land. They won a name among the nations. They traded with the surrounding countries and even minted coins—these are the coins with the inscription, "Mieshko king of Poland" or "Moshe Król Polski" (the Poles call the king *król*). When they were in that country, they discovered a forest of trees, and a tractate of the Gemara was carved into every tree. This is the forest of Kewczin, near Lublin. They said to one another: "Behold, we have come to the land where our ancestors lived of old." Why was it called Polin? Because the Jewish people said before the Holy One, Blessed be He: "Master of the Universe, if the hour of our redemption has not yet arrived, lodge here [*po lin*] through this night of exile with us, until You bring us up to the Land of Israel." (Agnon 1966, 353)

It should be noted that "Antecedents" was not Agnon's first version of the legend. In the first Hebrew version, entitled "Polin" (published in *Hatequfah* in 1920, 23–24), the story deals with refugees from the Rhineland (Ashkenaz). An even earlier version was published in German in 1916, under the title "Erste Kunde" (Agnon and Eliasberg 1916, 1–3); here, too, the story is told of refugees from the Rhineland: "wie Israel aus dem Frankenreiche nach Polen kam und sich dort niederließ."[18]

In all three of Agnon's retellings, it is a note that falls from the skies that directs the refugees to Poland. The divinely mediated migration to Poland also appears in "The Annals of Our House," told as a family saga. In this story, "our great-great-grandfather, Rabbi Shmuel from the Rhineland (Ashkenaz)" attains high distinction. In the wake of the jealousy this arouses, the following scene ensues:

> The astrologer waxed wroth and shoved our great-great-grandfather, who slipped and fell from the top of the tower. Raising his eyes toward heaven, our great-great-grandfather called out: "To Your hands I commit my soul."

A hand materialized, took hold of him as he floated in the air, and carried him to a forest that was a day's journey from Ashkenaz. That forest was in Poland. It's just as we wrote at the beginning of the story, that as things worked out our great-great-grandfather was forced to flee to Poland, but not of his own accord; a hand appeared and carried him there. (Agnon, Ha'Esh Ve'Ha'Etzim, 1967, 28–29)

The slip of paper that falls from heaven was not Agnon's invention. Here he was faithful to folk versions that must have been transmitted orally. One of these stories was printed by Gershom Bader:

> If you want to know how it suddenly occurred to these Jews in Germany to seek refuge in Poland, legend has it that after the Jews had decreed a fast and beseeched God to save them from the murderers, a slip of paper fell from heaven. On it was written: "Go to Poland, for there you will find rest. . . . The Jews set out for Poland. When they reached it, the birds in the forest chirped to greet them: "*Po lin! Po lin!*" The travelers translated this into Hebrew, as if the birds were saying: "Here you should lodge. . . ." Afterwards, when they looked closely at the trees, it seemed to them that a leaf from the Gemara was hanging on every branch.[19] At once they understood that here a new place had been revealed to them, where they could settle and continue to develop the Jewish spirit and the age-old Jewish learning. (Bader 1927, 2–3)

In Yiddish literature, the legend is recounted by I. L. Peretz in his *Reise Bilder,* first published in 1891: "The stillness of a summer night. At the edge of the sky, the nearby forest grows dark. On its trees our ancestors engraved the names of the Talmudic tractates they finished studying on the road. Not far from there they once encamped in the evening, and the Exilarch said: *Po lin!* And to this day, the country is called Polin; but the Gentiles can't explain why!" (Peretz 1947, 170).

Echoes of this legend also resound in the poem by Noach Pniel, "Po-lin":

> Po lin! chirped the birds from your trees.
> Indeed, my ancestors lodged in you for a thousand years
> And thrust my roots deep into a land that is my step-mother:
> I hung Gemaras in the top of every tree in your forest.
> *(Pniel 1970, 53–54; first published in* Hapoel Hatza'ir *1968, 29)*

In all these legends, Poland is recreated as a Jewish land. It is the Jews who name it to commemorate the role it plays in their history. The crux of the matter, though, is that their arrival and residence in Poland receives a divine stamp of approval, whether in the form of a heavenly voice that guides the refugee or a slip of paper that falls from Heaven and guides them to sanctuary in Poland. It is important to emphasize the different bent of the folk versions vis-à-vis Agnon's "Antecedents." In the former,

Max Fabian, "Auswanderer." Painting. Published in the anthology by Agnon and Eliasberg (1916).

the midrashic exposition of the latent meaning of the name *Polin* is oriented toward the Jews: Here they will lodge and find rest; according to the legend, the rationale for their settlement in this place is that here they will be able "to continue to develop the Jewish spirit and the age-old Jewish learning." That is, the legend glosses the Hebrew word *lin* in the sense given it by the medieval commentator David Kimhi, who writes, in his commentary on "where righteousness dwelt" (Isa. 1:21): "[Here] *yalin* does not have the literal meaning of 'spending the night,' but refers to perseverance and persistence in doing something." This version of the legend seeks to give a sense of continuity and permanence to the Jews' residence in Poland;

the ability to preserve the Jewish spirit and engage in Jewish scholarship in this new place are the justifications for settling there.

In the first Hebrew version of his story "Polin," Agnon remains faithful to the folk versions; the name-midrash is addressed to the Jewish community. "The homilists said: This is why it was called Polin, because when the Jews came to the land they said, '*Po lin!*' That is, 'here we will lodge until we merit to go up to the Land of Israel.'" The same explanation appears in "Erste Kunde." In "Antecedents," however, Agnon returns to the sense of the midrash in the elegy on the pogroms of 1648–49,[20] where the name of the country is expounded in relation to God: Poland is "the glory of the earth, . . . a place of Torah learning–here God lodges." In "Antecedents," too, it is God who lodges in Poland: "The Jewish people said before the Holy One, Blessed be He: 'Master of the Universe, if the hour of our redemption has not yet arrived, lodge here [*po lin*] through this night of exile with us, until You bring us up to the Land of Israel.'" These versions, even if understood metaphorically, endow Poland with an added measure of sanctity as the residence of the Holy One, Blessed be He Himself. Both Agnon's story and the elegy, however, conspicuously emphasize the transient nature of that sojourn. In general, in all versions of the legends, the name-midrash conveys the temporary nature of the sojourn in Poland; but this transience is given greater prominence in the elegy and in "Antecedents." In the elegy, it is depicted as a direct consequence of the destruction of the Jewish communities of Poland. For Agnon, it is the night of exile, which the Lord spends with his people until the dawn of redemption, in keeping with the idea that the Divine Presence followed the Jews into every place of their exile (BT Megillah 29a)[21] and that God accompanies every Jew in every place.[22] This conception of Poland as a temporary domicile is a recurrent theme in Agnon's collection *Poland: Legendary Tales* and is developed to its fullest extent in the last story in that collection, "The Emissary from the Holy Land, May It Be Rebuilt and Restored." The change points to the existence of the antithetical tendency, expressed in folk legends that reflect the Polish Jews' enormous pride in their synagogues and Torah scholars– and, in Agnon's version, even the assertion of their country's superiority to the Land of Israel (ibid., 394–402). We shall return to this later in this chapter.

No less important are the lines selected by Agnon to serve as the epigraph for his stories "Erste Kunde" and "Polin," and later for the entire collection *Poland: Legendary Tales:* "Poland the delicate, ancient in Torah and scholarship, ever since the day that Ephraim separated himself from Judah." These lines come from a penitential prayer by R. Moshe Katz of Narol in Poland,[23] a survivor of the pogroms of 1648–49 who later became head of the rabbinical court in the city of Metz. The stanza introduced by these two lines, which glorify Poland, concludes with the catastrophe that befell Polish Jewry in the pogroms of 1648–49.

> Poland the gentle, ancient in Torah and scholarship,
> Ever since the day that Ephraim separated himself from Judah
> Sealed in Torah study;
> But now exiled and disdained, bereaved and barren.
> It is in this penitential prayer that we read, inter alia:
> What can I take as witness or liken to you, O land of Poland? [Lam. 2:13, with Poland replacing the Jerusalem of the original]
> You pored over the [Talmudic] chapter "These are liable to death by burning" and the chapter "How does one roast?";
> You studied: "These are liable to death by strangulation" and the chapter "They hang,"
> The chapter "These are liable to be flogged" and the chapter "These are liable to be exiled."[24]

Agnon takes the etiological legend that endeavors to provide a theological justification for the Jews' initial settlement and long sojourn in Poland and inverts it, presenting Poland as a place of temporary residence, a night of exile. In and of itself this emphasizes the importance and centrality for him of the Land of Israel.

Another writer who drew on the *Po-lin* legend was Aaron Zeitlin, in his dramatic mystery *Estherke*. In it, the rabbi is recounting the legend to King Casimir the Great:[25]

THE RABBI:

We prostrated ourselves, we refugees from the sword, on the warm heart of the soil of Poland. *Po lin*—Here you must pass the night, said the angel, when once, in the night, we refugees arrived, with wives and children, in your fields. The ground still trembled under the soles of our feet as if we had only just now debarked from a demon ship. It seemed to us that the night was sharpening black knives; evil winds were stifling the slumbering birds and wanted to strangle our children too. A cloud opened above us, splitting asunder—and from its midst there peered out, rocking on a strand of lightning, an angel, and with a silver finger he pointed: *Po lin!* spend the night here! All was silent. And, just as in the past, through the gates of the Canaan, we entered the land in the morning.

CASIMIR:

Yours is a wonderful story, old man. Why only to spend the night? Your brethren have already spent more than one night on my land.

THE RABBI:

It is written: For in Your sight a thousand years are like yesterday that has past, like a watch of the night.[26] So too is the night to the people of Israel. The night of our exile will last a thousand years on your soil—but it is only

37

one night, O King. Until the day of Jerusalem dawns again, we will sleep here one night–those who came here earlier, and we, too, who arrive now, fleeing from wickedness and confusion. *Po lin!* spend the night here![27]

The rabbi's story, along with his dialogue with the king, makes Zeitlin's meaning clear. Here, too, it is divine intervention that guides the refugees to Poland. The entire cosmos participates in the revelation whose focus is the appearance of the angel. Zeitlin makes an explicit analogy between the entry into Poland and the entry into the Land of Canaan. As in the folk versions, here, too, the name-midrash is directed toward the refugees. Yet Zeitlin, like Agnon, emphasizes that the Jews' residence in Poland is a passing phase, invoking the relativity of the terms *night* and *watch*: a thousand years is the term set for the Jews' sojourn in Poland, as a variation on Psalms 90:4.

The *Po-lin* legends are the legends of wanderers, dealing with a community that has left its former home and with its reestablishment in a new place. It follows naturally that space should have a special significance in these legends. In fact, three distinct spaces are invoked. The first space–the country that has been left behind–hardly appears. The need to abandon it suffices to characterize it as a perilous place. The narrators do not bother to describe it, since its mere mention awakens the terror latent in the collective memory.

The second space is that of the passage, the places through which the refugees wandered while searching for a new haven. Providence does not forsake the wanderers and directs them to Poland, the sanctuary where they can find repose.

The descriptions of the landscapes of their refuge, their cynosure, the land of their desires–the third space–are typified by allusions to and associations with sacred Jewish concepts. The birds in the Polish forests chirp in Hebrew; the boughs of the trees bear leaves from the Gemara. This association appears in Agnon's retelling, too: "When they reached the land, they discovered a forest of trees, and a tractate of the Gemara was carved into every tree. This is the forest of Kewczin, near Lublin. They said to one another: 'Behold, we have come to the land where our ancestors lived of old'" (Agnon, 1966, 353).

The Jewish legend borrows its spatial apparatus from the world of wonder tales. In wonder tales, however, the boughs of the marvelous trees that grow in the wondrous space bear leaves of gold or fruit of precious stones, whereas in the Jewish legend the sparkling jewels of the material world are replaced by the priceless gems of the spiritual world. The legend cited by Bader does not refer to any specific place; Agnon, by contrast, draws on a local tradition and specifies the Kewczin forest near Lublin.

Legends describing idyllic landscapes were common in various Jewish communities. Here we shall examine two stories set in the area of Sczebrzeszyń: the first one is found in the YIVO collection; the second was recorded and transcribed in Israel as part of the IFA collection.

The Cave Leading to the Land of Israel

The path leading to the village of Kawenczynek, in the Shebershin district, goes through a steep valley between high mountains, almost as deep as a pit. In the valley there is a cave, which the locals call the *Żydowska Szkoła* or "Jewish House of Study." The story is told that when the Jews made their way from Spain to Poland they camped for a while in this valley; during their stop they studied and prayed. You could see traces of Hebrew words carved into some of the trees in the area, which were to be read: "Here we finished studying the tractate *Shabbat*." There is also a brook there, which is still known as the Brook of the Prophet Samuel.

In the same area there is a cave which, so tradition has it, leads to the Land of Israel. People say that roughly a hundred years ago there lived in Shebershin a righteous man, who was known as the "White Rebbe" on account of the white garments he always wore. He is still renowned throughout the district for the wonders he worked. He very much wanted to bring the Messiah. Once he went out to the forest and said he was going to the Land of Israel. All the young ragamuffins went with him, as did a few pious women. He came to the cave and stopped outside. First he sent a kid into the cave—and waited three days. When he saw that after three days the kid had not returned, he said that this must certainly be the path to the Land of Israel. Then he went into the cave and never came out again.[28]

The House of Study in the Shebershin Forest

The Jews of Shebershin were persecuted by the landowners, who did not allow them to learn Torah. They went out to study in the nearby forest, outside the village of Kawenczynek, and carved the names of the Talmudic tractates on the trees. The villagers always protected the Jews and considered the forest to be a holy place. They called it *Żydowska Szkoła,* which is Polish for "the Jewish Synagogue."

After the expulsion of the Jews from Spain, some of them settled in Shebershin. Back then they were forbidden to learn Torah. Every morning before dawn the Jews got up and at an agreed-upon sign silently stole out of the town and proceeded to a distant village, which they called Kawenczynek.

This village was surrounded by high hills and deep valleys, green and fragrant, full of hidden and extremely deep caves. The Jews would gather in one of these hidden caves to learn Gemara. Whenever they finished a tractate they would carve its name on a tree, so they would know which tractate they had finished and which ones they still had to learn.

The Polish villagers of those days were friendly to the Jews and kept watch over the place. When they learned that the authorities were on their way to catch the Jews, they warned them of their peril. On more than one occasion the villagers hid the Jews and saved them from cruel persecutions. The head of the yeshiva gave them his blessing: in recompense for this good deed he would protect them with every good word.

The Poles considered the spot to be holy. Whenever they found themselves in distress or if someone was seriously ill, all sorts of cripples and handicapped persons–the blind, the deaf, the lame, and victimized people from the whole area–came there to pray. They called it *Żydowska Szkoła*.

This name was attached in particular to the mountain whose recesses contained a deep cave, where the Jews learned Torah in those days. All this happened in the olden days.[29]

In these stories, a forest in Poland becomes a landscape of the Jewish Study. The cave of Kawenczynek becomes an ancient Jewish house of study, while the trees in the forest are consecrated by Hebrew inscriptions indicating which Talmudic tractates the Jews studied en route. In the second legend, the narrator emphasizes the sanctity of the spot by adding that the Polish Gentiles made it into a place of pilgrimage and prayer.

This application of sacred Jewish iconography to Polish landscapes is troubling. The legends ought not to detract from the myth of redemption, in which the Land of Israel plays the central role. In other words, such landscapes should be reserved for the Land of Israel, the cynosure of the future redemption. As I have shown elsewhere, in Diaspora folk narratives the Land of Israel is treated as an extension of supernatural space that penetrates into human space (Bar-Itzhak 1992). The folk legends of Polish Jewry, like those of other diasporas about their own places of residence,[30] construct spatial devices that link Poland to the Land of Israel. In these two stories the device involves well-known motifs of Polish Jewish folk legends–the cave and the kid.

In other stories (see Chapter 5), the spatial connection between Poland and the Land of Israel occurs via a subterranean passage that leads from synagogues in the Diaspora to the Land of Israel, or through the medium of stones from the Holy Temple that are incorporated into the walls of the local synagogue.[31] In all these cases the Land of Israel remains the sanctified space for which the Jews yearn; it radiates a measure of sanctity on the landscapes and synagogues of their present abode.

As noted above, the stamp of approval on residence in Poland as an act of divine choice ought not to detract from the myth of future redemption or come at the expense of the Land of Israel, the site of that future redemption. In the legends, space and time join forces to express the problem and to solve it. In the folk legend, Poland is recreated according to the Jewish archetype: the sacred Jewish world inheres in its essence, name,

"Mizrah" landscape and symbols from the collection of An-Ski's expedition. Reproduced in Rivka Gonen, ed., *Back to the Shtetl: An-Ski and the Jewish Ethnographic Expedition 1912–1914* (Jerusalem: The Israel Museum, 1994). With kind permission of Mr. Nicolas Ilin, Frankfurt.

and landscapes. The archetype of settlement–the exodus from Egypt, the wandering in the wilderness during which God accompanies and guides His people, and the entry into the Land of Canaan–is repeated in the settlement of Poland; but an awareness of the myth of redemption informs the depiction of space and time. The Land of Israel remains the Holy Land, the navel of the world, the lost paradise, and thus the cynosure and object of desire. The name-midrash on Poland associates it with rescue from persecution and with repose–but also with night, darkness, sleep, and transience; whereas the Land of Israel is associated with eternity. The

41

spatial devices that link the two countries–especially the subterranean passage–constitute a sign that the Land of Israel remains the region of absolute reality and holiness; through this link it emanates a portion of its sanctity onto Poland. The road to the holy precinct is always arduous and fraught with perils (Eliade 1991, 18); in our story it assumes a garb that recalls the subterranean labyrinth found in so many myths, which symbolizes the difficulties of every quest. This arduous path represents both the aspiration toward and the difficulties of the transition from the profane to the sacred, from the temporary and illusory to the real and eternal, from death to life, from man to godhead.

In Yiddish literature, it was Sholem Asch, in *Kiddush Hashem,* who stated this problem by linking two legends–*Po-lin* and that of the Polish synagogues and houses of study that will be magically transported to the Land of Israel in the days of the Messiah. Reb Mendel is talking with Reb Jonah:

> "Do you think, Reb Jonah, that there will ever be a settlement here with Jewish towns and synagogues?"
>
> "Of course! How, then? The place is specially intended for Jews. When the Gentiles had greatly oppressed the exiled Jews and the Divine Presence saw that there was no limit and no end to the oppression and that the handful of Jews might, God forbid, go under, the Presence came before the Lord of the Universe to lay a grievance before Him, and said to Him as follows: 'How long is this going to last? When You sent the dove out of the ark at the time of the flood, You gave it an olive branch so that it might have support for its feet on the water, and yet it was unable to bear the water of the flood and return to the ark; whereas my children You have sent out of the ark into a flood, and have provided nothing for a support where they may rest their feet in their exile.' Whereupon God took a piece of Eretz Yisroel, which He had hidden away in the heavens at the time the Temple was destroyed, and sent it down upon the earth and said: 'Be My resting-place for My children in their exile.' That is why it is called Poland (Polin) from the Hebrew *po lin,* which means: 'Here shalt thou lodge' in the Exile. That is why Satan has no power over us here, and the Torah is spread over the whole country. There are synagogues and schools and yeshivas, God be thanked."
>
> "And what will happen in the great future when the Messiah comes? What are we going to do with the synagogues and the settlements which we have built up in Poland?" asked Mendel as he suddenly thought of Zloczew.
>
> "How can you ask? In the great future, when the Messiah comes, God will certainly transport Poland with all its settlements, synagogues, and yeshivas to Eretz Yisroel. How else could it be?" (1919, 63–64)

As Asch recounts in the legend, Poland is a piece of the Land of Israel, which the Holy One, blessed be He, set aside for His children as a place of repose in their exile. This explains why the Jews flourished in this land

and, in particular, why it became a center of Torah study. The tension between Poland and the Land of Israel, the site of the future redemption, is expressed in Mendel's question: "And what will happen in the great future when the Messiah comes?" The miraculous transport of Poland, with all its towns and houses of study, to the Land of Israel, invoked alongside the *Po-lin* legend, reflects a problem that troubled the Jews of Poland and their legendary solution to it (see also Druyanov 1945, 792).

At the same time, every case of settling down in the exile harbors the possibility that the reflection may replace the real. We have already suggested that throughout *Poland: Legendary Tales* Agnon tried to emphasize the centrality of the Land of Israel against the opposing tendency so prominent in the consciousness of the Polish communities and their legends.

The echoes of Biblical verses in both of Agnon's Hebrew versions, but especially in "Antecedents," represent a consummate artistry that conveys a subliminal message to this effect. Through the background resonance of phrases from the Book of Esther and the story of Joseph–such as "the Lord had mercy on them and caused the king and ministers to show mercy to them" (cf. Gen. 39:21, Esther 1:16); "the king protected them against every foe and adversary" (Esther 7:6); "and to worship the lord according to the tenets of their religion" (Esther 3:8)–Agnon reminds his readers that Poland is indeed an exile. On the other hand, through the many allusions to the episode of the spies (Num. 13–14), Agnon hints that, for the Jews, Poland has replaced the Land of Israel. Witness such examples as "to trade throughout the length and breadth of the country," "we have come to the land where our ancestors lived of old", as well as the echoes of verses that in their original Biblical context refer to the Israelites' residence in their own land, but are applied to Poland in Agnon's story–such as "the Lord ordained blessings for them and blessed them in the land" (compare Gen. 12:3 and Isa. 19:24) and "Israel dwelled in safety in Poland" (cf. Lev. 25:19–20, Deut. 12:10, Ezek. 39:26). Agnon's use of the phrase "foe or adversary"–"the king protected them against every enemy and adversary"–hints that the Jews' exaggerated sense of security in Poland had no basis, as is emphasized by the echo of the Book of Lamentations, where we read: "The kings of the earth did not believe, nor any of the inhabitants of the world, that foe or adversary could enter the gates of Jerusalem" (Lam. 4:12).

Naive readers may see Agnon's story as an attempt to preserve a well-known folk legend of previous generations. If we may rely on Yehudit Halevi-Zvik's survey of the critical articles that appeared when *Poland: Legendary Tales* was first published, many did react in this way (Halevi-Zvik 1984). Kimhi, for example, read the stories as "a symbol of the past and a symbol of the present," because they constitute as a monument to the past. Silman saw Agnon as the spokesman for the past generations, feeling himself one with them, rather than above them or alongside them, which Silman believes is how Mendele Mokher Sfarim, Sholem Aleichem, and I. L. Peretz felt. But the naive readers are not Agnon's intended public. The readers he has in mind have the ability to accept ancient traditions while also juxtaposing and comparing them, as the juxtaposition appears in the relationship between text and subtext.

Folk legends are not static creations; they are dynamic works that have a role to fulfill in the present. Writers who recreate legends in their own unique style are using them to work through a problem that resonates in the cultural space of their own society and age. Agnon's text rests on a double foundation. On one side, it builds on the remote context—a Polish Jewish folk legend justifying the Jews' settlement and residence in Poland. On the other side, it is embedded in the present context—the Zionist awakening that sets the Land of Israel and its resettlement as its main objective, as well as Agnon's personal decision to settle permanently in Palestine. This double affinity is reflected in the intertextuality of Agnon's text, an intertextuality that, according to Gershon Shaked, is "the most important literary essence in his work" (1989, 25). Agnon is using a folk legend to realize his own historiographic predisposition.

Returning to the folk versions and the beginning of our discussion, where we enumerated Weinryb's five themes in legends of origin, we see that the *Po-lin* legends—like other stories built on a name-midrash and seeking to characterize the landscapes of Poland—require us to add a sixth theme to Weinryb's list: Legends of origin endeavor to provide an internal Jewish theological *imprimatur* to the Jews' settlement and residence in Poland. The rhetorical and poetical devices employed in these legends promote the adoption of the new land by associating it with sacred Jewish concepts. In this way, the geography of Poland becomes the geography of the Jewish imagination, and its landscapes the landscapes of its most heartfelt desires.

2

Legends of
Acceptance

SEGREGATION VERSUS INVOLVEMENT

In Chapter 1 we discussed legends whose objective was to give a theological stamp of approval to the Jews' residence in Poland. Now we shall consider legends of acceptance–legends that recount how the Jews were greeted when they arrived in Poland and accorded permission to settle there.

Legends that seek to give a theological and spiritual imprimatur to Jewish residence in Poland, like those discussed in the previous chapter, focus on finding a justification for settling there in the Jews' own spiritual apparatus and in the relationship between human beings and God, which is the source of their ethical system. Clearly, the relations between Jews and Gentiles are not the central axis of the legend, since this is not the problem that engages it. On the other hand, legends of acceptance are indeed built around this problem. Through them the guest nation that creates and tells the story expresses its relations with the host nation and reshapes the latter's reaction. Legends of acceptance are key legends of origin for Diaspora communities, which had to live among alien nations and depend on their goodwill. To use the terminology of Claude Lévi-Strauss (1963, 206–231),[1] these legends express the fundamental opposition between Jews and Gentiles which engaged Polish Jewish society throughout its existence.

As we shall see, these legends express all the mediating contraries that derive from this fundamental opposition, as depicted in Figure 1.

In expressing the process of mediation, a legend constructs a model of Jewish-Gentile relations that reflects the narrating society's outlook and aspirations for the substance of these relations. Although legends of acceptance are set in the distant past, the legend itself, as a work of folklore, is a dynamic creation subject to continual change and expresses the problems that trouble a society at a given time. The "springtime" of the community in which the plot unfolds, the era of its arrival in Poland, is portrayed in a manner that reaffirms the community's way of life in the generation that recounts the story. The legend expresses the present in which it crystallized and was told. Stories that coalesced and were told and transcribed in different periods construct different models because they responded to the sociocultural problems that concerned society then. Thus the totality of the extant legends transcribed in various periods reflects the changing cultural awareness of Polish Jewish society.

THE SEGREGATION MODEL

The oldest written story I have found dates from the eighteenth century. Here we should once again note Yisrael Zinberg's remarks about the important role that Jews played as mediators in the field of European folklore and as artists who wove their hopes into the legends and wonder tales of the folklore heritage they received from earlier generations. Nevertheless, "almost everything that remained is 'oral tradition'; it is only by chance that elements of this folklore material have been preserved" (Zinberg 1958, 4:89). Thus the student of folk culture has no choice but to rely on written material that was transcribed and preserved "by chance." The place where this material is transcribed and preserved becomes the context that shapes the text itself; hence it too must be taken into account, like the performance situation of oral texts. The oldest legend of acceptance I have found is incorporated into *Divrei binah* by Dov-Ber Birkenthal (or Berezover), who was born in Bolichow in southeastern Galicia in 1724. *Divrei binah* was never printed; the manuscript wound up in the archives of Yoseph Perl.[2] Pages from Birkenthal's memoirs found their way to the library of the Rabbinical Seminary in London and were published by Mark Wischnitzer in Berlin in 1922 as the *Memoirs of Reb Dov of Bolichow*.[3] Excerpts from *Divrei binah* were published in Jerusalem in 1956 in Avraham Ya'acov Brawer's *Galicia and Its Jews: Studies in the History of Galicia in the Eighteenth Century.*

A few prefatory words are in order about Dov-Ber Birkenthal, who, as a representative of an "important and insufficiently known" stratum of *maskilim,* deserves to be the subject of a monograph in his own right, according to Brawer (1956, 200). There is a striking difference between

46

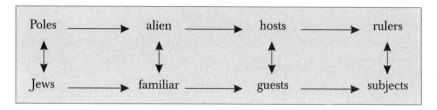

Figure 1

him and his Western contemporaries who were standard-bearers of the European Enlightenment. Like all well-to-do sons of his generation, he was educated in the Talmud and pious tomes. But he was also acquainted with non-Jewish culture; he studied Polish, German, Latin, and even French; and he could mix with the Polish intellectuals in their own language. He served as an interpreter and took an active part in the debate over the Lwow blood libel in 1759. Birkenthal was thoroughly convinced of the superiority of Jewish culture over the Gentile in everything related to its spiritual resources. As Brawer puts it: "He displays none of the self-abnegation of the *maskilim* before the brilliance of European culture" (1956, 200). It should be remembered that Polish-Jewish *maskilim* before the period of Ben Menahem were not differentiated from the masses, neither in their practices nor in their outward appearance. Jewish society did not blackball them, as it did the "Berliners" (Brawer 1956, 201).

Now for the story recounted by Dov-Ber Birkenthal:

> Jews came to Poland, an empty and desolate land, empty of attractive merchandise and of gold and silver; they brought with them every manner of fine thing and many treasures. They reached an agreement with the dukes and princes and councillors of state in Cracow, for in those days there was no king in Poland. Twelve *woiewodim*[4] ruled, and these accepted the Jews, showed them everything, and also borrowed thirty million in gold from them. . . . They made it an explicit condition that the Jews always wear the garb in which they came to the country. This was the custom until our time. In no wise did the Jews intermingle with the Gentiles in this country; they rejected not only their clothes, but also their language. . . . The pious ones of our people were accustomed to don special attire during prayer—the *letnik*, with a *breitel* on their heads. (Brawer 1956, 203)

As in other legends of origin, the plot is set in the distant past (the first of Weinryb's themes; see Chapter 1), in a period when "there was no king in Poland. Twelve [provincial lords] ruled." The country is described as "an empty and desolate land, empty of attractive merchandise and of gold and silver." The Jews are credited with having made over the country by bringing with them "every manner of fine thing and many treasures." Poland, as known to the narrating society in Birkenthal's time, is contrasted with Poland as it was, according to the story, when the Jews first arrived, as evidence of the Jews' contribution to changing the face of the country in which they settled.

The right of settlement was purchased: they even "borrowed thirty million in gold from them." Relations between Jews and hosts were purely a matter of mutual benefit and commercial interests. It is important to note that the story lacks a significant element found in legends of acceptance— namely, the reason the Jews came to Poland. Other legends mention some catastrophe that compels the Jews to seek the mercies of the Polish ruler or people; the ruler's or inhabitants' agreement endows them with the traits of graciousness and mercy. The omission of this element in Birkenthal's legend is compatible with its general bent: the Jews' were not in a bad way when they first came to Poland; hence their hosts hold no particular merit for admitting them to the country, and the Jews are not obliged to show their gratitude to them. Brawer, who was certainly acquainted with other legends of acceptance published in historical studies, expresses his astonishment at the absence of this sense of gratitude.[5] In fact, there is an inversion of sorts here, with the Jews characterized as donors more than as recipients. To use the terminology of Propp (1968), in his attempt to construct a morphology of the fairy tale, here the Jews are playing the role of donor.[6]

The legend builds a model of segregation between Jews and Poles, derived from their initial encounter and expressed in the etiological section that deals with Jewish costume. The segregation is mutual. Although primarily and originally imposed by the host society, which "made it an explicit condition that the Jews always wear the garb in which they came to the country," this segregation also expresses the will of the Jews in Poland over the ages: "they rejected not only their clothes, but also their language."[7] The conclusion—"This was the custom until our time"—refers to the narrator's own generation, of course. Birkenthal lived and was active in a transitional period when two contrasting Jewish streams were coalescing and spreading throughout Poland: Hasidism, coming from the east, and the Haskalah, penetrating from the west. Birkenthal, as a strictly pious Jew and a *maskil* of the previous generation, was strongly opposed to the innovators.[8] It is not surprising that, as in his twilight years he had chosen to justify his studies of Gentile lore by citing the rabbinic dictum "Know how to answer the freethinker" (BT Sanhedrin 39a), he would choose to create a model of segregation based on a legend of origin that was circulating among the people.

The system of relations described by the legend yields the model of segregation and alienation described in Figure 2. Thus a lifestyle oriented toward segregation and noninvolvement constructs a legend of origin that justifies this model. In this context it is important that the story was written in Hebrew and was clearly intended to remain within Jewish society only. The work was never printed. The rabbi of Lwow, Zvi Hirsch Rosanis, refused to approve the book for publication because of its insulting remarks about Christianity; he even advised the author to revise these passages.

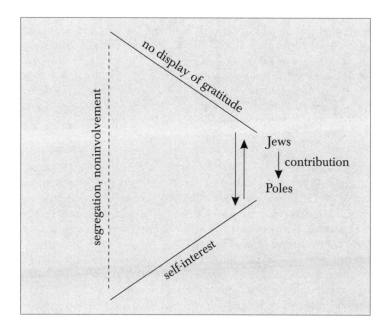

Figure 2

THE MODEL OF COOPERATION

Another legend of acceptance, which we shall call "The Legend of the Emissaries," creates an antithetical model. This legend was first published in Berlin in 1801 in an anonymous work entitled *Phylacterium oder Argenton und Philo im Schooße der wahren Glückseligkeit* (hereinafter Anonymous 1801).

The legend was published again in 1849 by Leon Weil (1849, 143–155, 159) in *Der Orient,* a weekly edited by Julius Fürst that appeared in Leipzig in 1840–50.[9] It resurfaced a number of times, in somewhat abridged form, in histories of Polish Jewry in German, Polish, Yiddish, and Hebrew in both the nineteenth century (Sternberg 1878; Kraushar 1862,

43; Lelewel 1851–56, 3, 417) and the twentieth century (Wiernik 1901, 199–200; Dubnov 1916, 40; Eisenstein 1934, 6–7; Mahler 1946, 18–19; and others).

All these versions credit Weil (1849) and the anonymous 1801 publication as their sources. The text published in *Der Orient* is as follows:[10]

The first Jews to settle in Poland came from Germany in the last decade of the ninth century.[11] The Catholic Church had already penetrated Germany. Its advance was paved in blood, for the cross bore with it the torch of war and destruction. The barbarian tribes of the German forests did not want to submit to Christianity; many who did so returned to paganism and let loose a rampage of fire and murder against those who accepted baptism. The believers in the cross were no less cruel than those who worshipped Wotan. The fire of war erupted from every volcano. Each side took an oath to cause death and imprecation. The loveliest lands were destroyed. Millions were annihilated by fire and sword.

Caught between the two camps was a small and unfortunate people, known for the magnitude of their suffering and the fortitude they displayed in every age and place. They were a small people who had been exiled from the land which they still proudly called their land. They were a people who, wherever they turned, were the object of scorn and derision, hated, persecuted, enslaved, trodden under foot. Until the modern age they were considered unworthy of enjoying what all human beings merit and should not be denied to any born of woman.

Between the two camps that were annihilating each other in Germany, fate interposed a handful of Jews. These Jews had come from the south, seeking refuge, protection, and security. That had indeed been their lot here for a long time; but no longer. The tempest that raged throughout Germany did not spare the innocent huts of the children of Jacob and assailed them with a terrible might. Even when the Jews displayed neutrality, they were swept up by the war between the two camps. Their peaceful conduct and neutrality made them the enemies of both sides, who coveted the aliens' gold and riches. When they did not hand over their gold and riches voluntarily, they were dispatched to the axe and the stake.

Like a fire that rages with nothing to stop its spread, and, out of control, mercilessly consumes everything that lies in its path, so it was here. The German vandals assaulted the Jews even when they had nothing or had already handed over everything they owned. These cruel men, whose wrath knew no bounds, did not spare children or women, the aged and the infirm. Nothing was sacred to the attackers; they pillaged, raped, beat, murdered, and burned—on one side in the name of the cross, on the other, to the glory of Wotan. Every day brought fresh suffering; every day brought new pain. What could the miserable orientals do? They had to find themselves a new and more secure abode; and this they did.

They did not turn to the west, where the war raged even more fiercely

Der Orient.

Berichte, Studien und Kritiken

Zehnter für Jahrgang.

Das Abonnement auf ein Jahr ist 5 Thlr. Man abonnirt bei allen löbl. Postämtern und allen solid. Buchhandlungen auf ein Jahr.

jüdische Geschichte und Literatur.

Herausgegeben

von

Dr. Julius Fürst.

Von dieser Zeitschrift erscheinen wöchentlich das Literaturblatt mitgerechnet, zwei Bogen, und zwar an jedem Sonnabend regelmäßig.

№ 31. Leipzig, den 4. August 1849.

Inhalt. Deutschland's vereinigte Staaten Aus Mähren. Das Komité für eine jüd. Gemeindeordnung. Lehrerversammlung. Die jüd. Lehrer in Loschitz und Auffee. Aus dem Regbisirikt. Das Schulwesen im Gh. Posen. Von der Lübbow. Die Chrisilichkeit als Merkmal. Hamburg. Extravaganzen gewisser Mitglieder der kons. Versammlung. — Beitrag zur Geschichte der Juden in Polen, von L. Weyl. — LB. d. Or.

Front page of the periodical *Der Orient* (no. 31), 1849.

than in Germany; nor to the south, whence the demon of antisemitism glared at them from a thousand eyes that sowed terror; nor to the north, with its marshes and forests populated by wild animals. Instead they gazed longingly eastward, to the young but flourishing kingdom of Poland. They decided to choose men renowned for their excellence in wisdom and experience and to send them to the king of Poland, to ask him to grant a refuge to the oppressed Israelites of Germany. They selected five men: R. Akiva Estremaduri, the scholar R. Hezekiah the Spaniard, the mathematician R. Emanuel of Ascalon, the orator R. Levi Bakhri, and R. Nathanel of Barcelona.[12]

On the throne of the Piasts in Gniezno in those days sat Leszek IV, who was known for his good heart, wisdom, and moderate rule. The delegation of Jews from Germany arrived in Gniezno[13] in the month of Shevat of the year A.M. 4653 [893 C.E.]. They presented themselves to the ruler as the emissaries of an unfortunate oriental people that had been expelled from its homeland and requested an audience to submit their petition orally. This was granted. The strangers were admitted to the king's presence and greeted him according to the tradition of those days. One of the delegation, R. Levi, delivered a short speech in Latin, full of good sense and information, describing the suffering of those who had sent him.[14] He petitioned the king to deliver them from their suffering and show them favor in the land of Poland.

51

Leszek was amazed. The speech spoke to his heart. He marveled at the stranger's modesty and manners. The horrifying picture of suffering and distress, which the speaker had described with such skill, touched him to the core. The young king of Poland passed on his inner feelings to the many courtiers who were standing about him. By his demeanor and the look on his face he gave the waiting emissaries to understand that they had not appealed to the grandson of Piast in vain. Encouraged by this, the strangers laid forth their requests: (1) that they be permitted to settle in the kingdom of Poland; (2) that the immigrants be allotted large tracts of land to farm;[15] (3) finally, that they be permitted to engage in crafts and trades as they requested.

Growing increasingly friendly, the king asked the Jews a number of questions about their religion. They replied with insight and always to the ruler's full satisfaction. The reader will allow us to present some of the king's questions and the Jews' responses.[16]

To the first question: "What is the essence of the Jewish religion?"

They replied: "The Jews believe in an unseen, eternal, and omnipotent entity that cannot be divided, Who created everything, rules over everything, and directs everything."

When the delegation was asked: "What do the Jews believe with regard to the soul?

They replied: "We believe that the power of thought resides in the soul. We believe it is immortal and independent of the putrefaction of the visible body."

To the king's question: "Are Jews, according to their belief, subject to divine vengeance when they transgress against other persons?"

The strangers replied: "Certainly. The smallest sin against innocent persons is written down against us and we are punished severely for it."

To the question: "Do the Jews consider those who totally disagree with them to be human beings?"

They replied to the royal investigator: "Anyone who can think and speak is a human being and must be treated as such."

The king: "But such a person is totally at odds with your opinions and rules of conduct."

The emissaries: "As human beings we can judge and decide regarding acts that involve human beings, but not those that relate to God. In those matters God alone has the right to judge."

The ruler of Poland asked next: "How did you behave when persons of foreign birth asked to be accepted in your ancient homeland?"

The delegation: "In the manner that God and mankind demand of us."

The king: "Is there anything in your law codes about tolerance?"

The delegation: "Absolutely. Permit us to present to you, on this matter, a number of passages from our Writings."

Leszek consented. The delegation proceeded:

"You shall not wrong a stranger or oppress him, for you were strangers in the land of Egypt. (Ex. 22:20)

"You shall not oppress a stranger, for you know the feelings of the stranger, having yourselves been strangers in the land of Egypt. (Ex. 23:9)

"When a stranger resides with you in your land, you shall not wrong him. The stranger who resides with you shall be to you as one of your citizens; you shall love him as you love yourself, for you were strangers in the land of Egypt; I the Lord, am your God. (Lev. 19:33–34)

"[The Lord] upholds the cause of the fatherless and the widow, and befriends the stranger, providing him with food and clothing. You too must befriend the stranger, for you were strangers in the land of Egypt." (Deut. 10:18–19)

They also cited Deuteronomy 24:19 and 26:11.[17]

Leshek was extremely satisfied and ended the audience, saying that he had to consult with the priests of his Gods. After that he would convey his final decision to them.

Three days later the delegation was summoned into the king's presence again. He informed them that he would be extremely happy to admit a people like the Jews to his kingdom. As for allowing them to live in separate settlements, he could not allow this for certain reasons, but he would allow them to settle wherever they wished, to engage in agriculture, to raise livestock, and to engage in crafts and trades.

After they prostrated themselves at the feet of the noble ruler, they thanked him and his councillors in heartfelt words that expressed their profound gratitude. Then the jubilant emissaries hurried back to Germany to bring the good tidings of their mission as fast as possible to their brethren, who were waiting for it with bated breath.

When the Jews heard the good news, life returned to their encampment. The dirge vanished from their lips, the tears disappeared from their eyelashes, their brows were no longer furrowed. Everything had changed. The suffering turned into joy, the pain into hope, the agony into comfort. When fortune's wheel turns upside down, one is well-advised to lay aside the pen and allow readers to ponder for themselves. And so we do here. . . .

A year later, in A.M. 4654 [894 C.E.], a large contingent of Jews arrived in Poland. The strangers' oriental garb sparked interest. Everyone crowded around the immigrants and stared in amazement, from their feet up to their heads and back again down to their feet. The superstitious Poles thought them beings from another world. Wherever the Jews went they were ogled and stared out. Every place they were greeted kindly. People offered to help and serve them and were hospitable.

Some eleven years later, in A.M. 4665 (905 C.E.), the Jews in Poland were accorded the following privileges: (1) freedom of settlement; (2) freedom of worship;[18] (3) the right to maintain their own courts of law; (4) an unlimited right to transport and occupations; (5) independence of the nobles;[19] (6) strong protection against hostile attacks.

On the basis of these privileges the Jews built houses, farmed, and engaged in many occupations, crafts, and trades. Little by little they forgot the pain and suffering of the bygone times.[20]

This legend preserves, for the most part, the poetics of the folk narrative, as reflected in the dialogue, repetition, tripling, characterization, and other details. One can only conjecture about the form in which the oral legend circulated in Jewish society. The transcription, for its part, has historiographical pretensions. Names and dates are given—the date of the emissaries' departure from Germany, the date of the Jews' arrival in Poland, and the date when they are supposed to have received the first privileges. Historical research rejects most of these dates for the initial settlement of Jews in Poland. Even Kraushar, who would like to view the Jews of Poland as autochthonous, states that there is no evidence that Jews were granted privileges in Poland before Bolesław of Kalisz did so in 1264 (Kraushar 1862).

It is important to note that the first sources of this story were transcribed in non-Jewish languages—German and Polish. The German texts, like the story above, describe the situation in Germany before the Jews fled and the reason for their emigration. Here a legend of origin is contained within another legend of origin: incorporated in a legend of origin about the Jews' reception in Poland is a legend of origin about the Jews' arrival in Germany from the south, their peaceful life in Germany before the arrival of Christianity, and the subsequent end of this tranquility. The story also includes some of Weinryb's basic themes of legends of origin: the antiquity of the Jews' settlement in the country, their enjoyment of equal rights in the past, and the abrogation of these rights in a later period (see Chapter 1). It may be assumed that this section was intended for the German audience and was accompanied by implications for Jewish emancipation, appropriate to the time and place.

In contrasting Germans and Poles, the legend commends the latter, who accepted the Jews. Leszek receives the Jews cordially and unconditionally, though only after an inquiry into the tenets of their religion and their customs and after consultations with his priests. He does not ask for anything in return, in contrast to the tale cited by Birkenthal (see above). The legend is clearly imbued with a Jewish sense of gratitude toward the Poles.

The Jews, too, are depicted in a respectful manner. A key factor contributing to this is the emissaries' high rank and occupations.[21] Historians have cited their Spanish names as evidence of tale's fictional nature. Indeed, where do they come from? Were the narrators seeking to add an

Michał Stachowicz, "Lech the First Announcing Gniezno as the Capital of Poland." Originally a wall painting that was destroyed by fire in 1850. Lithography according to a copy by Zygmunt Bogusz Stęczyński. From Julian Máslanka, *Literatura A Dzieje Bajeczne* (Warsaw: Państwowe Wydawnictwo Naukowe, 1984).

exotic oriental element to their tale? Do they represent an attempt by refugees from the Iberian peninsula who settled in Poland to forge a link between Spain and the origins of Jewish settlement in Poland by giving the refugees from Germany a south European origin, thereby increasing their own prestige and asserting their common origin with the Jews already living in Poland? We shall return to these questions later. The chief speaker's mastery of Latin and his oration, which makes an impression on the king, elevate his image and that of the community that he represents. The presentation of the main tenets of the Jewish religion and especially the Biblical passages relating to non-Jews seek to highlight the social elements, aesthetic elements (the Jews would like, inter alia, to engage in crafts), and principally the humanistic elements of the Jewish religion, so important in the nineteenth century to those who sought to integrate into non-Jewish society.

The story incorporates a number of Weinryb's themes: the Jews settled in Poland in pagan times, during the reign of the legendary King Leszek of the House of Piast (on the House of Piast, see Chapter 3); the king granted the Jews permission to settle there; in the past they enjoyed many privileges and friendliness from the Poles, which is described hyperbolically in the story; the Jews brought with them the traditions of an older center of Jewish life–in Germany and perhaps even Spain.

In this tale the fundamental opposition between Jews and Poles is augmented by additional elements, as shown in Figure 3. Here we have a model of associates and cooperation between two peoples, in contrast to the model in Reb Dov-Ber Birkenthal's story, as seen in Figure 4.

In contrast to the segregationist model presented by the eighteenth-century Hebrew legend, the legend first published in non-Jewish languages by nineteenth-century historians presents a model of interaction and co-operation. This suited the historiography of the nineteenth century, which was influenced by liberalism and progressive ideas and especially by the struggle for emancipation, whose cause it served. The legend of origin provided additional ammunition in the general arsenal wielded to achieve political and social benefits within the Jewish community and in the ties between the Jews and the outside world. And, as Shatzmiller notes in his discussion of origin myths, in certain periods the story was more effective and more attractive than a factual and historical discussion because it gave it an aura of eternity (Shatzmiller 1985, 49–61).

"FIRST ACQUAINTANCE": FROM INDULGENCE TO EQUALITY

Located somewhere between these two models–the segregationist model represented by the legend of Dov-Ber Birkenthal, in which only the Jews act as donors, and the model of interaction and cooperation represented by the legend of the emissaries, in which only the Poles act as donors–is a third legend of acceptance, also from the nineteenth century. Transcribed by Marek Dubs, it appeared in 1861 in the Polish-language Jewish pe-riodical *Jutrzenka* (Dubs 1861, 7:50–52; 8:58–60). Dubs was a Jew who attained many honors for the period. He was a delegate to the Galician Sejm (parliament), a member of the council of the Agricultural Com-pany, and a member of the urban department. He was frequently called to consult with the authorities on public affairs. An editor's note states that the tale is part of a larger work and that the story about the Jews' arrival and reception in Poland is a typical Jewish legend. Introducing the story, Dubs notes that it is a folk story full of innocence and good-heartedness which merits attention. As stated, the story was published in Polish. The question of the language and venue of publication will be treated below.

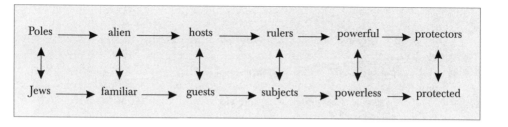

Figure 3

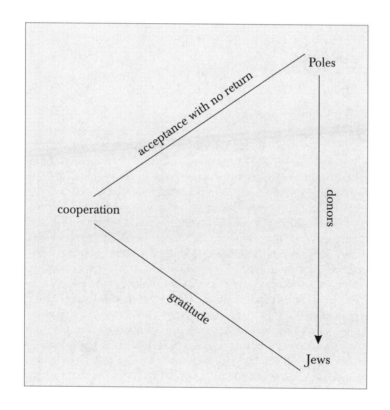

Figure 4

First Acquaintance

It was from Germany—so relates the folk tradition—that the Jews came to Poland. The hand of God guided the Jewish people and preserved them in their wanderings from valley to mountain and mountain to valley, through forests and across rivers. When they left Germany, this community, which, though large, possessed much gold and silver, took along its scholarly rabbi, the cantor of the synagogue, and a number of craftsman. With great care they wrapped several copies of the holy books of Moses, written on parchment, and wrapped in cloth of gold, to serve the new community that would be established. Each scroll was ornamented with a silver crown, a silver breastplate, and a silver hand to guide the reader. Beyond these, they made do with a single copy of the midrashic writings and a copy of the Mishna and Gemara. Several carts laden with merchandise bore the private property of a number of these Jews. One cart, shared by all, contained goods to be given as a present to the prince. When they drew near to the place where the Poles lived, they unfurled a white banner, which bore on one side a lion with the Hebrew inscription, "Judah is a lion's whelp" [Gen. 49:9] and, on the other side, the Hebrew inscription "the standard of the camp of Judah" [Num. 2:3].

A horseman clothed in white, riding a white steed and bearing the white banner in his hand, addressed the prince and asked him to receive the delegation of the Jewish community that was approaching. The prince, who practiced the hospitality of the patriarch Abraham, consented. He dispatched an elderly grandee and six young courtiers to greet the delegation. The nobles stationed themselves under the shade of a large linden tree, which was in flower just then, to wait for the approaching visitors. The horseman with the white banner rode back to the Jews' camp with all his strength. When they heard the good tidings that the prince had sent lords to greet them and they were waiting for their envoys, the men considered it to be the dictate of conscience and prudence to select three of their most dignified fellows, fluent speakers of Polish, to serve as their representatives and meet the noblemen, and also to study the mood of this people, about whom they knew nothing.

The three emissaries were joined by the rabbi and the cantor of the synagogue. The white-bearded rabbi carried the Torah scroll, with its ornaments described above. This was the only weapon carried by the delegation, which lacked all other means of defense. There was actually an important reason for choosing three emissaries. The newly arrived community wanted to ask three crucial questions. For each question they appointed a separate envoy. The first and oldest among them was to raise the question of murder— an important question indeed! For this reason he was called the emissary of murder. The second, somewhat younger than the first, was to ask about robbery. He was called the emissary of robbery. The third and youngest was told to ask about settlement. He was called the emissary of settlement. The envoys selected were best suited to the task among all the community, on account of both their sumptuous garments and their attractive appearance.

The procession set off. At its head was the horseman garbed in white, astride the white horse and bearing the white banner. The emissaries, the rabbi, and the cantor marched in stately order behind him.

When the rabbi gave a signal, the cantor began to sing in Hebrew the 114th Psalm, which was appropriate to the situation of the small community. For it reads:

When Israel went forth from Egypt, the house of Jacob from a people of strange speech, Judah became His holy one, Israel, his dominion. The sea saw them and fled, Jordan ran backward, mountains skipped like rams, hills like sheep. What alarmed you, O sea, that you fled, Jordan, that you ran backward, mountains, that you skipped like rams, hills, like sheep? Tremble, O earth, at the presence of the Lord, at the presence of the God of Jacob, who turned the rock into a pool of water, the flinty rock into a fountain.

It was a wonderful song. The birds stopped flying and left off chirping in order to hear it better. The people in the fields laid down their tools when they saw the strangers. If at first they were gripped by fear, this quickly gave way to amazement. They did not understand a single word of the Hebrew psalm, but nevertheless sensed that it was a prayer intended to extol the Almighty.

When the song was over the procession halted, for the rabbi gave a sign that he wished to speak. All turned toward the speaker and listened attentively to the following sermon: "Almighty God created weak man, breathed a soul into him, and gave him the earth as his inheritance. He gave him commandments to guide his life in this vale of tears. Furthermore, he left him the freedom to choose between good and evil, the freedom to cast himself into the abyss of sin and the possibility to rise with his good deeds and merge his spirit with that of the Almighty.

"Our fathers, who had this freedom of choice, sinned and are no more, and we suffer for their transgressions. On account of these transgressions our ancestors were banished from their land, the land that is holy to God. They witnessed the burning of the Temple of the Lord and the delivery of the Jewish people into the pitiless hands of the cruel Romans.

"From that time and until today we live among alien nations. The vicissitudes of fate toss us about like chaff in the wind. We saved almost nothing from the ship of our sovereignty when it ran aground, except for our faith. Do you think that belief in God is a small matter? I say to you, when we save our faith we save everything. What value is there to property, which the hand of chance can destroy? What value is there to treasures, which the first brigand can steal from us? But let all the rulers of the world try to deprive believers of their faith—will they succeed? Let all the forces of Satan unite, let them seduce and charm, let them act in anger armed with an iron scourge, let them gather all their forces; they cannot turn good into evil. And so it is, dear brothers: hidden in our Talmud, which was saved, there is might, the might of belief. Let us choose our path to God as we were taught by Moses and the prophets.

"We are going to meet a new people. Let us endeavor to be accepted by them, and even more. By living exemplary lives of labor and modesty we can acquire the inhabitants' friendship. Let our exemplary conduct add new luster to the tarnished name of Israel. Let us raise our souls to God and all difficulties will vanish. The sea of hatred will not cover us; no, it will flee from us. The Jordan of persecution will flow backward. Every type of obstructing mountain will skip like rams to clear a path for us, and so will the small hills of evil, which have not yet grown to the height of mountains. The kids that, were we lost, would turn into rams, they too will retreat from our path. Should you ask what miracle can work this, make the sea of hatred part, the Jordan of persecution flow backward, the mountains and hills of hostility skip? I will answer you in the words of the psalm: 'Tremble, O earth, at the presence of the Lord, at the presence of the God of Jacob,' He who turns the rock of a hard heart into a pool of mercy and the flint of evil into a fountain of love for one's fellows."

Here the rabbi's voice fell silent. His audience, strongly moved, wept, whether from joy or sadness they could not say. "And now let us go in the name of God," continued the rabbi after a moment's pause. "Let us go and the Almighty will guide our steps."

The procession continued on its way. When the emissaries saw from afar the great linden tree, with several armed knights standing in its shade, they asked the rabbi in what manner the encounter would take place. "With prayers and blessings," replied the rabbi. He added, "The prayers and blessings will be recited aloud and translated into Polish by the first emissary."

As they drew near the linden tree, their hearts, except for the rabbi's, pounded ever more forcefully. You could read their fear on every face. They certainly had cause to be afraid. An encounter between the defenseless and those who are armed, between weak and strong, can expose the former to great danger. As they approached and could make out from close up the expression on the faces of the waiting knights, though, each felt an upsurge of hope at the sight of the magnanimity and benevolence reflected in the men's faces. The elderly Polish nobleman who stood at the head of the group looked sympathetically at the approaching strangers.

When they were only a few dozen paces away from the linden tree, the rabbi recited a short prayer, and the first emissary translated it aloud into Polish. The end of the prayer was: "Magnified and sanctified be His great name in the world that He created according to His will. May His kingdom be established in your lives and your days and the life of the whole house of Israel, speedily and soon. Now say: Amen."[22]

"Amen," replied the emissaries.

"Amen," said the old nobleman, followed by the others. It would be hard to describe their astonishment at the sound of the Jews' prayer in Polish, a prayer that reminded them of their own daily prayers.

After this the rabbi recited a blessing in Hebrew and the first emissary translated it aloud. One could see joy on the noblemen's faces when they heard the words of the Torah: "May the Lord bless you and protect you! May the Lord make His face shine upon you and be gracious to you. May the Lord bestow His favor upon you and grant you peace." [Numbers 6:24–27]

"Greetings to the best people on the face of the earth," called the old nobleman. The elderly Pole's festive salutation breathed new hope into the emissaries, who, along with the rabbi, marched ceremoniously up to the nobles. The emissaries fell at their feet, while the rabbi, the Torah scroll in his arms, gazed on the scene without moving, for the word of the Lord does not bow or bend down before any man.

The elderly nobleman extended his hand to the messengers and bade them stand up. They rose, and the first one addressed him as follows:

"I was sent to you, honorable lord from a race of heroes, by my brothers, the children of Israel. Mine is an important mission–to ask you the first question. I am the emissary of murder."

When he heard these words, an unpleasant expression appeared on the old man's face. He had already made a gesture as if he was about to take hold of his weapon, but, fortunately, the emissary's next words reassured him completely.

"It's this way," he continued. "I must ask you an important question. Will you murder us? We are the descendants of the patriarchs, Abraham, Isaac, and Jacob. We bear with us the Holy Law of Moses. We believe in God who created the heaven and the earth. I repeat my question: Will you murder us?"

"The nobles of Poland are not murderers," replied the old grandee solemnly.

The first emissary withdrew and the second one took his place.

"I was sent to you, noble lord, by my brothers, by the people chosen by God. Once we had our own land, our own law, and our own king. But in the fullness of time we lost our homeland. Since then we live modestly among the nations, supporting ourselves from trade and crafts. We wish to trade with you. We have various goods and gold and silver coins. But covetousness is part of human nature, so we and our possessions are exposed to great danger. Therefore I was charged to ask this important question: Will you rob us?"

"The nobles of Poland are not brigands," the old man answered without losing his patience.

The second emissary withdrew and his place was taken by the third.

"Most powerful lord," he addressed the old man, "my two predecessors found favor with you. Please allow me, as the third emissary of the community of Israel, to ask you a third and last question. To carry on our crafts and commerce we need a place, a permanent residence. I make bold to request an answer to the following question: Will you allow us to settle among you?"

"The nobles of Poland practice hospitality toward strangers," replied the honest old man.

"Long live the nobles of Poland!" acclaimed the newcomers and signaled the horseman on his white steed to gallop back to the rest of the community with the news of the positive outcome of their mission.

The emissaries, accompanied by the rabbi and the cantor, proceeded on to the prince. After they were presented to him with due pomp, they received his confirmation of the promise given by the nobles.

The next day the small community settled down in peace and freedom among the Polish people. They made the prince a gift, the cart laden with fabrics, as a memento of their first encounter. Thus was struck the pact between the Jews and the land of the Piasts.

This story is quite similar to that of the emissaries with regard to its model of Polish-Jewish relations and is the antithesis of the model created by Birkenthal's story. Nevertheless, there is a material difference between the two related stories: whereas the story of the emissaries creates a model of cooperation based on the Jews' gratitude at the favor extended them by their hosts in bygone days, the model advanced by the later story is one of greater equality. Here, too, Polish society is characterized by nobility of spirit. The men are God-fearing, handsome, and, most important, hospitable. In the answers of the Polish noblemen from the period of initial settlement, the nineteenth-century legend conveys the model of conduct that the Jews expect of the Polish people—that is, the Poles of the nineteenth century, like the Polish aristocracy of the past, should not murder, rob, or act in contradiction to the custom of hospitality toward the Jews. In this story, too, no considerations of profit enter into the decision to accept the strangers. Alongside the Jews' gratitude, the legend creates a more even balance between the two peoples. The Jewish community is imposing, distinguished by its wealth; this hints at its potential contribution to their new home. It is also distinguished by its spiritual life, as reflected in the description of the holy books, the figure of the rabbi, the psalm that is chanted, and the sermon, prayer, and blessing. The narrator lingers over the Jews' handsome faces, describes the horseman in his white raiment and the banner with its ancient Jewish symbols, the festive nature of the procession, and the pride of the rabbi, who does not bow before princes. All of this produces a further analogy between the two peoples. Even the Jewish prayer reminds the Poles of their own daily liturgy.

Although the Jews are accepted unconditionally, they make the king a generous gift as a token of thanks for the graciousness of their reception. The words of the rabbi promise that they will lead an exemplary life among the host nation: "We are going to meet a new people. Let us endeavor to be accepted by them, and even more. By living exemplary lives of labor and modesty we can acquire the inhabitants' friendship. Let our exemplary conduct add new luster to the tarnished name of Israel."

The legend depicts Jews and Poles as both donors and receivers and lays the ground for equal cooperation between the two nations (see Figure 5).

Another important element in this story is the division of the emissaries into two categories with different roles to play. The emissaries of the Jewish religion, represented by the rabbi and the cantor, are presented as the authorized representatives of the Jewish faith; none disputes their authority and leadership. The second category of emissaries is chosen by virtue of outward appearance and garb—that is, the ability to win favor—as well as by command of the Polish language, which enables them to communicate with the ruling nation. This is even encouraged by the rabbi, who says, "The prayers and blessings will be recited aloud and translated into Polish by the first emissary."

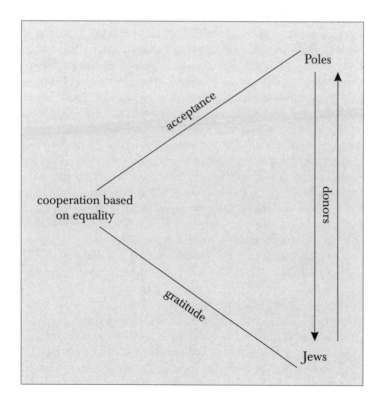

Figure 5

The legend characterizes the community as God-fearing, stately, dignified, and proud of its traditional spiritual leadership. But it also stresses the importance of adaptability and understanding and emphasizes that knowledge of the language and culture of the ruling nation is a prerequisite for cooperation and equality with it. This message is directed internally. The legend creates a narrative metaphor for the world view of the journal in which it was published.

As early as 1841, Jacob Tagendhold gave voice to the aspirations of the Jewish *maskilim* to publish a Polish-language periodical, which, in his words, "would help disseminate among Polish Jews a genuine moral enlightenment as well as love for the social virtues and productive labor" (Zinberg 1971, 52). It was only in the aftermath of increased social ferment in Poland and the rise of national aspirations among the Polish nobility and intelligentsia (which led to the second Polish insurrection against the Russians in 1863) that "the problem of the Polish-Jewish nation" surfaced in the Polish press as well. The justice minister in Warsaw, Prince Wielopolski, formally declared that the Jews should be granted equal rights.

This was the background for the decision by the Warsaw Jewish intelligentsia to publish a periodical with the objective, in the words of Marcus Jastrow, of "influencing the Jews and weakening the prejudices against us in the society around us" (Zinberg 1971, 53). The first issue of *Jutrzenka*, edited by Daniel Neufeld (1814–74),[23] appeared on 5 July 1861. It favored the Polonization of Polish Jewry (Shmeruk 1978, 262). The inaugural editorial noted that *Jutrzenka*'s goal was to increase the productive forces among the Jews in science and the arts, commerce and industry, and crafts and agriculture. It would also seek to spread the language of the homeland among all strata of the Israelite population (Zinberg 1971, 54).

From the remarks of Jastrow and Neufeld, we learn that the periodical had two target audiences: Poles, among whom it wished to weaken anti-Jewish prejudices, and Jews, to whom it wished to convey the message of Polonization. In their discussions of *Jutrzenka,* both Zinberg and Shmeruk note that the language to be used for Jewish literature and journalism became a key issue and the major focus of the journal and its editor, Daniel Neufeld. This sentiment was reflected in *Jutrzenka*'s campaign against Yiddish, which it deprecated as the "detestable jargon," the "worthless dialect," and "babbling" (*szwargot*); only its total abandonment could permit the Polonization of Polish Jewry (Shmeruk 1978, 261–262).[24]

The version of the legend of acceptance published in *Jutrzenka*, which, according to Marek Dubs, embodied the innocence and magnanimity of the Jewish people, expressed the historical situation of the conflict of forces in Jewish society, the cultural problem of the time and place, and the world view that the periodical sought to disseminate through the medium of a folk legend. The legend conveys the message of Jewish involvement in Polish

JUTRZENKA

TYGODNIK DLA IZRAELITÓW POLSKICH.

POD REDAKCYĄ

Daniela Neufelda.

ROK I[szy]

NUMER 1 — 26.

WARSZAWA.

GŁÓWNY SKŁAD W KSIĘGARNI H. Natansona.

1861.

Front page of the periodical *Jutrzenka*.

society on the basis of equality. The message is intended not only for the Jews but also, and perhaps mainly, for nineteenth-century Polish society: the legend depicts relations of this sort and presents them as stipulated, in the early years of Poland, by the dignified Polish nobility. The author appends to the legend his own wish, with rhetorical flourish: "Would that this enchanted moment of first love might blossom forever!" The legend incorporates another important message for Jewish society, however. It seeks to reassure the general Jewish public about the Jewish intelligentsia, who recognize the central place of the traditional religious leadership but realize that, without the existence of a mediating agency in Jewish society–one integrated into the culture and language of the country–the kind of communication that can guarantee the tranquil life the Jews long for is impossible in Poland.

CONDITIONAL ACCEPTANCE:
THE JEWS AS RAIN-BRINGERS

In Menaḥem Naḥum Litinski's *The Book of the Annals of Podolia and Jewish Antiquities There,* published in 1895, we find another story of acceptance. In its main details, this story corresponds with the legend of the emissaries presented above. There is a substantial difference between them, however: a condition. The king agrees to allow the Jews to settle in Poland on condition that they bring the rains in due season. The condition alters the model presented in the legend of the emissaries, where there is an unconditional favor and gratitude toward those who offer it. Litinski's story runs as follows.

> In the year 893, emissaries of the Jews of Germany–Rabbi Hezekiah the Spaniard, Rabbi Akiva Estremaduri, Rabbi Emanuel of Ascalon the ge-ometer, Rabbi Levi Bakhri the orator, and Rabbi Nathanael of Barcelona–arrived in the city of Gniessin, which was the seat of Duke Lesek of Poland (he was the second duke from the House of Piast), seeking refuge and shelter in his land for their fellow Jews, because of the wars of religion that had just broken out in Germany and from which they had suffered greatly. After the duke consulted with his priests in the temple of his gods, he showed them favor and told Rabbi Levi Bakhri, who was the chief speaker in Latin, that he would give them permission to come to Poland and live wherever they wished on condition that they would undertake to bring the rain in due season through their prayers. The next year, in 894, many Jews came to Poland from Germany, and in 895 Duke Lesek granted them privileges according to which they had the following rights:
>   1. To live in all the duke's dominions, wherever they saw fit;
>   2. To worship their God according to their religion, without hindrance;
>   3. To judge their community according to Jewish law;

4. To deal in every craft and profession;

5. To be subject to the king alone and not to the princes and lords of the country.

6. The government will shield and protect them against all foes and adversaries.[25] (Litinski 1895, 18–19).

Two explanations for the discrepancy presents themselves: (1) The rain-bringing theme is a supplement to the story of the emissaries; or, more plausibly, (2) the legend of the emissaries, as it circulated orally, included the condition of bringing rain, but it was removed from the version published in foreign languages for the twin reasons that a sacred legend is incompatible with a historical chronicle and that it did not suit the world view of the retellers. We shall return to this question later.

Stories about rainmaking constitute a well-known Jewish oicotype about which much has been written (Hirshberg 1945, 46–54; Patai 1939, 251–286; Noy 1959b, 34–45; Schwarzbaum 1993a, 84–95; Bar-Itzhak 1978, 62–68). In most cases the rain falls through the merits of a righteous man, a *tzaddik,* usually a hidden *tzaddik.* The folk narratives of Polish Jews, however, include legends that associate rainmaking with a request by the Polish ruler. In these legends we find a motif similar to that in the legends of acceptance. This is the case, for example, in the story told by Pinhas Guterman from Michow in Poland (IFA 2550).[26] His tale, set in the time of Casimir the Great, the last ruler of the House of Piast[27]–that is, in a period later than the story of acceptance–deals with a severe drought in Poland. When the Poles' prayers are not answered, Casimir the Great dispatches a decree to the Jewish town, ordaining that "the Jews go to the synagogues to recite a prayer for rain to the God of Israel." The Jews comply with the king's order and proclaim a public fast. After they have recited the prayer for rain and the evening service, it begins to drizzle, and the shower turns into a downpour that continues day and night.[28] All acknowledge that the rains are falling because of the God of Israel and because of the Jews who put their trust in Him. The conclusion creates a clear link with the legend of acceptance: "Since then the rains have begun in Poland on time; to this day, the rains fall in due season."

Folk legends also present the association between the Jews' prayers and the fertility of the fields as a belief prevalent among the Gentiles. We find this, for example, in "The Man Who Prayed in the Water Channel," reprinted by Ben-Yehezkel from *The Works of Righteous Men,* published in Warsaw in 1898. The story involves a non-Jew who comes to Rabbi Abraham the tavernkeeper:

"You have been the tavernkeeper in the village for years," the Gentile began.

"You certainly know the custom of the farmers, that we sow our fields

67

Artur Markowicz, "Prayer." Painting. With kind permission of the Jewish Historical Institute, Warsaw.

during your Days of Awe, that is, on the two days of the New Year and on the Day of Atonement, because we have found it to be tried and proven: If we sow when the Jews are standing close together, the grain will stand tall and close together and be blessed. (Ben-Yehezkel 1961, 281)

Later we shall see how Agnon used this motif in his version of the legend of acceptance, "Rain." We see, then, that one of the legends of acceptance of Polish Jewry linked their admission to Poland with the condition that they bring rain at the appropriate time. The same motif is found in their legends that are not directly associated with their arrival in the country, as is the association that their neighbors make between the Jews and the fertility of the fields.

Most elements of this legend of acceptance are identical to those in the legend of the emissaries, including the favor displayed by the Poles when they admitted the Jews to their country. But the conditional acceptance of the Jews–they must bring rain in due season–moves the legend closer to the world view embodied in the story presented by Dov-Ber Birkenthal, namely, that the Jews were admitted conditionally and because it was

ספר

קוֹרוֹת פֶּאדָאלִיָא וְקַדְמוֹנִיוֹת הַיְהוּדִים שָׁם

או

חֹמֶר לְדִבְרֵי יְמֵי הַיְהוּדִים בְּרוּסְיָא

כולל

עניינים רבים הנוגעים לקורות מדינת פאדאליא מראשית ימי הוסדה
עד עתה, ולקורות בני ישראל שם מיום האהזם בה עד ימינו אלה,

חֻבְּרוּ בשלשה חלקים

עפ"י כתבי-יד עתיקים מדורות שעברו, כתבי-העדה והרשות, המפיצים אור על
קורות בני ישראל בפאדאליא, ויסדו על אדני החקירות בדברי-הימים להפלך
ההוא, לתועלת "דברי ימי עמנו" בארצנו, – וְעֻטְּרוֹ בהערות והגהות יקרות
מאת גדולי הוקרי עמנו בזמננו.

מנחם נחום בר' אברהם ז"ל ליטינסקי.

אדעססא, תרנ"ה.
בדפוס מ"א בעלינסאן.

"КОЙРОСЪ ПОДОЛІЯ",

Къ исторіи евреевъ въ Подоліи и очеркъ извѣстій
о Подольской губ.

или

Матеріалъ для составленіе "Исторіи евреевъ въ Россіи",

Составилъ по историческимъ источникамъ въ трехъ частяхъ

М. Н. ЛИТИНСКІЙ.

(часть I.)

ОДЕССА, Типографія, М. Бейленсона.

1895.

Title page of M. N. Litinski, *The Book of the Annals of Podolia and Jewish Antiquities There* (Odessa: M. A. Belinson, 1895).

profitable to do so. The condition is a metaphor for the Jews' insecurity and uncertainty in the host country. Each year they must prove afresh that they have fulfilled the condition and show that their tolerance is worthwhile.

Why should the condition be to bring rain in due season? Is this legend unique to the Jews of Poland or was it adopted from another source? A study of various Jewish legends of origin preserved in writing reveals that the admission of the Jews on condition that they bring rain (and the concomitant belief in their ability to do so) is found in another Jewish center–Spain. Here, too, we should recall Zinberg's assertion about the folk creation of Spanish Jewry: "There is no doubt that throughout this time original folk creation never ceased among the masses, not only for the people but also by the people. . . . The masses created legends, fairy tales, and songs in their vernacular. . . . But all this was oral" (Zinberg 1958, 7:13). Because the copying of manuscripts was expensive and had to be supported by the wealthy, writes Zinberg, "it is easy to understand why we do not find vernacular folk art. At the same time, folk works sometimes made their way into written literature, albeit in a changed form. . . . Because folk creation is essentially oral, almost all of it has been lost in its original form" (ibid., 14). Hence students of folk culture must rely on whatever written material has been preserved and on stories circulating today by word of mouth (if such stories are still part of the oral tradition). In a note to the story he presents, Litinski says that in the matter of bringing rain in due season he relies on a book by Epstein, *Chronicles of the Kings of Russia,* published in Vilna in 1873. According to a note in that volume, "the learned rabbi, our teacher Mordechai Plongien, told me that the book *Yad Avi-shalom* (weekly portion of *Emor*) cites in the name of *Zeror hamor* (weekly portion of *Behukkotai*) that when the Jews came to settle in Poland they undertook to bring the rains in due season with their prayers; otherwise the priests refused to admit them to that country" (Epstein 1873, 189). Epstein relies, then, on an oral communication or tradition that draws its source from the book *Zeror Ha'Mor* by Abraham Saba (d. 1508), who had been among those expelled from Spain.

An examination of *Zeror Ha'Mor*–first printed in 1567 and cited as the original source for the rainmaking theme–reveals, as we might have expected, that Poland is not mentioned at all. The story is related in general terms about the status of the Jews among the Gentiles; the only Diaspora specifically mentioned is the Iberian. Here is the relevant passage:

> He said, "I will grant your rains in their season" (Lev. 26:4), not "I will give you rains." This teaches that the rains are ours, as we read elsewhere: "The water is ours" (Gen. 26:20). *This was our glorious strength when the nations took us in, because we knew to bring the rains in due season.*[29] This is the meaning of the verse, "that great nation is a wise and discerning people" (Deut. 4:6).

70

They see the cantor wrapped in his prayer shawl and reciting the Thirteen Divine Attributes to bring the rain. This is why it says "your rain"–they belong to you. When He gives rain He is not doing you a favor. He said that they are yours. The favor is that the rains come in due season. This is [the meaning of] "I will grant your rains in their season." This signifies that they are ours because we accepted the Torah, which is called water, as it is written: "Ho, all who are thirsty, come for water" (Isa. 55:1). But the nations of the world, who did not want to accept the Torah, are not worthy of water; this is why it says, "your rains." (p. 32)

It says "your rains," because the rain is important. This is why [the Sages referred to the phrase added to the *Amida* prayer in the rainy season, "He causes the wind to blow and the rain to fall" as] "the might of the rains," namely, that they fall by virtue of His might, from the Holy One, blessed be He, and no other. As it says, "Can any of the false gods of the nations give rain?" (Jer. 14:22) They come down at the decree of the King and not according to the nature of the world, as was attested by Elijah, who said, "there will be no dew or rain except at my bidding" (1 Kings 17:1). This is the meaning of "I will give them water" (Num. 21:16). I give them, not you. According to this, then, the rains ought to belong to us, not to some other nation. This is why the verse "if you follow My laws"–rules that surpass human reason–is followed by "I will grant your rains in their season," for they too are the decree of the King and surpass human reason. And [the passage continues] that if you observe the Sabbatical year, it too a commandment surpassing human reason, then I will repay you measure for measure by granting your rains in their season. For it is appropriate that they be your rains and not another's. Because the rains are the epitome of all good, in this passage [the Torah] enumerates all of the good things that derive from them, namely: "the earth shall yield its produce and the trees of the field their fruit" (Lev. 26:4). That is, because you observe the Sabbatical year, the land will produce everything good for you–"the earth shall yield its produce and . . . your threshing will overtake the vintage . . . and I will grant peace in the land." If you observe the Sabbatical year you will not behold exile from the land and will have peace, for its peace will be your peace. (p. 32)

We have the power to bring down the rains in their season through our prayers. This is well known, *for it was on this condition that we were accepted in the Gentile land when we were exiled from our land. Something like this happened once in the kingdom of Aragon during a drought.* They threw the Jews out of the city and shut the gates in their faces until they brought water. (p. 34)

The midrash on the verse "I will grant your rains in their season" asserts that the rains belong to the Jews and not to any other nation because Jews are the only ones who accepted the Torah, which is compared to water. That the rains fall in due season, however, is a favor granted by the Holy One, blessed be He, to Israel. The favor is dependant on whether "you

71

follow My laws," that is, the observance of the Torah and commandments. From this ensues the Jews' ability to bring rains in due season by means of their prayers. *Zeror Ha'Mor* states that the Gentiles, too, believed in the Jews' rainmaking powers. Their ability was known among the Gentiles, "for it was on this condition that we were accepted in the Gentile land when we were exiled from our land." The specific case mentioned is a drought in the kingdom of Aragon. Nevertheless, the general stipulation concerning acceptance among the Gentiles permitted other communities to adopt the story for themselves.

Incidentally, *Yad Avi-Shalom*,[30] cited by Epstein's informant, does not mention Poland either. Its author, relying on *Zeror Ha'Mor*, writes:

> It is written in *Zeror Ha'Mor* for the weekly portion of *Behukkotai*, on the verse "I will break your proud glory" (Lev. 26:19), that Israel has the power, through prayer, to bring rain, and that it was on this condition that the Gentiles accepted them in their land. Once there was a drought and an elder admonished them. He began: "The water is ours"—we have the power to bring them down with our prayers. The explanation is that the nations did not want to admit us to their lands, saying, "they have no portion in this world." But they accepted us because we could bring down rain, and there is no life without water. So they get more benefit from Israel than Israel gets from them. (ibid., weekly portion of *Emor*, p. 46)

Further investigation reveals that *Zeror Ha'Mor*, to which Litinski and Epstein refer, is not the only source for a Spanish Jewish story that makes the Jews' ability to bring down rain a condition for their acceptance by Christians. The notion appears several times in Shlomo Ibn Virga's *Shevet Yehudah*, where we read about the dispute between King Alfonso of Portugal and Don Joseph Ibn Yahya. The latter begins:

> "With regard to the matter of bringing rain, our Talmud tells of several righteous men who did this. In addition, the Christians ask the Jews of Toledo to bring rain, and they do so through their prayers. . . ."
>
> After this the king asked: "Why was David chosen to be king rather than Saul? The latter displayed extraordinary compassion when he did not want to kill the Amaleqite children. He also displayed holiness: even though Samuel told him that he and his sons would die on the morrow, he did not hesitate to go out like one going to his wedding canopy."
>
> Tomas replied: "Had he asked and pleaded, the Lord would have turned him away. But if David wept, the Lord would have forgiven him at once."
>
> The king said, "*now I know why the Jews are answered when there is a drought!*"
>
> The viceroy replied, "I do not think so. Rather, the Lord hates them. He grants their request so that they will not return to stand before him again." (Ibn Virga 1946–47, 142, 158)

According to Shimon Bernstein, in his study of the *diwan* of sacred poetry of Shlomo Ben-Meshulam Da Pierra:[31]

> Historians of the Jews in the Hispanic lands have noted that the Jews of Spain were in the custom of praying frequently for rain. Some saw this as representing an attempt by the Jews to have something in common with the Catholic majority, who conducted many religious processions to ward off drought–a custom still to be seen there today. It is known that the Jews in Spain sometimes prayed for rain at the request and perhaps even the *demand* of their Christian neighbors, who believed that the Jews' prayers had some special power to bring rain. (Bernstein 1945–46, XIX: 5)

Here Bernstein cites the passage from *Shevet Yehudah* about the residents of Toledo who asked the Jews to bring rain, which they did through prayer.

We see, then, that the story about the Jews' power to bring rain in due season, the Gentiles' belief in this capacity, and the Jews' acceptance by the nations because of this power was part of the folk tradition of Spanish Jewry. Folk tales circulating orally today still preserve this tradition, though with no substantial link to legends of origin (IFA 3841, 9236, 10620).

Did the story develop independently in the two diasporas or was it brought to Poland from Spain, either in written sources known to Polish Jewry[32] or through stories recounted by Spanish exiles who reached Poland? Although we cannot provide a definite answer to this question, the Spanish names of the emissaries and the speaker's command of Latin lend weight to the latter hypothesis.[33] Even so, specifying the source of the legend cannot explain its vitality among Polish Jewry. Here I accept the statement by Sara Zefatman, who writes, in her discussion of the legends of foundation of the Jews of Spain and Germany: "Even though we must not reject out of hand the possibility that familiarity with a particular narrative form, imported from one society to another, may spawn its sporadic repetition in the receiving society, this is not enough to maintain a long-living narrative tradition. Certainly it is not enough to nurture its repeated retelling–an essential action if folk creation is to survive and remain vital" (Zefatman 1993, 129). The same argument applies to legends of origin (within which legends of foundation are a subcategory): only social and cultural problems common to the two communities can engender common poetic solutions (Zefatman 1993). This joins up with Weinryb's analysis (see Chapter 1), which points to the similarity in the legends of origin of various Diaspora communities and ascribes it to their comparable positions–the need of a minority group settled among another people to deal with dangerous situations.

The peril looming over the Jews in Christian countries stemmed not only from their being a minority that adhered to its religion in a period of Church intolerance, but also from the fact that in medieval Christian

Europe, dominated by a dread of sorcery and magic, the Jews were seen as magicians or sorcerers endowed with supernatural knowledge and mastery of charms and talismans. This belief did not disappear from Europe in later centuries; the Jew, as the embodiment of the Other, was still being accused of magical practices even in later periods, albeit with decreasing frequency (Trachtenberg 1939, 1–10; 1993, 57–76). That the Jews could not avoid dealing with their neighbors' belief in their preternatural powers is reflected in Jewish folk narrative as well. Consider, for example, the famous legend cited by Natan Nata Hanover in his book *Yeven Mezulah* (Hannover 1968, 39): Here the maid of Nemirov exploits the Cossack's belief that she knows a charm against bullets; she tricks him into killing her, thereby avoiding a forced marriage.

The story of acceptance on condition of bringing rain in due season represents a Jewish response to the Gentiles' belief. In both Spain and Poland the Jewish legend traces the source of the power to observance of the Torah and commandments. It is also associated with the third theme in Weinryb's scheme, namely, that the Jews contribute to the country and rescue it from disasters (including plague, drought, and the like). It seems to me, though, that the latent significance of the legend goes beyond the theme of contribution and rescue. Weinryb sees no further, as I have already noted, because he examined the legends of origin as directed outward, toward the majority before whom the Jews must justify their residence in its land. Hence Weinryb gives short shrift to the inward-directed meaning intended for the narrating (minority) society.

What is the latent meaning of the rainmaking story as a legend of acceptance? What social and cultural problems does it represent? Unlike the other legends of acceptance, this one has a distinctly theological core, built on the link between the Jews and their God. True, the other legends, especially "First Acquaintance," also radiate a holy atmosphere; but their plots do not involve supernatural occurrences such as rainmaking. This legend aims to give the narrating society a sense of power and superiority. The rains are "ours" and fall in due season as a direct result of the special bond between the Jews and their God, a bond of faith and observance of the commandments that allows them a charm denied the ruling nations. The legend reinforces the ego of the narrating society by giving it a sense of spiritual superiority. That a people dependent on the good graces of another and persecuted for its faith need such reinforcement is obvious and comprehensible.

The rainmaking story deals not only with spiritual superiority but also with this-worldly matters–the relations between the Jews and their neighbors and hosts, who wield the power in day-to-day affairs. Rainmaking involves controlling the forces of nature and the capacity to give life to human beings. The Jews' power to bring the rain in due season turns them into "donors," without whom the very life of the host nation is imperiled. In the words of *Yad Avi-Shalom,* "There is no life without water. So they get more benefit from Israel than Israel gets from them."

In addition to creating a sense of spiritual superiority, the legend conveys the message that the Poles must make sure that the Jews remain in their country and concern themselves with the survival of the Jewish religion, for this is a condition for rain in due season—"if you follow My laws," that is, if the Jews observe their religious injunctions.

Nevertheless, as we noted, conditional acceptance of the Jews creates a metaphor of an insecure life, of perpetual uncertainty. The Jews must demonstrate their skill anew, year after year, proving that they are fulfilling the condition and that it is worth tolerating them. An unequal relationship between the two peoples is constructed a priori, a situation in which the Jews are inescapably humiliated. All this expresses the sociocultural problem common to the two diasporas and explains why the legend circulated in both of them.

The inequality and humiliation latent in the perpetual need to prove themselves was certainly not to the liking of the Jewish intelligentsia of the nineteenth century in the debate it sought to conduct with the ruling society. Hence it is not surprising that these circles—who wanted to apply the legend of acceptance to the context of their demands for emancipation, in the spirit of nineteenth-century liberalism and progressive ideas—omitted this element from the versions of the emissary legend published in non-Jewish languages.

"RAIN": AGNON'S LEGEND OF ACCEPTANCE

As I mentioned in the Introduction, the most important author to add his unique voice to the legends of origin of Polish Jewry was Shmuel Yoseph Agnon. Any discussion of the legend of acceptance must consider Agnon's version, "Rain," and examine its interactions with the folk versions.

We have already looked at several versions of the legends of acceptance of Polish Jews—that of Dov-Ber Birkenthal, the legend of the emissaries, "First Acquaintance," and the story of acceptance on condition of bringing rain. There is no way to know whether Agnon was acquainted with "First Acquaintance" as published in *Jutrzenka.* It seems likely, however, that he did know the other versions. The tale of the emissaries enjoyed wide circulation in histories of Polish Jewry; Brawer's *Galicia and Its Jews: Studies in the History of Galicia in the Eighteenth Century,* in which Dov-Ber Birkenthal's story appeared, was dedicated to Agnon. On the assumption, then, that Agnon was acquainted with several versions of the legends of acceptance, it is significant that the variant he chose to retell was the story of conditional acceptance and rain. Agnon's choice indicates that he saw this version as expressing, more than the others, the life of Polish Jewry and its relations with the surrounding society. Oral traditions known to Agnon may also have contributed to his decision, but this is only a hypothesis.

Not only did Agnon choose the version of acceptance on condition of bringing rain, he gave the title "Rain" to both of his published texts on this theme. Agnon first published the legend in German in the anthology on Polish Jewry he edited with Eliasberg in 1916 (Agnon and Eliasberg 1916, 5–8), under the title "Regen" ("Rain"). The same title ("Geshem" in Hebrew) was given to the Hebrew version when it first appeared in 1925 and was retained through the final publication in *Poland: Legendary Tales,* included in *Elu Va'Elu* (hereinafter Agnon 1967, 355–356). This contrasts with Agnon's practice of changing the titles of many of his other Poland legends. For example, the German version of the story of Casimir the Great and Esther is called "Estherke's House," whereas the Hebrew version is "Heart and Eyes" (see Chapter 4). His adherence to the name "Rain" indicates the centrality that Agnon attributed to this element in the legend of acceptance.

As a first step in our consideration of Agnon's legend of acceptance, let us compare the German text (the first version) with the Hebrew version. As is known, Agnon was in the habit of revising his stories. Comparing the final version with the earlier one may reflect changes in the story during this process of final coalescence and may indicate various links to earlier folk versions.

Table 1
Textual Comparison of S. Y. Agnon's "Regen" and "Geshem"

"Regen"	"Geshem"
In that day I will respond–declares the Lord–I will respond to the sky, and it shall respond to the earth. (Hosea 2:23)	"I will grant your rains in their season," not "rains." This teaches that the rains are ours. This was our glorious strength when the nations took us in, because we knew to bring the rains in due season. (Zeror Ha'Mor, weekly portion of Behukkotai)
The rabbi, author of Yad Avi-Shalom (weekly portion of Devarim), recounts, based on the book Zeror Ha'Mor (weekly portion of Behukkotai), that when	

Table 1 cont.

"Regen" (1916)	"Geshem"
the Jews came to live in Poland they undertook to bring the rains through their prayers, since otherwise the pagan priests would have refused to accept them in their country. This is the story of the rain!	
In the year 4653, emissaries of the Jews came from the kingdom of the Franks; they were Rabbi Hezekiah the Spaniard, Rabbi Akiva Estremadura, Rabbi Emanuel of Ascalon the mathematician, Rabbi Levi Bakhri the orator, and Rabbi Nathanael of Barcelona. They all came to the city of Gniessin, the residence of Prince Leszek of the House of Piast, the king of Poland, to entreat him to grant their fellow Jews refuge in his country, the land of Poland, since in Franconia they found no resting place.	Now certain Jews came to Leszek, king of Poland seeking a resting place for their brethren in his land, for living in Germany they found no resting place.
They addressed him as follows: You know all of the hardships that have befallen us. Our ancestors went down to the land of Franconia and we dwelt there many days. But the people dealt harshly with us and our ancestors. Now we are in Gniessin seeking a resting place in your land. This is our request: We wish to live in your country, but we wish to serve our God; we shall obey the king's commands and not turn aside to the right or the left, until the spirit from on high has mercy on us and leads us erect back to our land."	

Table 1 cont.

"Regen" (1916)	"Geshem"
The prince sat in his pagan temple and showed them favor. He answered Rabbi Bakhri, the chief spokesman, and said: "Wait three days, and then I shall reply to you as my gods instruct me"–so the emissaries of Israel stayed with Leszek.	Now Leszek was sitting in the temple of his gods and showed them favor. Leszek answered them, "Stay here for a few days and I will respond to you." So they stayed with Leszek.
The pagan priests came to Leshek and said, "Who are these men with you?"	The priests came to the king and said, "Who are these men with you?"
Leszek replied to the pagan priests: "Israel has sent to me: Behold, we have been a shame and disgrace for the nations around us. This is our request: We wish to live in your country, but we wish to serve our God; we shall obey the king's commands and not turn aside to the right or the left."	Leszek said to the priests: "Israel sent to me: We have been the spoil of the Gentiles all around. Let us dwell in your country but serve our God. We will keep the king's ordinances. We will not turn aside to the right or the left until the Lord has mercy on His people and restores them to the land of their fathers.
The pagan priests said to Leszek: "Do not let them come into your kingdom unless they bring the rain in due season through their prayers."	The priests said to Leszek: "Do not let them come into your territory unless they bring rain in due season, for they have the power to bring the rains with their prayers."
On the morning of the third day, Leszek got up and spoke to the Jewish emissaries: "Behold, my land is before you. Live where you please. I will make a covenant of peace with you. You shall dwell in security in the land of Poland and bring down the rain in due season, abundant rain with your prayers."	Leszek got up on the third morning and said to the emissaries of the Israelites: "On this condition we shall agree: if you bring rain in due season."

Table 1 cont.

"Regen" (1916)	"Geshem"
The emissaries answered, saying: "Deliverance is the Lord's."	They replied, "Deliverance is the Lord's."
He made a covenant of peace with them and gave them good statutes and ordinances to live by. They left the prince with their privileges in their hands. They went back to their brothers and told them what had happened to them. They said: "Arise and let us go, for we have seen the land; behold, it is very good, and the heart of the inhabitants of the land has no malice toward us. They do not know the God of Heaven; they fear their idols.	He made a covenant of peace with them and gave them good statutes and ordinances to live by. They left Leszek with privileges in their hands. They went back to their brothers and told them all that had happened to them. They said: We have seen the land and it is good. The inhabitants of the land, too, are well-disposed toward us. They do not know the religion of the surrounding nations; they fear their own idols.
"But they do believe in the God of Israel, that He has the power to help His sons when the heavens are sealed and no rain falls. When His children pray to Him, he grants rain on the earth."	
	We also saw Jews there.
They told them everything that the prince had said to them: "Behold, my land is before you. Live where you please. I will make a covenant of peace with you. You shall dwell in security in the land of Poland. But entreat the Lord your God to bring down the rain in due season."	This is how the king answered us: "My land is before you; dwell where you please. But entreat the Lord to bring down the rains in due season.
They added: "We also saw Jews there who came from Kiev and from the land of the Khazars.	

The entire community raised its voice aloud [and said] as follows: "Blessed be the Lord who has given a resting place to His people Israel."	The entire congregation raised its voice and said: "Blessed be the Lord, the God of Israel, Who has given a resting place to His people Israel." They put their trust in God that He would respond to them and cause it to rain on the earth.
They asked what had happened to their brothers and said: "Come, let us go there." So the Jews left Franconia and came to find sanctuary in the shade of the kings of Poland. They brought with them the language of their country, the language of the Germans, and the customs of Israel. The Jews dwelt in security, a blessing in the land. They served the God of their fathers and the land gave its bounty."	The Jews with their families set out and came to find shelter in the shade of the kings of Poland. Israel dwelled in security, a blessing in the land. They served the God of their ancestors, Who gave rain on the earth in due season, and the earth gave its bounty.
This is why the peasants in Poland to this day scatter their seeds in their fields on Rosh Hashanah and Yom Kippur, to commemorate what their ancestors did. For their ancestors did this: When the Jews stood before their Father in Heaven, bent over and with empty bellies, they went out and scattered their seeds in their fields. For if the fields were sown at the same time as the Jews were standing before their Father in Heaven, bent over and with empty belly, the ears of grain that came out of the ground were full, the earth gave its bounty, and the field was blessed. They are maintaining their ancestors' customs.	This is why to this day the Gentiles sow their fields near the date of the Eighth Day of Solemn Assembly, the day when the Jews say the prayer for rain. They are maintaining their ancestors' customs.

Comparison of the two texts reveals a number of differences between them:

80

1. The epigraph of the German version, taken from Hosea 2:23, has been replaced in the Hebrew version by the passage from *Zeror Ha'Mor*. The German version has an introduction in which the narrator cites *Yad Avi-Shalom* and *Zeror Ha'Mor* as his sources. The Hebrew version omits this; evidently the epigraph from *Zeror Ha'Mor* is considered sufficient to tell readers that this source is the key to understanding the message of the story, as we shall see below.

2. The German text is faithful to the chroniclers' versions and reminiscent of the text published by Menaḥem Naḥum Litinski. The year of the Jews' arrival in Poland is specified, along with the names of the emissaries, their destination—the city of Gniessin (Gniezno)—the name of the Polish ruler, and the origins of the Jews already living in Poland before the arrival of Jews from the west. In the Hebrew version, all that remains of this is the name of Leszek and the passing allusion that there were already Jews in Poland. As is known, Agnon was in the habit of rewriting his stories, frequently using an older version as the nucleus of a new story (Shaked 1973, 137). This is conspicuous in our story, where he moves away from the style of the chronicles in which he evidently first encountered the legend. Agnon viewed the legend as expressing a different existential truth from that expounded by the chroniclers. He probably decided to leave out of the Hebrew text most of the pseudo-historical details that constituted the focus of the historians' debate about the reliability and antiquity of the legends—a debate he wanted to keep far away from his story.

3. Unlike the German text, written in a broad epic style with detail and repetition, the Hebrew version is concise and brief. This is most conspicuous in the address to Leszek requesting the right of settlement and in the description of the situation of the Jews in Germany. In the German version all this is recounted twice, once by the Jews to the ruler and again by the ruler to the pagan priests. In the Hebrew version it is reported only once. Note that Agnon chose to report them as related by the prince to the priests rather than by the Jews to the ruler, which seems to be the more logical procedure. The most likely explanation for this is his desire to indicate that the message conveyed by the emissaries' petition—"We have been the spoil of the Gentiles all around. Let us dwell in your country but serve our God. We will keep the king's ordinances. We will not turn aside to the right or left until the Lord has mercy on His people and restores them to the land of their fathers"—was conveyed in an unequivocal manner and so understood by the ruler when he greeted the new arrivals. Putting the words into the king's mouth demonstrates this. The Jews undertook to be loyal to the king of Poland on condition that they be permitted to observe their religion and hold on to the vision of redemption. (This pulls the rug out from under the charge of Jewish disloyalty to Poland, frequently voiced against this background.) That the

king reports their remarks to the priests indicates that when he accepted the Jews in his land he understood their way of life and faith. Hence if there was any breach or denial of the pact between the two people, it was not on the part of the Jews.

4. In the German version, the Polish peasants sow their fields on Rosh Hashanah and Yom Kippur, and the description resembles that in "The Man Who Prayed in the Water Channel" (cited above). The Hebrew text speaks of "near the date of the Eighth Day of Solemn Assembly, the day when the Jews say the prayer for rain." We may surmise that here Agnon was guided by the desire to coordinate the two times—the sowing season and the annual prayer for rain.

To uncover the meaning of Agnon's story we must do more than merely compare Agnon's versions with each other and with the folk versions; we must also be aware of the echoes of Biblical verses—the cultural code required to decipher any Agnon text. Let us concentrate on the Hebrew version. As we have already seen, Agnon uses the epigraph of the Hebrew version to direct us to *Zeror Ha'Mor*. Scrutiny of that work (see above) indicates that Agnon is using the epigraph to bring in the Jews' own view of their rainmaking ability. Jews and Gentiles both believed in this ability, on account of which the latter were willing to allow the former to settle in their land. In the Jewish view, as expounded in *Zeror Ha'Mor,* the rains are "ours" because of the Jews' acceptance of the Torah. Rainfall in due season is understood as being an act of grace by the Holy One, blessed be He, to His people, an act of grace that depends on "if you follow My laws"—that is, on observing the Torah and commandments. Hence the ability to bring rain in due season is a function of religious and ethical conduct. Indeed, this builds the central theme of the story, which is the gap between the Jewish world and the pagan Polish world.

The opening sentence of the story presents the background and characters—Leszek, king of Poland, and the emissaries who come to find refuge for their brothers, the Jews of Germany, who cannot find rest in their own land. The Hebrew word *manoah*—"rest" or "resting place"—appears twice in this sentence: "seeking a resting place for their brethren in his land, for living in Germany they found no resting place." The repetition is no accident; it focuses our attention on the word with its range of Scriptural connotations: cosmic catastrophe (after the Flood, "the dove could not find a resting place for its foot" [Genesis 8:9]); national disaster; and the disaster of exile, as described both in Lamentations 1:3 ("Judah has gone into exile because of misery and harsh oppression; when she settled among the nations, she found no rest; all her pursuers overtook her in the narrow places") and, chiefly, in Moses' rebuke when he speaks of the nation's fate if they do not adhere to the Torah:

The Lord will scatter you among all the peoples from one end of the earth to the other, and there you shall serve other gods, wood and stone, whom neither you nor your ancestors have experienced. Yet even among those nations you shall find no peace, nor shall your foot find *a place to rest*. The Lord will give you there an anguished heart and eyes that pine and a despondent spirit. The life you face shall be precarious; you shall be in terror, night and day, with no assurance of survival. In the morning you shall say, "If only it were evening!" and in the evening you shall say, "If only it were morning!"–because of what your heart shall dread and your eyes shall see" (Deut. 28:64–67)

The associations aroused by the allusions to Biblical verses build a sense of the dread in which the German Jews live, the existential dread of life in exile.

Leszek greets the emissaries seated in the temple of his pagan gods. This hints at the antiquity of the period–pre-Christian Poland–as will be made explicit later: "they fear their idols." The king's attitude toward them is described in the phrase "he showed them favor." On the overt level this characterizes the king, but the Biblical associations of the phrase (Gen. 39:21, Ezra 9:9) remind us of the Jewish notion that the favor of Gentile rulers depends on divine intervention. Just as favor on the part of a powerful figure in the Bible–such as "the Lord was with Joseph: He extended kindness to him and disposed the chief jailer favorably toward him"–is interpreted as divine intervention on behalf of the hero, so too the attitude of the king of Poland toward the German Jewish emissaries is orchestrated from on high.

The next section of the story is strewn with verses and fragments that link it with the *Parashat Balak* (Balak pericope) and the previous section in the Book of Numbers, which relates the Israelites' request to pass through the land of Sihon, king of the Amorites. Later, the king's instruction to the delegation, "Stay here," alludes to Balaam's words to Balak's emissaries: "Spend the night here" (Num. 22:8). Still later, the priests' "Who are these men with you?" echoes exactly the Lord's question to Balaam concerning the Moabite envoys (ibid., 9). The emissaries' remarks, as reported by the king to his priests ("Israel sent to me: We have been the spoil of the Gentiles all around. Let us dwell in your country but serve our God. We will keep the king's ordinances. We will not turn aside to the right or left") echo the words of the delegation to Sihon ("Let me pass through your country. We will not turn off into fields or vineyards, and we will not drink water from wells. We will follow the king's highway until we have crossed your territory" [Num. 21:22]) and the delegation to Edom in 20:17 ("we will follow the king's highway, turning off neither to the right nor to the left"). The priests' reply, "Do not let them come into your territory," echoes Sihon's refusal: "But Sihon would not let Israel pass through his territory" (Num. 20:23).

83

Why did Agnon incorporate the first part of the story, which deals with the arrival of the Jews in Poland and their acceptance on condition that they bring rain in due season, with verses from the Balak pericope and the previous section in Numbers? The answer seems to be that Agnon was attempting to underlay his surface text with a subtext that would highlight the disparity between the Jewish and Gentile perceptions of the Jews' special capacity to bring rain in due season. The Sihon and Balak pericopes deal with a wandering foreign nation that penetrates a settled pagan land and sows panic among the inhabitants, sparking off an urgent appeal to sorcerers and magical practices. The condition on which the Jews are admitted to pre-Christian Poland, namely, that they bring rain in due season ("for they have the power to bring the rains with their prayers"), indicates—if we read the subtext—how the Jews were really viewed by their new hosts: as sorcerers with magical rainmaking powers. Agnon contrasts this with the Jews' own view of their "skill" by means of the epigraph, which tells us that this power is the Lord's special favor to His people and depends on their spiritual and ethical status—their observance of the Torah and commandments. The emissaries' response to Leszek reinforces and underscores this: "Deliverance is the Lord's." This echoes Joseph's "interpretations are the Lord's" (Gen. 40:8). Like the Balak pericope, it signifies that human beings can do nothing through magical means that contravenes the divine will. Later, in their report to their brethren in Germany, the Jews explain Leszek's words in their own way: "But entreat the Lord to bring down the rain in due season." The community's response ("The entire congregation raised its voice and said: 'Blessed be the Lord, the God of Israel, Who has given a resting place to His people Israel.' They put their trust in God that He would respond to them and cause it to rain on the earth") and the narrator's closing words, where he associates worship of God with rainfall in due season ("They served the God of their ancestors, Who gave rain on the earth in due season") emphasize the Jewish perspective. The many echoes of the Balak pericope raise to the level of principle what Balaam states there as part of the narrative—"Lo, there is no augury in Jacob, no divining in Israel" (Num. 23:23)—and make plain the discrepancy between the Jewish and pagan views.

The story is also strewn with verses, fragments, and allusions to two deceitful Biblical covenants—the episodes of Joshua and the Gibeonites and of Jacob's daughter Dinah, where in the latter the Israelites deceive the local inhabitants and in the former become the victims of the fraud. In the story of Dinah, Shechem, son of Hamor, the "prince of the land," rapes Jacob's daughter Dinah and afterward asks for her hand in marriage. He sends his father to Jacob with this request. Jacob's sons, Simeon and Levi, deceiving Shechem and his father, agree to the betrothal on condition that the city-dwellers undergo circumcision. While the city-dwellers are recovering from the operation, Simeon and Levi attack the town and massacre the menfolk. The pact with the Gibeonites, too, involves deception: The Gibeonites trick Joshua into making a pact with them that allows them to remain in the country unharmed.

Leszek's response to the Jews–"On this condition we shall agree: if you bring rain in due season"–echoes the words of Jacob's sons: "Only on this condition will we agree with you; that you will become like us in that every male among you is circumcised" (Gen. 34:15; both use the extremely rare Hebrew verb *ne'ot* 'agree'). The king's pact with the delegation: "I will make a covenant of peace with you," alludes to the treaty with the Gibeonites ("Joshua made peace with them; he made a pact to spare their lives" [Josh. 9:15]). The emissaries describe Poland to their brothers as follows: "We have seen the land and it is good. As for the inhabitants of the land, too, their heart is well-disposed toward us." In addition to the echo of the episode of the spies, this reminds us of the story of Dinah: "These people are well-disposed towards us" (Gen. 34:21). The king's words, quoted by the emissaries, "Behold, my land is before you. Live where you please," again echo lines from the story of Dinah: "You will dwell among us, and the land will be open before you; settle, move about, and acquire holdings in it" (Gen. 34:10).

By interweaving his text with Biblical verses associated with deceitful pacts, Agnon constructs another subtext. On the overt level of the plot, the Jews are accepted in Poland. Although this acceptance is conditional, it is accompanied by good intentions. The subtext hints at what has proven to be true throughout the history of the Jews of Poland–that the pact is destined to be breached because of the disparity between pagan-Polish materialism and the Jewish view that real life depends on the life of the spirit. It necessarily follows that the agreement cannot long endure, because it contains latent elements of deception, fraud, and violence. We should note that the king's invitation–"Behold, my land is before you. Live where you please"–also echoes the story of Abraham and Abimelech (Gen. 20:15) and the story of Lot and the angels, with its threats of violence and terror (Lot tells the people of Sodom, who mean to harm the angels, "Look, I have two daughters who have not known a man. Let me bring them out to you, and you may do to them as you please; but do not do anything to these men, since they have come under the shelter of my roof" [Gen. 19:7–8]).

This element grows stronger as we continue. The Jews' arrival in Poland is described as follows: "The Jews with their families set out and came to find shelter in the shade of the kings of Poland." This passage echoes Jotham's parable: "Then all the trees said to the thornbush, 'You come reign over us.' And the thornbush said to the trees, 'If you are acting honorably in anointing me king over you, come and take shelter in my shade; but if not,

85

may fire issue from the thornbush and consume the cedars of Lebanon!'"
(Judg. 9:14–15). Finding shelter in the shade of the king of Poland, or in
that of idolatrous Egypt–"Who set out to go down to Egypt without asking
Me, to seek refuge with Pharaoh, to seek shelter under the shade of Egypt"
(Isa. 30:2)–is like seeking shelter in the shade of the thornbush.

In this way, living in the shade of the kings of Poland–"Israel dwelled
in security, a blessing in the land"–takes on an ironic tone. The irony is
reinforced by the fact that Agnon takes verses that are associated in the
Bible with residence in the Land of Israel and applies them to Poland. In
the Bible, dwelling "in security" refers to living in the Land of Israel as
opposed to exile: "you shall eat your fill of bread and dwell securely in
the land" (Lev. 26:5); "When you cross the Jordan and settle in the land
that the Lord your God is allotting to you, and He grants you safety from
all your enemies around you and you live in security" (Deut. 12:10); "they
shall no longer be a spoil for the nations, and the beasts of the earth shall
not devour them; they shall dwell in security with none to trouble them"
(Ezek. 34:28); "Judah and Israel from Dan to Beer-sheba dwelt in security,
everyone under his own vine and under his own fig tree" (1 Kings 5:5).
The associations with Biblical verses that oppose residence in the Land of
Israel to residence in the Diaspora create an ironic contrast to the plot of
the story.

The overt plot of Agnon's acceptance story "Rain" resembles that of the
folk legends that condition the Jews' acceptance on rainmaking, such as
that cited by Litinski. As we noted above, Agnon's choice of precisely
this version of the legend of acceptance is significant: Agnon chose a
version that leads to a life of insecurity and uncertainty, in which the
Jews, year after year, must prove their skill and fulfill the condition,
as a metaphor for Jewish life in the Polish diaspora. On the surface,
Agnon's legend, like its folk forebears, expresses gratitude for the Jews'
admission to Poland in their time of distress. As I have shown, however,
the Biblical echoes create a subplot that evolves through its contrast with
the surface plot. If the folk legend of acceptance depicted the past as a
period of acceptance, rights, and privileges, and sought to use this past
to ameliorate the community's lot in the present, Agnon's subplot insists
that this ancient pact of toleration and privileges could not endure. It,
too, involved deception and fraud accompanied by violence–not because
of any evil intent on the part of the host society, but because of an
unbridgeable gap, the non-Jewish world's fundamental inability to accept
the spiritual essence of Judaism. That world could not comprehend this
essence even when it benefitted from it (with rainfall in due season); it
could understand the relationship only in the material, tangible terms of
primordial paganism. Hence dwelling in security, as reported by the story,
can be taken only ironically.

Nevertheless, Agnon is at pains throughout the story to stress that the Jews fulfill the condition laid on them and the condition they themselves set. This is reflected in the means by which he builds the message that the conditions set by the Jews for settling in Poland—that is, being allowed to worship their God and adhere to their vision of redemption—were clearly stated and understood by their hosts. The conclusion, too, which recounts the peasant custom of sowing the fields when the Jews prayed for rain, is another expression of the Jews' meeting their commitment. If so, the Jews not only receive; they also give to the society that took them in. Or, in the words of the author of *Yad Avi-Shalom,* to whom Agnon alludes in the German text, "so they get more benefit from Israel than Israel gets from them."

Taken as a whole, the acceptance legends discussed in this chapter reflect the changes that took place in such stories as a result of changing currents of thought and the problems that preoccupied Jewish society in a particular age. Even though the oldest legend was written down in the eighteenth century by Dov-Ber Birkenthal, we may assume that the earliest acceptance legend is that about the rains in due season, which is found among both the Jews of Poland and the Jews of Spain, even though our earliest recorded version dates only to the nineteenth century. The condition for the acceptance of the Jews is a metaphor for a life without security, a live of perpetual uncertainty for the Jews who must prove each year that they have met the condition and that it is worthwhile for the host country to continue to suffer their presence. In this way the legend expresses the essential inequality between two peoples and the abject state in which the Jews lived. This legend is certainly not trying to be a model of either segregation or cooperation—of the sort found in other legends—because in its world, where there is total separation, a discourse of this kind is not possible. The gap and separation are givens that cannot be bridged.

Only in the eighteenth century did Dov-Ber Birkenthal, a *maskil* of the previous generation who was opposed to innovations and feared the penetration of the Western European Enlightenment, relate a story that creates a model of segregation, because of his fear that this situation was about to change. In the nineteenth century, by contrast, those who wanted emancipation and Polonization told stories that described the earliest web of relations between the two peoples as one of cooperation based on compassion or equality.

Agnon's legend deals with a totally different message. It uses the acceptance legend of the Jews of Poland in a unique way to reflect on quite a different problem, one that was in the cultural air of his period and which eventually brought him to emigrate to Palestine. Agnon selected the folk legend of the conditional acceptance of the Jews—they must guarantee the annual rainfall—because it expressed the insecurity and abject state of

CHAPTER 2

life in the Diaspora. He does so not in order to derive some consolation from the Jews' superior ability to bring down rains and their Gentile hosts' dependence on them, but to undercut and totally reject this kind of existence. The legend depicts the alliance between the two peoples as one that could not endure; those who wanted to see Poland as a land in which the Jews lived in security were thereby delusional. In this way he conveys the message that security is possible only in the Land of Israel, as part of a return to national life–the Zionist vision.

3

The Legend of Abraham the Jew, King of Poland

Two figures appear in the folk legends of Polish Jewry who, according to the legendary chronicles, served as kings of Poland. One of these was Saul Wahl,[1] a known historical personage of the sixteenth and seventeenth centuries. We shall not deal with the legends of his reign here; in Chapter 5, however, we will consider legends of origin having to do with the synagogues he founded. The other figure was Abraham, known as "Prochownik" on account of his occupation as a merchant of gunpowder (*proch*). This legend is set in the ninth century and is linked to the ascension to the throne of the legendary King Piast (c. 860), the founder of the Piast dynasty that ruled until 1370. Thus the plot antedates the acceptance legends discussed in Chapter 2. Some believe that the legend was not created until the thirteenth or fourteenth century, when gunpowder first appeared in Europe; others hold that it dates from no earlier than the eighteenth or nineteenth centuries, when it was invented to fulfill apologetic needs (Weinryb 1962, 1–11; Weinryb 1973, 18).

What can we learn from the legend of Abraham Prochownik, the Jew crowned king of Poland? What poetic devices inform it? What does it tell us about the cultural mentality of Polish Jewry and the roles it fulfilled?

What process does a legend pass through in being transformed from oral tradition to written literature? The present chapter will deal with these questions.

The legend of Abraham Prochownik is a legend of origin set in the ninth century, the period when, according to some historians, Jews first appeared in Poland (Bałaban 1948, 1–5; Schipper 1926, 15; Kraushar 1865, 57; Lelewel 1851–56, 18). In the absence of written sources about the origin period, historians were drawn to transcribing this legend; they incorporated it into their publications, thereby preserving it. True, some of these historians rejected this legend as offering unreliable evidence about the date of the Jews' first appearance in Poland, whether because of the historical anachronism (a ninth-century hero who sells gunpowder) or other reasons (Weinryb 1973, 18). None of them demonstrates any interest in its poetics. Nevertheless, the chroniclers of Polish Jewry deserve credit for transcribing and preserving the legend.

Most of the historians are content to give a précis of the legend.[2] The oldest complete version that preserves many elements of folk legend is included in Herman Sternberg's histories of the Jews of Poland (Sternberg 1860, 6–8; Sternberg 1878, 4–5). It runs as follows:

> Upon the death of King Popiel, who belongs to the legendary period, the royal throne of Poland was vacant. In their conclave in Kruszwica, the electors were unable to agree on the choice of a new ruler. At the suggestion of the oldest among them, it was decided that whoever entered the city first at daybreak on the next morning would be crowned king.
>
> Four guards were stationed at the corners of the bridge leading to the city in order to report who entered the city first.
>
> It happened that the Jew Abraham, who was bringing gunpowder to the city and for this reason was called Prochownik was hurrying to the city at dawn. The guards greeted him jubilantly and accompanied him to the city, where he was acclaimed king. But Abraham refused to accept the proffered crown. When he saw that the electors remained steadfast in their decision, he requested one day to think the matter over and to pray to his God for advice. He absolutely forbade anyone to disturb him in his devotions.
>
> Two days and two nights passed and Abraham did not appear. When he did not appear on the third morning either and the patience of the waiting throng was at an end, the farmer Piast called out loudly: "Brothers, we can't go on this way. The country cannot manage without a head, and since Abraham is not coming out, I shall go get him." He brandished his axe and broke into the house where Abraham was sequestered.
>
> "Poles," said Abraham, coming out, "do you see this farmer Piast? Elect him as your king. He is intelligent, for he saw that it is impossible for a country to remain without a king for a long time; and he is brave, for he

disobeyed my order in order to save the fatherland. Crown this man and give thanks to God and to Abraham Prochownik."
So Piast was proclaimed king.

This is clearly not a folkloristic transcription. We may presume that the legend has undergone some kind of redaction. For example, the note that King Popiel dates from the legendary period of Polish history is a comment added by Sternberg the historian. All the same, the story preserves elements of folk-narrative poetics, such as repetition, tripling, dialogue, and the description of the confrontation, as well as motifs characteristic of folk tradition, such as the selection of the first person who chances to come to a particular place.[3]

Like legends of origin, this legend, too, is etiological. First and foremost, it seeks to provide a foundation for the Jews' right to live in Poland. The plot is laid during the first consolidation of the kingdom of Poland, in the pre-Christian period; the implication is that if Jews were already living and accepted in Poland then, their right to live there cannot be called into question. The legend also legitimizes their occupation in trade by showing that this was their livelihood in Poland from days of yore. Principally, however, the legend relates the Jews' unique contribution to Polish society—responsibility for the ascension of the glorious Piast dynasty, whose most august scion, Casimir the Great, expanded the Jews' right of settlement in Poland and, according to legend, was personally involved with Jews through his beloved Estherke (Shmeruk 1981; Bar-Itzhak 1989, 65–76; and see Chapter 4 below).

The legend implies that the Jews are essential to Polish society: when the Poles were unable to decide who should be king, the insight of a Jew brought them to select the appropriate monarch, a man endowed with intelligence and courage. This contribution legitimizes the Jews' residence in Poland, both externally and internally. Externally, the right to live in Poland was granted as their due because they contributed to its commerce, to the election of its kings, and to making proper decisions. That is to say, the Jews were wise and resourceful precisely in those domains where the natives' incapacity was most apparent. In fact, the legend was used for apologetic purposes. Weinryb notes that, in 1868, Smolka, a member of the Polish sejm, used the story of the "Jewish king Abraham" to defend the Jews of Galicia in the Polish Sejm and demand equal rights for them (Weinryb 1973, 336).

The legend has another important message—namely, that the Jews, once admitted to the country, did not seek a dominion that was not theirs. Internally, speaking to the Jews themselves, the legend indicates that Poland is a homeland adopted for a limited period of time and that the Jews living there are not interested in assimilation; they remain loyal to their religion and will return to their land in the Messianic era. The Talmudic sage Rabbi Yose states that the Israelites were given three commands when they entered the Land of Israel–to select a king, to destroy the seed of Amaleq, and to build the Temple–and inquires as to the order in which they should be fulfilled (BT Sanhedrin 20b).[4] All agreed, however, that a Jewish kingdom could exist only in the Land of Israel.[5] Should a Jewish monarchy arise in a foreign country, it would lead to assimilation. The latent message of the legend is that, despite the Jews' adoption of Poland as a temporary homeland, they must not surrender their essence and their national-religious uniqueness to satisfy a passion for distinction and power.

As mentioned, Sternberg's text preserves some aspects of folk-narrative poetics and conveys the chief points of the tale, the skeleton of the plot, and the latent messages. But it is not a full documentation of the oral story.

A transcription that does presume to document an oral story is found in the works of Roman Zmorski (1822–67), who transcribed the legend in Polish in 1854 (Krzyżanowski 1965, 10) as he heard it from Jews or, as he put it, from "the descendants of Abraham." Zmorski, who also signed his name Zamarski,[6] was a student of Polish folklore, particularly of the Pomorze district and the Kashubians.[7] The legend was first published in 1854 (under the name Zamarski). The posthumous *Pisma orginalne i tłumaczone* (Original and Translated Tales; Zmorski 1900) contains the full text of the folk legend. Zmorski's humoristic preface and Krzyżanowski's remarks about it (1965, 10) make it clear that the legend of Abraham Prochownik was unfamiliar to Polish society and sparked amusement.[8] The Polish tradition about Piast's election is quite different. The three most important Polish chronicles present the story as follows: Piast and his wife Rzepicha, who have an only son Ziemowit, provide a hospitable reception in their hut to two travelers who had previously been expelled from the palace of King Popiel. The travelers participate in the ceremony of the son's haircut, where they perform a miracle so that the food and drink do not run out. Thanks to them, Piast and his wife can host many guests. After the festivities, Piast is chosen king (Anonim Gall 1965; *Kronika Wielkopolska* 1965; Kadłubek 1974). Many have studied the Polish; some have noted a resemblance to the Biblical story of Abraham and the angels, only to reject it, too rashly in my opinion (Maślanka 1984).

The Polish legend is extremely different from the Jewish legend of Abraham Prochownik. Hence Zmorski's humorous preface to the Jewish legend comes as no surprise:

> Our earliest history has been ignored for so long that it is not astonishing if today we have amazing revelations and, what is more, from sources where no one would expect to find them. With no merit, blind fate brought to my

hand, albeit not from such an ancient source, a detail relating to an ancient and important period. This detail sheds new light on the shadowy legend of Piast's ascension to the throne of the Lechs[9] and enriches our historical gallery with the patriarchal figure of Abraham Prochownik.[10]

Zmorski's text runs as follows:

The Legend of Abraham Prochownik
(as told by his descendants)

In ancient days, very ancient, when people still knew nothing of brandy and tobacco, there was a large city in Poland on the shores of a lake called Gopło–Kruszwica. The city is still there today, but it has fallen so far that a leasehold[11] hardly brings in even a thousand zloty. Still, it used to be such a large city! Like Brody or Warsaw. At the water's edge there stands an old tower where no one can live any longer. Only the owls nest there.

Once there was a king whom they called Popielnik. They called him that because he was extremely lazy and very fond of sleeping. He didn't think about anything in the world except gluttony and boozing. After he had gorged himself and got drunk, he would lie down in the chimney nook, in the warm ashes. What a life! It was also his end, if my masters will be so kind as to listen.

One day at supper Popiel gorged himself on eels. To keep his belly from hurting him during the night he proceeded to drink an entire gallon of old mead. So, even though he was used to drinking, this was too much for him. When he got up from the table he could scarcely find his way to his chimney corner. The moment he lay down in the ashes he fell asleep like a log. He would always take a cat to sleep with him at night, to keep the rats and mice from biting his nose, because there were so many of them there. But that evening he was so drunk that, to his misfortune, he forgot to take it with him. If my masters will just listen to what happened to him!

After everyone in the tower had gone to sleep and it was quiet, the rats and mice came out of their holes and began to scamper all about. When they realized that there was no cat in the fireplace, at once–hop! hop!–they jumped one after another and began to sniff at whatever it was that was lying there in the ashes. Popielnik was sleeping so deeply that the fat was almost oozing from him. "It's a ham!" they thought, and began to nibble to see how it tasted. Popielnik was so drunk that he didn't feel anything and didn't move. So! He was so delicious they ate and ate until they had gobbled him all up.

Early the next morning the cook came to bring Popielnik his breakfast. He looked–"Oy vey! [Woe is me!]" Only the bones were left. Panic-stricken, he began to cry bitterly. The others heard and began to yell too. So they all cried bitterly until the entire town was shrieking loudly. So! The dirges and weeping began when they found out that the rats had eaten their Popiel. Not that they were particularly sad about Popielnik; it was only that he

93

Ignacy Gołębiowski, "Popiel the Second Eaten by Mice." Originally painted on stone. From *The Beginning of Polish Kings and Princes* (Lwow, 1855).

hadn't left an heir. So people were extremely upset because they didn't know where to find themselves a king. How can one live without a king? Then there's no government and no rule and no order.

Then the Poles gathered from all corners of the world and began to consult among themselves as to whom they should choose. Oh, it got them so excited, just like today when our lords assemble for consultations. They ate, they drank a lot, and they talked and screamed until their ears hurt, but they could come to no conclusion. When some wanted to crown such and such a person as king, ten others at once responded that they were no

94

worse than he was. God knows how much longer they would have talked on, but the butchers didn't know where they were going to find meat for them and the merchants ran out of wine. Then one very old Pole, who was evidently more intelligent than the others, climbed on the table and began to speak. "You cannot," he said, "agree about your king. Let me advise you what you should do. Tonight, post guards at the entrance to the city. The first person who enters the city tomorrow morning, we'll make him our king. At least there won't be any more dissension. Now all of you must take an oath that you will tender absolute obedience to whomever God brings on the morrow."

After he had spoken, everybody liked his idea and took an oath to obey whomever God would bring them. They posted four soldiers on the bridge at the entrance to town to watch and see who would be the first to enter the city the next morning. Now listen, masters, here comes our great-great-grandfather Abraham!

Our great-great-grandfather Abram was, like most Jews, a merchant. He smuggled gunpowder and distributed it in Poland to various shooters, in exchange for the skins of rabbits and foxes. On this day he got up early, when the stars were still shining, took his pack on his back (the gunpowder he carried under his shirt), and started off on the road for Kruszwica. Here, no sooner had he climbed onto the bridge than four ruffians jumped on him, grabbed hold of him, and cried out, "Hail! He's ours!"

He was so frightened he almost fainted, because he thought they wanted to take him into a room and inspect him. He trembled and couldn't utter a word. Now the cannons began firing and the bells ringing and the trumpets blasting. Ten lords, as handsome as angels, dressed in white, marched forth, followed by many Poles dressed in their finest and waving banners.

Our great-great-grandfather thought: "Some sort of procession is under way here. This is my chance to run away, with God's help." He tried to free himself from the soldiers, but they held him tightly. When he looked he saw that the procession was marching straight toward him and all the people were kneeling before him and calling out, "Hail!"

Abram didn't understand what was happening to him until they told him the whole story and started to lead him off toward the tower.

"You see,"[12] thought our ancestor, "it won't be bad. I'll live in such a tall tower that no student[13] will be able to hit it with a rock. Every day there will be noodles and kugel with honey and carp with egg, like on the Feast of Tabernacles! So, but what will happen when there is war?"

The moment he thought about war he was terrified. Even though he traded in gunpowder, his was a merciful heart without peer and he fainted when he barely nicked his finger. So he turned down the proposal to become king and said so to the Poles. But when they heard this they entreated him to have mercy on them, because without him there was no salvation for them. He kept saying that he wouldn't be a successful king, that he couldn't go to war because he was a great coward. They answered him that if he didn't want to fight there wouldn't be war. But he thought–he was smart–that the other side could start a war and when he was king he would have to command the army. And he stubbornly insisted that he didn't want to be king.

When Abram saw that there was no way out, he turned to his intelligence. "So, he said, "if you've taken an oath to obey me, listen to what I'm ordering you to do now! Even if you kill me, I don't want your crown. I must pray to the Lord[14] to advise me what to do. Build me a booth in the marketplace, bring me carp and kugel and a gallon of mead–but not too strong–and I will go into seclusion there and pray. When I finish I will be your king."

The Poles obeyed him. They built a booth for him in the marketplace and brought him kugel and carp and mead. Abram closed himself up inside the booth and sternly forbade them to disturb him until he came out by himself.

Abram sat there for a day and a night. He sat there another day and a night. In general it was very pleasant for him there, like a doughnut in the fat. The Poles sat in the market street and waited for their king, but they were afraid to call him, since he had strictly forbade them to do so. So, you will see, my lords, at once, how it all ended.

The third morning came and Abram didn't move. The Poles didn't know what to do. There was one wheelwright there from the suburb who was known as Piast, a strong lad and quick on the uptake. Finally, tired of waiting, he grabbed an axe and stood in front of the booth. "Brothers!" he said. "It can't go on this way! The country simply can't manage without a leader for such a long time. If he doesn't come out on his own I'll bring him out to you, even if he hangs me for it." He smashed in the door of the hut with the axe, took Abram by the hand, and pulled him out to the people.

They all thought that Abram would command that he be executed then and there. But Abram merely stroked his beard and gestured for silence. So, they all grew quiet, and our ancestor began to speak.

"Poles!" he says. "Do you see the wheelwright Piast? He will be your king. You crowned me and now I am crowning him. He is intelligent and saw that the country cannot remain without a king for such a long time. He is brave, for he was not afraid of my ban when all of you were afraid. Place the crown on his head and give thanks to God and to Prochownik."

So, when our ancestor spoke with such wisdom, they couldn't oppose him. They did what he said and led Piast to the tower, placed the gold crown on his head, and gave him a golden scepter. In this way he became king. He lived for a very long time and ruled with strength and wisdom. And just as Abram said, all the Poles gave thanks for him to God and to Prochownik. To our ancestor he gave the privilege that in all of Poland, only he could trade in gunpowder.

So, why are my lords laughing? My lords think it isn't true? By the love of God, that's how it was! My father heard the story from his grandfather, who heard it from his grandfather. . . .

The epic expansion is prominent here, in contrast to Sternberg's version. This legend preserves the mode of oral transmission, including direct address to the audience ("If my masters will just listen"), the narrator's reaction to the responses of his audience ("So, why are my lords laughing?"), repetition, tripling, dialogue, rhetorical questions, contrasts, and more. The legend is replete with humorous passages and even satire.

Zmorski states that he presents the legend as it was related by the descendants of Abraham–that is, by a Jewish narrator. Even if he did not add or change anything in an attempt at parody,[15] though, one must relate to the legend as if told in an extracultural context, to Polish "masters," as the narrator terms them. Elsewhere I have discussed a story told outside its natural context[16] and investigated the narrator's responses to the extracultural listener and how the responses of such a listener affect the nature of the text (Bar-Itzhak 1998). I noted that, in the narrative process in folk literature, the audience is an element that contributes to the shaping of the text (Bar-Itzhak 1993). Narrators *recreate* whatever they have received from their tradition. The audience's expectations, modes of absorption, and responses are also significant partners in the evolution of the work. Narrator and audience engage in a process of quasi-negotiation, set in a context in which signals are exchanged at various levels between narrator and audience, who consolidate them into patterns of insight. Because both narrator and audience are part of the direct communicative process during the story, there is a two-way flow of information: both sides are simultaneously addressing and addressed. The legend we have here was told to Poles who were not familiar with it, as we know from Zmorski's testimony and Krzyżanowski's introduction. It is clear from the text that they are skeptical about the tale and consider it to be absurd or amusing, as is reflected in the narrator's concluding words: "So, why are my lords laughing? My lords think it isn't true? By the love of God, that's how it was!"

The question of absurdity and amusement is made more complex by the genre with which the story is affiliated–the legend. This genre has historical and geographical pretensions; what it relates in these domains is accorded credence by the narrating society even if, like sacred legends, it contains supernatural elements.[17] Legends of origin, which are a sort of historical myth, may be sanctified even more. Legends present a value system with which the narrator identifies. If the audience rejects the values presented in the text or has reservations about them, the underlying fabric of the legend is strained; or, as Werses puts it, "The factor of belief in what is related is decisive in determining the genre image of the folk tale, which is in no way stable: a legend can turn into a fairy tale or a joke or shrink to a mere rumor. It all depends on the elements of transmission by the narrator and the response of the audience" (Werses 1987, 232–233).[18] The narrator in an extracultural context, alert to the listeners' response when they broadcast skepticism and amusement, feels the rug being pulled out from under his feet and hastens to provide a seal of authenticity to what he relates by calling as witness the memory of the generations: "My father heard the story from his grandfather, who heard it from his grandfather. . . ." This fact of transmission in extracultural circumstances is crucial for understanding the story; we shall return to it later.

The introduction is typical of a folk legend. The events take place in a remote but historical age and the setting is a specific and known place. To attract attention, a *soupçon* of mystery is mixed in at the beginning, in the image of the old tower where only owls live today. It is clear that the narrator is already attempting to add to the credibility of his story by invoking familiar geographical details such as the name of the city, its location, and the name of the adjacent lake. The reference to the condition of the city in the present also serves this objective. The description of the city's decline allows the narrator to describe himself and the livelihoods of the Jews, using leaseholds as a gauge for income.

Unlike the story presented by Sternberg, which is related in skeletal and concise form, here every action that moves the plot forward is expanded almost into a complete episode. The story comprises four scenes. The first deals with Popiel and his death, to which Sternberg devoted a single line. With regard to what is related, the character sketched is compatible with the Polish traditions; this indicates that the traditions were familiar and exploited, among other reasons, to win over the audience. The Polish chronicles portray Popiel as a hated ruler who died a shameful death and was eaten by rats. Some add to the list of his transgressions the murder of family members and describe him as lazy and despotic (Anonim Gall 1965, 15; Kadłubek 1974, 93; *Kronika Wielkopolska* 1965, 63).[19]

The narrator describes Popiel and his sorry end humorously and even satirically. The nickname "Popielnik" suggests an association with *piekielnik,* someone condemned to hellfire. The description of his gluttony and of the rats who think him a ham is truly comic. But the narrator aims his shafts of derision not only against the hated king but also against the Poles, through the satire he uses to depict their great mourning for such a worthless king. The use of *oy vey* to express a dirge reflects the narrator himself, of course.

The second scene deals with the convocation of the Poles to elect a new king. Here we have a humorous description with a contemporary ring: "Oh, it got them so excited, just like today when our lords assemble for consultations. They ate, they drank a lot, and they talked and screamed until their ears hurt, but they could come to no conclusion." The possessive in "our lords" legitimizes the satire. Their utter inability to reach an agreement is suggested by the fact that the assembled throng would have remained there forever had the food and drink not run out. The joy felt by the members of the assembly when they hear the old man's advice to choose the first person to enter the city is explained more as a fear of remaining without food and drink than as a desire to choose a king. At the end of the episode, the narrator anticipates future events in a direct address to his audience: "Now listen, masters, here comes our great-great-grandfather Abraham!" This anticipation increases the tension of waiting for the central character and the event that is the keystone of the story.

The third episode deals with Abraham's acclamation as king. The hero is described as a merchant who barters smuggled gunpowder to Polish hunters for furs and skins. The acclamation scene is painted in comic tones by the disparity between the expectations of the Jew, who is preparing himself for disaster and attempting to run away, and the true situation, in which he is greeted by salutes and kingship. When we consider Abraham's reasons for rejecting the crown we must again remember that the tale was related in an extracultural context. A Polish audience cannot be told the real reasons why a Jew must not accept the Polish crown and why such a gesture of generosity is in fact a bear hug. The narrator adopts the method of irony at his own expense (considered in the context of Jewish humor by Noy [1962]), in this case the self-deprecation of the Jew who lacks precisely those qualities that the Poles rate highly, such as martial skills and bravery. In this way, the narrator converts his weakness into strength and uses it to justify the refusal while avoiding a possible confrontation with his audience.

Abraham's weighing of the pros and cons, accompanied by an enumeration of the culinary delicacies of the Feast of Tabernacles, is amusing. The narrator avails himself of this opportunity to express the imaginary yearning to cut the powerful down to size, through the description of the Jew who sits in the booth like "a doughnut in fat," while the Polish nobles wait outside in the street for three days.

The fourth and final scene brings Piast on stage and concludes with his coronation at the end of the story. The narrator provides biographical details about Piast: his occupation and origin are in keeping with the Polish tradition (see above).[20] This increases the credibility of the story for Polish audiences and reflects the narrator's familiarity with Polish traditions. In this episode the narrator conveys the important message that the Jew does not seek a crown that does not belong to him. He knows his place in his adopted country. Most important, though, is that the Jew's contribution and the benefits he brings to the people are incalculable. Twice the narrator repeats that the Poles must offer thanks to God and to Abraham. The formula is first spoken by Abraham when he proposes that Piast be made king: "Place the crown on his head and give thanks to God and to Prochownik"; it is repeated by the narrator as an ongoing tradition: "And just as Abram said, all the Poles gave thanks for him to God and to Prochownik." In other words, this gratitude must be kept in mind by all

99

who acknowledge the contribution that the House of Piast made to Poland.

There is one more addition in the story beyond Sternberg's version: the grant of the exclusive right to trade in gunpowder to the Jew, in recognition of his service—a relevant detail that the narrator will not omit when he tells the story to a Polish audience. It should be noted that in the Yiddish version of the story, printed by Wiernik in 1901, the gratitude is expressed immediately, though in a slightly different manner: "and it is easy to understand that Abraham had an important position under his rule" (Wiernik 1901, 199).

The story concludes, we noted, with the narrator's attempt to overcome the amusement that the story arouses in the audience by calling on past generations—on the Jewish memory—as witness.

Now we must compare Zmorski's extracultural transcription of the story with the Hebrew text printed in *Ha'Nesher* in 1861 (the oldest written version in Hebrew):

Upon the death of the last Popiel in 860, the nobles of Poland gathered in the town of Kruszwica to anoint a king but could not reach agreement. Each man voted for the one who seemed best to him. Some of them said, "The crown should be ours." All agreed unanimously that "come morning and the Lord will tell us![21] Whoever enters the city tomorrow at first light is the holy one whom the Lord has chosen to be ruler over Poland!" They stationed guards around the city and gave them their orders: "Stand by the watchtowers all night. At dawn, greet whoever enters the city first and say to him, 'Peace unto you, our Lord King!' Then accompany him into the city with the celebrating throng."

All night they stood at their posts. The moon and stars grew dim and, with dawn, a star rises from Jacob![22] When they looked up, here comes Abraham the gunpowder merchant. They prostrated themselves and said: "Be blessed in your arrival, O King!" Then they accompanied him into the city, and everyone they met cried out, "Long live the King!"

Abraham said, "Who am I and who is my family? I am a gunpowder merchant, and you would anoint me your ruler? What is this dream you have dreamed?"[23]

When Abraham saw that the princes of Poland were holding him to their word, he answered them: "Give me the space of a night and a day, and I will pour out my complaint before my Lord.[24] Perhaps a spirit from on high will be poured out on me[25] and I will become fit for kingship." They said, "As you will, our King!" Then Abraham went to the house of prayer to prostrate himself and ask for help from Him Who enthrones kings. He ordered his men not to let the people break through and disturb him at his prayers. Then he closed the door behind him and locked it.

A day passed and a night elapsed and the door of the temple remained firmly closed. They waited a long time[26] for him to come out. A day and a night passed again. It was morning and it was evening on the second day and Abraham remained standing before his God.[27] The townspeople, the men of Kruszwica, gathered about the House of the Lord.[28] Finally Citizen Piast could no longer control himself before all those present.[29] He raised his voice and called out, "Brothers! It is not good for the land to be without a king, 'without a ruler a nation is ruined';[30] as for that man Abraham, we do not know what has happened to him.[31] I will open the door and bring him out to you." Then he did just as he said.

Abraham came out and said to them, "Do you know this man Piast, princes of Poland? He is imbued with a valorous spirit. Listen to me and anoint him king, for he has wisdom and intelligence. He understood that it is not proper for the inhabitants of Poland to be like sheep that have no shepherd.[32] You see that to save his homeland he donned valor as his armor and did not obey the king's orders.[33] Now anoint him and it will be good for you. And with the bounty that you enjoy, remember Abraham the gunpowder merchant!"

They heeded his voice and anointed Piast to be their ruler. (*Ha'Mevasser/ Ha'Nesher* 1861, 1(14): 109–110)

Any discussion of the story must consider the periodical in which it appeared. *Ha'Nesher* was a supplement to *Ha'Mevasser,* the first Galician Jewish weekly, which was published in Hebrew in Lemberg (Lwow) from 1861 until 1867. The editors were Abraham Isaac Menkes (*Ha'Mevasser*) and Joseph Cohen-Tsedek (*Ha'Nesher*). The latter edited *Ha'Nesher* throughout its career.[34] The story was printed as part of a monograph entitled "Annals of Poland," serialized for more than an entire year starting with the second number of the periodical (19 June 1861). Although the monograph is not signed, it seems likely that the editor of *Ha'Nesher,* Joseph Cohen-Tsedek, compiled the material, as he did in other numbers with reports on Jewish news from around the world. A note appended to the report on events in various countries stated that "the political section and the supplement *Ha'Nesher* are edited by me, Joseph Cohen-Tsedek."

The monograph is written in high-flown language (see also Werses 1989, 119); A. I. Papirna has written about the florid style of the entire periodical (Papirna 1952). The monograph has a clear slant and unambiguous message: asserting the antiquity of Jewish settlement in Poland and defending the Jews against "those who blot out the name of Israel and will not write it in their books" (*Ha'Mevasser/Ha'Nesher* 1861, 1[14]: 109). The author is displeased even with the Polish historian Lelewel, who believed that the Jews reached Poland in the ninth century, because of the latter's assumption that they arrived as slave-traders. Feeling defamed, he criticizes Lelewel sharply: "Is it not far-fetched to believe that the Jews traded in this loathsome trade and bathed their footsteps in the blood of human lives?" (ibid.).

101

ה נ ש ר

יפרוש כנפיו להביא מרחוק ומקרוב דברי תורה וחכמה .

ואשא אתכם על כנפי נשרים ואביא אתכם אלי (שמות י"ט ד)

The masthead of the periodical *Ha'Nesher* (1861).

The author himself was convinced that the Jews had indeed been living in Poland for around a thousand years. He cites the legend of Abraham to prove this: "Indeed, if the ancient story called 'The Story of Abraham the Gunpowder Merchant' is true, as is attested by ancient authors, we know that already a thousand years ago there were Jews in Poland. We transcribe it here" (ibid.). The author does not name "ancient authors" or the source from which he is transcribing the story. From what he wrote previously, it would seem that his chief written source was Sternberg, whose book had appeared the year before. The author of the monograph praises that volume: "With regard to the time when our ancestors first came to the land of Poland, there are arguments among the historians. Some blot out the name of Israel and will not write it in their books. . . . Until there arose in our generation the scholar and talented writer Herman Sternberg and began writing the annals of the Jews of Poland. Even though only the first part has reached us, it is a great help to us, like the other books of the nations, who were not reluctant to bear the name of Israel on their lips" (ibid.). In other words, he was also familiar with Lelewel. Of greatest interest, though, is his attitude toward Zmorski's version: "He recounts the story with overflowing fury and it seems he would like to hide something. But what can he do when there are faithful witnesses?" (ibid). The "witnesses" he cites are coins with Hebrew inscriptions found in Poland, a topic that was much discussed, and not necessarily in connection with the legend of Abraham (see, for example, Schipper 1926, 50–51). By "witnesses" he may also have been referring to oral folk traditions, but he does not state this explicitly.

Whereas the story published by Sternberg was incorporated into a historical work in German and was also accessible to non-Jews, and Zmorski's

102

version is an example of an extracultural transcription intended for a non-Jewish audience, the story in *Ha'Nesher* is clearly intracultural. It was published in a periodical intended for Jews only; the use of Hebrew turns it into a story in the private code of the social reference group. The narrator invokes it to prove a historical thesis to those who may be assumed to know it already, both from written versions and from oral legendary history. It is not surprising that the narrator uses Biblical language to lend the story an aura of antiquity, as is appropriate for a legend of origin of the narrating society. The most conspicuous difference from the other versions involves the character of Abraham. Zmorski's hero is quite frank about his fears; here, though, the narrator echoes Scripture to create a metaphorical analogy between Abraham and the heroism of Israel: "with dawn, a star rises from Jacob! When they looked up, here comes Abraham the gunpowder merchant." The phrase borrowed from Balaam's blessing—"a star rises from Jacob, a scepter comes forth from Israel; It smashes the brow of Moab, the foundation of all children of Seth" (Num. 24:17)–alludes to both future greatness and valor. The respect for the character is also expressed by the other characters' extreme reaction when they meet him: "They prostrated themselves and said: "Be blessed in your arrival, O King!" When Abraham decides to go into seclusion, it is not food and drink that top his interests, as in Zmorski's humorous description; the place where he secludes himself is not an ordinary house (as in Sternberg and Wiernik) or a hut in the marketplace (Zmorski), but a house of prayer. Inherent in this is the key difference between this version and the others: in the Hebrew version, Abraham goes into seclusion in a house of prayer in order to request assistance from "Him Who enthrones kings." The very use of this term indicates the character's scale of priorities and his attitude toward earthly kingship vis-à-vis the Kingdom of God. The term "the house of prayer" links up with the etiological element of the Jewish claim for the antiquity of the Jewish settlement in Poland: if the Jews already maintained a house of prayer in Kruszwica in the time of Popiel, the implication is that there was a permanent Jewish presence there, not just traders passing through the country.

The scene in which the townspeople surround the "house of the Lord," waiting for their king, could by no means have been presented in this fashion in a story intended for a non-Jewish audience, especially since the Poles are assimilated to the people of Sodom! It expresses a pride that, in the condition of Jewish life in Poland, can be expressed only within the reference group. The term "house of prayer" leads the narrator to change another detail. In the other versions (including Wiernik's Yiddish text), Piast breaks down the door of the house with an axe in order to drag Abraham out. But violence against "the house of the Lord" is inappropriate; the dramatic picture in the earlier versions is moderated into the pallid " 'I will open the door and bring him out to you.' Then he did just as he said" (ibid., 109).

The motif of the house of prayer also appears in Agnon's version of the legend of Abraham Prochownik, although in a different vein, as we shall see. Similarly, the theme of the gap between an earthly king and "Him Who enthrones kings," which is developed in Agnon's story, originates in this version. Perhaps the Galician Hebrew periodical was known to Agnon and he drew on it, as he almost certainly drew on other written and oral versions.

ABRAHAM PROCHOWNIK BECOMES ABRAHAM THE VILLAGER: AGNON'S VERSION OF THE LEGEND

The story of Abraham Prochownik, king of Poland, is no longer a living legend transmitted orally by Polish Jews. The 2,600 Polish Jewish folktales collected in Israel, starting in the 1950s, and preserved at IFA do not include a single version of the legend. In my fieldwork among Polish Jews in Israel I found that the story is still remembered, but I was unable to transcribe a single full version.[35] The informants related to it chiefly as informative or anecdotal. Some mentioned it in connection with the Jews' contribution to Polish society, in contrast to how the Poles recompensed the Jews during the Holocaust;[36] some dismissed the story as quite irrelevant to their lives today.

The story remains in the collective memory thanks to versions that have been transcribed, but also thanks to its metamorphosis into a literary work by Agnon.[37] As already mentioned, more than any other author, Agnon worked seriously at writing the legends of origin of Polish Jews. In *Poland: Legendary Tales,* the legend of Abraham comes second (after "Antecedents"), under the title "Watchers for the Morning" (Agnon 1967, 353–354).[38]

As I have already noted in earlier chapters, a close reading of Agnon's legend allows us to trace the process whereby a legend is transformed from oral tradition to a work of written literary art. It also permits us to appreciate Agnon's unique touch when he deals with folk legends.[39]

Watchers for the Morning

I was met by the watchmen who patrol the town.
"Have you seen the one I love?" (Cant. 3:3)

In those days there was no king in Poland: King Popiel had died when the rats invaded his palace and his bedchamber and his bed and ate him and he died, and there was no heir to the throne. All the elders of Poland gathered and came to Kruszwica to elect a king. After many days passed and they had not found the man after their hearts, they said: "The first person to enter the city tomorrow will be king over us." They stationed watchmen at all four corners of the city, saying: "The first person to enter the city tomorrow—the kingdom is his." They are standing at the corners of the city and Abraham the villager is climbing the ascent to the town to pray the morning prayer with the Hebrews. The watchmen saw a man coming to the city and they blew on their ram's horns and hailed him, Long live the King! They took him and rushed him to the council house and stood him before the princes and elders of the state and told him that he had been chosen to be their king. They proclaimed before him, "Long live the King!"

Abraham bowed low before the sons of Poland and said, "Who am I that I should come this far, when I was going to pray the morning prayer?" Abraham refused to place the crown of the kingdom of Poland on his head. He said, "Let me go, for dawn is breaking." They said, "We will not let you go unless you be our king." When he saw that they were endeavoring to make him their king, he said to them, "Listen to me and give me two days to think about the kingship. As for you, do not come to my house before I come out to you and call you." Abraham got up and went inside the house and sat there in the inner room for two or three days. When the people saw that their king was so long in coming out they cried out loudly.

Now Piast, a man of the soil, was standing at the front of the crowd. He called out, "Listen to me, all you men of Poland! How long will the land be desolate without a king to rule over the people? Now if Abraham is so long in coming, behold, I will go bring him out to you." Taking an axe, he raised it against the house where Abraham was and broke down the door. Abraham came out and stood in the doorway of the house and said to them: "I will not be your king, nor will someone else be your king. Piast will be your king. Choose him, for he saw that your country could not exist without a king and broke into the house where I ordered that no one should come. Now place the royal crown on his head and make him your king." The princes of Poland listened and crowned Piast and the kingdom was his. Abraham left the presence of the dukes of Poland and ran off in a hurry to the house of prayer. When he got there they were praying the morning prayer, standing in awe and saying in fear, "Eternal Lord who ruled as king before any being was created."

The main points of the oral tradition are preserved in "Watchers for the Morning": the tradition about the death of Popiel, who was eaten by rats, and the absence of an heir; the conclave in Kruszwica to choose a king; their distress because of their inability to reach an agreement and their decision to enthrone the first person who entered the city the next morning; the arrival of the Jew Abraham and his acclamation as king; Abraham's refusal and seclusion; the appearance of Piast, who breaks down the door in his concern for his country; Abraham's declaration that Piast should be king because of his concern for Poland; and Piast's coronation.

There are also differences, however: (1) the title of the story; (2) the character of the hero—the name Abraham remains, but the cognomen

Prochownik has vanished, and he is now called "Abraham the villager"; (3) those who assemble in Kruszwica are called the "elders of Poland," and the proposal to crown the first person to enter the city is reported as being a consensus decision; (4) in Agnon's legend, Abraham comes to the city to pray, not for commercial reasons; (5) there is no mention of the fact that the Poles should be grateful to the hero; (6) the story does not end with the coronation of Piast and the granting of trade privileges to the Jews, but with Abraham's rushing off to the house of prayer and the first verse of the liturgical poem "Adon Olam."

What is the reason for these changes and what is their significance? What message is the author attempting to convey? How is this message cast? As I noted in earlier chapters, answering these questions requires that, in addition to examining the changes vis-à-vis the folk versions of the legend, we also examine Agnon's use of Jewish sources and the various strata of the linguistic and cultural code thereby invoked. Deciphering the meaning of an Agnon text involves examining its interrelations with the various sources, which may be incorporated *en bloc* into the text, alluded to, or organically interwoven into it (Shenhar-Alroy 1989).

The story begins with an epigraph—a verse from the Song of Songs: "I was met by the watchmen who patrol the town. / 'Have you seen the one I love?' " The verse deals with love and the quest for the beloved. Traditional exegesis reads this love as that of the Jewish people for its God. The title of this story, "Watchers for the Morning," also relates to love of God. It comes from Psalm 130:6: "I am more eager for the Lord than watchmen for the morning watch for the morning," when they will be relieved of duty. The entire Psalm expresses a steadfast adherence to God and faith that the Lord will bring salvation to His people: "I look to the Lord; I look to Him; I await His word" (v. 5); "Israel waits for the Lord, for with the Lord is steadfast love and great power to redeem" (v. 7).

The epigraph and title create the first theme—the love of the Jewish people for its God—which, as we shall see, is a thread that runs through the entire story. Both epigraph and the title contain the word "watchmen/watchers": we shall see how this functions in the story.

The introduction, "in those days there was no king in Poland," is followed by a description of Popiel's death at the teeth of the rats and the note that there was no heir to the throne. The sentence echoes a refrain that the Book of Judges uses, in its last chapters, to designate a perilous situation of anarchy: "In those days there was no king in Israel; every man did as he pleased" (Judg. 17:6; the first clause recurs in 18:1 and 19:1). The stories in these chapters involve, inter alia, relations of hospitality. The first episode is that of Micah, who has an ephod made and persuades a Levite lad from Bethlehem of Judah to live with him and eventually to be his personal priest. The story also deals with idolatry and the violence of the

106

Danites against Micah and his family and later against the city of Laish. The second story of "hospitality" is that of the concubine of Gibeah, which also involves violence and idolatry. The echo suggests, then, that Agnon's story, too, involves the charged and sensitive relations between guest and host. The host does a good turn for the guest, welcoming him into his house, and expects that the latter will display gratitude. Such relations frequently lead to a situation in which the host, feeling his power, pressures his guest and exploits him to his own benefit or places him at risk against his will. In this way, the Biblical echoes produce a second theme that runs throughout the story—relations of guest and host, the relations between Jews and Poles in the pre-Christian period, with a consequent allusion to the possibility of violence.

In the absence of an heir, the Poles gather to elect a king. Agnon chooses to phrase it this way: "All the elders of Poland gathered and came to Kruszwica to elect a king," reminding us of the first institution of kingship in Israel: "All the elders of Israel assembled and came to Samuel at Ramah, and they said to him, '. . . appoint a king for us, to govern us like all other nations'" (1 Sam. 8:4–5). This approach—which, as we shall see, contributes to the message—entails omission of a detail found in the folk versions, namely, that it is the oldest member of the assembly who proposes crowning the first person who will enter the city the next day.[40] Here the proposal is reported as a general consensus. The association with the Israelites' first demand for a king creates a sense of the antiquity of the events, through the tacit analogy between the end of the period of the judges in Israel and the pre-Christian period in Poland. Agnon uses the association with Samuel to introduce a third theme—the kingdom of man and the kingdom of God. The kingdom of man is the kingdom of the Gentiles. The elders of Israel, who ask Samuel for a king, want to be like all other nations. Their act is condemned: "For it is not you that they have rejected; it is Me they have rejected as their king" (1 Sam. 8:7), says God to Samuel. Judaism is a culture of the dominion of God, not of the kingdom of flesh and blood.

Following the decision to crown the first person who enters the city the next morning at dawn, the conclave posts watchmen, as in the folk version. But in Agnon's story the word "watchmen" is charged by the story's title and epigraph. The verse that serves as the epigraph appears a second time in the Song of Songs, with a significant difference: "I met the watchmen who patrol the town; they struck me, they bruised me. The guards of the walls stripped me of my mantle" (Cant. 5:7). The association of the watchmen posted in Kruszwica with the watchmen from the Song of Songs hints that an encounter with them is apt to lead to catastrophe.

The watchmen posted to greet the future king—the first person to enter the city at dawn—are watchers through the night who look forward to dawn, when their mission will be accomplished. On the overt level, then, they tie in with the title of the story, "Watchers for the Morning." But the echo of the Biblical verse adds another level, on which the Jewish hero's eagerness for his God and King is more intense than that of the watchmen who long for the arrival of their flesh-and-blood king.

The chief difference between Agnon's text and the folk versions involves the characterization of Abraham. Agnon's protagonist is not Abraham Prochownik, who comes to conduct business, but "Abraham the villager . . . climbing the ascent to the town to pray the morning prayer with the Hebrews." Agnon's preference for "morning prayer" over "morning service," for "house of prayer" over "synagogue" or "house of study," and for "Hebrews" over "Jews" helps produce an aura of antiquity. The obtrusive present tense of "Abraham the villager is *climbing the ascent to the town*" is an exact echo of Saul's arrival in Ramah in search of his father's asses (1 Sam. 9:11). The analogy between Abraham and Saul prepares us for what will happen next. Just as Saul went in search of his father's asses and was involuntarily invested with the monarchy, so Abraham who went off to morning prayer will be called to kingship involuntarily. The salute "Long live the King!" is also an echo of Saul's coronation (1 Samuel 10:24).

Why "Abraham the villager" instead of Abraham Prochownik? I can offer two reasons for this change. One involves the dispute among historians about the discrepancy between the protagonist's occupation (gunpowder merchant) and the period in which the legend is set. Agnon wanted to avoid controversy about his story, since for him the legend expresses a profound truth quite different from what preoccupies the historians. Eliminating the occupational cognomen eliminates this debate. The main reason for the change, however, has to do with the message of the story and Agnon's desire to treat his people's power of spiritual endurance. For this he needs a figure who is sacred rather than profane. Agnon's Abraham is linked with the holy; the very reason he comes to town is a matter of piety. Abraham must be a villager because village Jews used to come to the city for public prayer. Coming to town for the morning service also ties in with the theme of the love of God and the title of the story. "Watchers for the Morning" was the designation applied to groups of pious men who rose for prayer before first light, very early in the morning, and who were in the habit of reciting Psalms at the conclusion of the penitential prayers. Natan Nata Hannover reports the existence of such groups in Poland: "At the head was a group who got up early, before first light, the "Watchers for the Morning," to pray and mourn the destruction of the Temple" (Hannover 1968, 94).[41]

Abraham is a man wrapped up in his prayer and love for God. What is more, in the general context of the sentence the phrase "Abraham the villager" recalls "Abraham the Hebrew," an association strengthened by the fact that he is said to be coming to pray with "the Hebrews."

The designation "Abraham the Hebrew" (Gen. 14:13) appears in the context of the war of the foreign kings.[42] Their presence in a Gentile environment creates an analogy between the two characters. The patriarch Abraham is associated with the discovery of faith in one God from within a pagan society and with the suffering he endured as a result of his beliefs. According to the Midrash, the nations twice attempted to make Abraham their king: "All the nations acknowledged his more than human achievement, and they fashioned a throne for Abraham, and erected it on the field of battle. When they attempted to seat him upon it, amid exclamations of 'Thou art our king! Thou art our prince! Thou art our god!' Abraham warded them off, and said, 'The universe has its King, and it has its God!' He declined all honors, and returned his property unto each man" (Ginzberg 1913, I, 232).

The herald of the Jewish faith cannot accept a human kingdom and repeatedly proclaims the kingdom of God, thereby distinguishing between the Jewish and pagan worlds. The analogy between the two figures produces an ideal Hebrew character among the Polish pagans and hints at Abraham's future rejection of the Polish elders' offer of the crown.

Abraham also has to deal with guest-host relations. Abraham's response to the princes and elders ("Abraham bowed low before the sons of Poland") also recalls the patriarch Abraham. The conduct of Abraham, the exemplary host, is described as "he *rushed* to greet them. . . . Let me *take* a morsel of bread. . . . Then Abraham *rushed* to the herd and *took* . . . and hastened. . . . He *stood* by them under the tree as they ate" (Gen. 18:2–8). Agnon uses different forms of similar verbs for actions that are done to the modern Abraham, rather than by him, as if he himself were the *pièce de resistance*. The Polish hosts "*took* him and *rushed* him to the council house and *stood* him before the princes." The change of verb form casts an ironic light on this hospitality and indicates the gulf between the Polish hosts' response and that of the patriarch Abraham–and hence between the two cultures.

Abraham repeats what the narrator has already told us, namely, that he is on his way to morning prayers. The repetition is no accident. Agnon wishes to emphasize his hero's scale of values and priorities. Abraham indeed refuses to place the crown of the kingdom of Poland on his head: "Let me go, for dawn is breaking," he protests. The verbal allusions here point up the hero's difficult struggle and the threatening atmosphere in which he finds himself. The very same words are uttered by the angel wrestling with Jacob (Gen. 32:27–28), and a slight variation is found in the episode of the concubine of Gibeah: "They raped her and abused her all night long until morning; and they let her go when dawn broke" (Judg. 19:25).

The Poles' stubborn insistence that he accept the crown ("we will not let you go unless you be our king") is reported in language that recalls the people's demand that Gideon, having saved them from the Midianites, rule over them (Judg. 8:22). This is followed by Gideon's refusal (which we will consider later) and, in the next chapter, by the parable of Jotham, which also reflects Judaism's negative view of the kingdom of man as compared to the kingdom of God.

The people's reaction to Abraham's prolonged seclusion again reminds us that we are dealing with a society of idolaters; here is the echo of the biblical episode during which Moses fails to come down from Mt. Sinai (Ex. 32:1–6) and the people embrace anarchy and worship of the Golden Calf.

Piast's appearance on stage and his conduct are reminiscent of that described in the folk legend. His designation as "man of the soil" draws on the folk tradition as well as on the biblical passage "Noah became a man of the soil" (Gen. 9:20)–which, according to the commentators (Rashi ad loc., David Kimhi in *Sefer hashorashim*), means that Noah was lord of the land. It is possible, however, that the phrase foreshadows what is about to happen: that Piast, the man of the soil, will become lord of the land of Poland and inaugurate a new royal dynasty. The point in the story when Piast breaks down the door with an axe is also associated with the theme of hospitality–in this case, with the story of Lot and his guests, whom the Sodomites demand be brought out to them: "they moved forward to break the door" (Gen. 19:9). Once again the reader is reminded of the threat and danger of the act of hospitality.

Abraham's words when he comes out, "I will not be your king, nor will someone else be your king. Piast will be your king," are reminiscent of Gideon's answer to the people's request that he rule over them: "I will not rule over you myself, nor shall my son rule over you; the Lord alone shall rule over you" (Judg. 8:23). The theme of God's kingdom versus the kingdom of man comes back, with the contrasting analogy between the pagan and Jewish worlds: for the Jews, the kingdom of God is enough. The host nation, sunk in idolatry, does require a king of flesh and blood.

The conclusion adds a final and extremely significant change from the folk versions. "Abraham left the presence of the dukes of Poland" echoes the verse in Esther: "Mordechai left the king's presence" (Esther 8:15). But in contrast to Mordechai, who emerges in royal robes and who, according to the Midrash, was the king's viceroy, Abraham comes out with empty hands. The Midrash criticizes Mordechai for becoming so preoccupied with royal affairs that he no longer had time to study Torah, as he had done previously. Abraham, who emerges with hands that hold nothing of the riches of this world, is the true winner who, like the patriarch Abraham, rejects the honor and riches that the nations would shower on him. He rushes off to the house of prayer for the morning prayer, instituted, according to tradition, by the patriarch Abraham, and through which the Jew enthrones his God each morning. The awe and fear are reserved for the morning prayer. The words of the liturgical poem "Adon Olam" conclude the story: "Eternal Lord who ruled as king before any being was created." The hymn continues: "When all came into being by His will, His name was proclaimed King. Even after all things shall have come to an end, He alone, awesome, will remain King."

This, finally, is the message of the spiritual kingdom of the Jews, which Agnon conveys by interweaving three themes: the love of God in Judaism as opposed to paganism; hospitality relations of guest and host; and the kingdom of God as opposed to the kingdom of man.

The story deals with the encounter between a people without a land—a people of the spirit, whose hallmark is love for its amorphous God—with the "people of the land," as Agnon calls them, a people that lives in its land, a people that is all earthliness and impulses. Here we should be especially careful. Agnon has no interest in condemning and criticizing. He wishes to conduct a poetic inquiry to understand the spirit of his people, which permitted them to cope and endure in a historic encounter that was difficult, even though accompanied by good will. Agnon uses the legend to treat historical phenomena and puts into practice his reading of Schlegel to unite poetry and philosophy. For the romantics, legend, as a folklore genre, reflected the pure spirit of the people (Herder 1968). In this way, the romantic Agnon could forge a link with the collective past of the first adventures of the Jews in Poland. The legend also made it possible for him to break through the barriers of reality and touch on the metaphysical—a characteristic of a genre that gives equal standing to the wondrous and the imaginary.

Agnon put bridle and saddle on the folk legend through his use of the classical language and verbal echoes that guide the reader. This transforms the legend from an etiological story that attempts to ground the Jews' right to live and trade in Poland— and their demand for gratitude on the part of the Poles—into a myth of the Jewish spirit. The abstraction from the world of matter freezes, as it were, the terrors and annoyances of profane time— just as happens to Abraham, who at the beginning of the story is on his way to morning prayer and reaches his destination at its end. When he arrives at morning prayer, in which man proclaims God to be king over him, there is a miraculous rupture of the chains of time; the profane time that intervenes between sacred times vanishes as if it had never been.

The folk legends about Abraham Prochownik are legends of origin, as we have seen, and incorporate a number of Weinryb's themes: The Jews settled in Poland in antiquity, which gives them a right to live there. They made a key contribution to the Polish people by helping to establish the glorious Piast dynasty. The treatment of Jews was better in the distant past, as expressed in the Poles' willingness to install a Jew as king of Poland and the granting of commercial privileges to Jews.

111

Kingship is a central theme of the story. In addition to the pleasure listeners could derive from a story in which the Poles want to make a Jew their king, other messages are conveyed. Abraham's rejection of the crown proclaims to the Gentile world that the Jews, as guests in a host country, are not out for power or authority that does not belong to them. This was an important message in every period, but especially at a time when Jews were trying to attain equal rights. But the issue of the crown also links up with a theme that I would add to Weinryb's scheme (see Chapter 1): the granting of an internal Jewish imprimatur, theological and spiritual, for living in Poland. As noted, Judaism recognizes a legitimate Jewish kingship only in the Land of Israel; accepting dominion in an adopted country is tantamount to assimilation. The rejection of the crown in the past, when the situation of the Jews was incomparably better (to the point that the Poles were willing to crown a Jewish king), transmits a message that living in Poland does not mean relinquishing Jewish identity—a message that was particularly relevant in the nineteenth century, when the Jews were asking for equal rights. In other words, attaining equal rights did not mean Jews should assimilate or surrender their religious and national identity.

Agnon's story offers an alternative interpretation of the Jews' reception in Poland. This is not an acceptance story meant to affirm and strengthen the Jews' presence in Poland, but rather a story that presents their reception as an event bearing a priori the seeds of the future catastrophe.

4

The Legend of Esther the Jewess and King Casimir the Great of Poland

The story of Esther and Casimir (Kazimierz) is a legend of origin from the folk tradition. It deals with the relationship between a Jewish girl, Esther or Estherke, and the king of Poland, Casimir the Great—that is, a relationship that violated a Jewish religious taboo. In normal circumstances, such relations would be condemned, but the absence of such condemnation, and even possible legitimation, is seen from the story of the biblical Esther on, when such relations are interpreted as being decisive for the survival of the entire community. The positive attitude toward the heroine is justified by an exegesis that interprets the heroine's act as self-sacrifice on behalf of her people. Thus the legends about Esther and Casimir are used in the folk tradition to explain the grant of settlement rights and the expansion of the privileges of the Jews in Poland by King Casimir. As we shall see, folk tradition uses the legend to explain why King Casimir expanded the Jews' privileges; in the words of the sixteenth-century chronicle *Zemaḥ David,* by David Ganz: "For her sake the king granted the Jews great privileges." Local folk traditions make use of the legend to explain place names, the establishment of synagogues, and more.

The story of Esther and King Casimir the Great, in Yiddish and Polish written literature, has been studied extensively by Chone Shmeruk (1981,

CHAPTER 4

"The Jews and Casimir the Great." Etching. From Jan Czynski, *Le réveil d'Israel* (Paris, 1848).

206–280). In his fascinating work, Shmeruk shows how a folk legend that circulated orally became the theme of many literary works in both languages, and he uses the story to examine the points of contact between the two literatures. In this chapter I will consider folk versions of the legend of Casimir and Esther that Shmeruk did not study, as well as Agnon's "Heart and Eyes."

Who are the heroes of this legend? Casimir (1310–70), the last king of the House of Piast, reigned from 1333 until his death. His name was linked with the Jews because he confirmed the privileges granted them by Bolesław of Kalisz and expanded them in 1334. Polish folktales relate that Casimir would visit peasant huts in disguise and reward the householders for their hospitality.[1] Etiological stories, relying on folk etymologies, link his name and deeds to place names in Poland, including the towns of Będzin, Czeladź, and Zagóże.[2] The tradition that interests us, and which was known to both Poles and Jews, deals with his relations with the Jewess Esther. Folk traditions also link place names with Esther. We hear of her house in Opoczno (many sources even include a picture of the house) and about fortresses that Casimir built for her in Łobzow near Cracow and in Bochotnica near Kuzmir (Kazimierz). Polish tradition locates her final resting place in a garden in Lobzow, which was a favored residence of

114

Casimir. We even hear that, in 1787, King Stanisław Augustus ordered the garden to be dug up in a vain quest for treasures and mementos.[3]

The legend of Casimir and Estherke circulated by word of mouth in various Jewish communities. In Radom, the legend of Esther was cited to explain the name of the city:

> Once, when the king was pursuing a gazelle in the forests of Solib, he encountered a wild beast of prey. He happened to be near a village at the time, and saw that the beast was threatening a young girl who was gathering herbs. He killed the beast before it could spring. The girl's name was Esther, the daughter of one of the Jewish residents of the place. The king was greatly impressed by her beauty and nobility, to the point that he brought her to the castle in Radom. At once he gave orders that it be repaired and expanded. He built houses and planted gardens there and made Radom into Estherke's residence. In the new quarter the king had built around the castle (Rawańska and Rynek streets), he had a special palace constructed for his beloved (Nos. 5 and 6 Rynek Street) and lived with her there. To this very day these houses are called "Estherke's House." Because the king had the new quarter built and frequently visited Estherke's house, the people called the place "Rad-dam," or "Happy about this house." (Benet 1961, 28)

In this story the name is explained in Polish, unlike the examples presented in Chapter 1, but the content is attributed to central events in the legendary annals of the Jews. The story attributes the Polish name of the city to the joy of the Polish king in his Jewish beloved. The growth of the city, too—the construction of its houses, the establishment of a new quarter, and the planting of gardens—is also traced to Casimir's love for the Jewish Esther. In addition to Weinryb's first theme, namely, that the origins of the Jewish community go back to the distant past (see Chapter 1), we also have a variation on the third theme: the Jews made a significant contribution to the general welfare—in this case, to the growth, expansion, and adornment of the city.

In Lublin there was a legend that Estherke was buried in the old cemetery there under a tombstone with her name engraved on it. When Berek, the narrator of Klemens Junosza's *The Miracle in the Cemetery,* describes the cemetery of Lublin, he exclaims: "Great personages are buried there, great leaders! There is even one stone on which no less and no more than one name is written! Does my master know who it is? It's Esther! Does my master know whose name that is? She was just a Jewess from the lower class, the daughter of a poor tailor, but later she became a Jewish queen" (Junosza 1905, 24).[4] This legend, which was transcribed at the end of nineteenth-century, seeks to glorify the Jewish cemetery of Lublin with the grave of Esther, a Jewish queen. The legend reflects the ancient Jewish tradition that Esther was married to Casimir and therefore also queen of Poland. This, of course, contradicts the Polish tradition that she was his mistress. Shmeruk believed this to be a key issue over which the two traditions differed (Shmeruk 1981). We should note that in folk Jewish versions written down later, especially those recorded after World War II, Esther is no longer described as a Jewish queen and is sometimes explicitly referred to as the king's mistress. This changed perception of the characters evidently stems from historical study of the episode as well as the narrators' familiarity with the Polish tradition.

Many legends linked Esther with the town of Kuzmir (Kazimierz). Mayer Kirshenblatt, born in the 1916 in Opatów and living today in Toronto, tells the following story:

> King Casimir ruled Poland about 800 years ago. Legend has it that he had a Jewish girlfriend and that she was instrumental in the King inviting the Jews to Poland to promote commerce. He used to entertain his lady under an ancient oak tree. When I was a young boy, we were told that the tree was still standing. Its branches, each one as thick as an average tree, were so huge they had to be supported. The tree was in the Jewish quarter on the outskirts of Cracow–in Kazimierz (Kuzmir, in Yiddish).[5]

The legend incorporates several of Weinryb's origin-legend themes: The Jewish community of Kuzmir has ancient roots. The Jews were invited to settle in Poland by the king. The Jews were invited to Poland because of their economic contribution to the prosperity of the country. According to the legend, it was Esther who persuaded the king to invite the Jews to settle in the country; this highlights her activity on behalf of her people and sets up an analogy with the biblical Esther, something we will see below in other legends. The oak tree–of which the narrator notes, "When I was a young boy we were told the tree was still standing"–is a literary device invoked to add credibility to the story. The size of the tree and thickness of its branches turn into a mythological spatial element and can be interpreted as a metaphor for the size, importance, and rootedness of the Jewish community in Poland. In Kuzmir there was a legend that Casimir the Great built the Great Synagogue as a gift to Estherke (Schneiderman 1970a, 12; Schneiderman 1970b, 14). According to another legend, a subterranean passage led from the tower there to the castle in Bochotnica, "which the king built for his beloved, Estherke. During her days and nights of solitude, when her hero and lover was in Cracow, on the Wawel, preoccupied with affairs of state, or when his armies marched to war against the enemies of Poland, the daughter of the Jewish tailor from Opoczno would embroider a curtain for the Holy Ark in the Kuzmir synagogue (Schneiderman 1970a, 14).

The legend, which was passed down from generation to generation in Kuzmir, attributed special powers to this ark curtain, whose central motif

Mayer Kirshenblatt, "King Casimir the Great Entertaining His Jewish Girlfriend Estherke" (1997). Acrylic on canvas. With kind permission of Barbara Kirshenblatt-Gimblett.

is a fire-breathing monster. The curtain survived wars and the many conflagrations that destroyed the wooden synagogue before a brick building was built in the early eighteenth century. The Jews of Kuzmir identified the monster with the serpent of the Garden of Eden, who seduced Eve to eat from the Tree of Knowledge, an interpretation suited to the figure of Estherke.

The ark curtain was hung in the old synagogue only on festivals, when it was guarded day and night by details from the burial society. The rest of the year it was stored, along with other ritual articles, by the merchant Reb Vevche Bromberg. The legend of Esther and Casimir and the ark curtain became a tourist attraction. Many tourists came to Kuzmir to see the ark curtain and hear the legend of Esther (Schneiderman 1970a, 15).

Thanks in part to this legend, relates L. Schneiderman, Kuzmir became a Polish tourist center: "The association with artists and authors who used to come to Kuzmir in the summer months stirred the imagination of the tour guides in the town. From year to year they expanded their repertoire

Maurycy Trębacz, "Landscape of Kazimierz." Painting. With kind permission of the Jewish Historical Institute, Warsaw.

of tales and anecdotes about the history of the oldest community in Poland. The central motif in all of their improvisations was the Estherke legend" (Schneiderman 1970b, 104).

Schneiderman tells of the two Yankeles, Yankel Schwarzman and Yankel Goldfarb, two tour guides who won the nicknames "Faktor" and "Yaponchik," respectively. Both spoke elegant Polish, which astonished visitors. Each had his own style and version of the legend.

Old Yankel Faktor's account of King Casimir's nocturnal trips to Buchotnica, where Estherke's palace was located on a hill overlooking the Vistula (Wisła), was dry and serious. He considered his story to be historically accurate in every particular. He referred to Casimir as "the king of the peasants," in accordance with Polish tradition, and related that the king brought Spanish goldsmiths to make the gold thread with which Estherke embroidered the ark curtain for the Kuzmir synagogue. By contrast, Yankel Yaponchik, who was a natural-born clown, would spice his tales with descriptions of the traditional Jewish foods, such as *cholent* and gefilte fish, that Estherke prepared for Casimir the Great.

In his story, "Ven Yash iz gekomen," Ya'acov Glatstein tells about a visit to Poland by someone who had left the country many years before and moved to New York. The Jewish tourist visits the remains of the palace and listens to a local guide relating the story. In an at once lyrical and grotesque style, Glatstein describes how the tourist viewed the folk legend and its characters.

> He said "Estherke's castle" so apathetically that I began to suspect him of feigning a special indifference in order to see how far the past would wound me. In fact, it wounded me like a golden arrow straight to my heart. On the top of the hill floated a Jewish folksong that shot a golden arrow straight into my heart, wrapped in velvet and silk. The folk song was, of course, "the golden peacock that flew away, flew away and sang."
>
> King Casimir was dressed in a paper Purim crown and had a silk beard. He was a bit foolish and somewhat resembled Ahasuerus, but he was a fiery lover who carried the Jewish girl back and forth, higher and higher, to the place where they had just finished building the light-towers.
>
> Mordechai stood below and scratched himself in his helplessness. Such an obsession to raise her so high, you could be left breathless from such an ascent. Estherke herself said nothing. She lay in a dead faint in the king's arms. She was perfumed like a spice-box. Submitting, she was naked, or three-quarters naked, while the last quarter Casimir with his own heart shuddered violently.
>
> During the long days when the king was being king somewhere far, far away, Estherke looked down with longing at the pump, at the dark houses and her brethren. At night she would loosen her tresses and sing: "I will go out on the balcony and look at the little town." In these sad longings for the king with the silken beard, she tied a note to the tail of the golden peacock. The note was written to the Jewish people, but the king's sorcerer made a sudden windstorm throughout the neighborhood. The golden peacock couldn't find a way through this terrible storm to the Jewish people, and the note fell off its tail and was lost. (Glatstein 1940, 258–259)

The associations with the Biblical Esther and the Purim holiday found in Glatstein's version also appear in a story transcribed in 1990 from a Warsaw-born Jew, Yehuda Herman, of Kibbutz Beit Keshet. He told the story as, he said, it was current in his home town:[6]

> The miracle of Esther and the wicked Haman took place only once in history; after the Biblical canon was sealed, there were no more miracles. But had the Biblical canon not been closed, they could have added the Scroll of Polish Esther. This is how it was:
>
> Once King Casimir the Great of Poland was traveling through his kingdom. In one town he saw a pretty young girl. "Who is she?" he asked the townspeople.
>
> "Esther," they replied.
>
> "Whose daughter is she?"
>
> "A tailor."

119

"And who is he?"

"A Jew."

"Bring her to me," commanded the king.

They did so. At once he fell in love with her and made her his mistress. As long as she lived, it was good for the Jews. Only after she died did the troubles begin.

That is why, had the Biblical canon not been closed, they could have added the Scroll of Polish Esther.

The plot of the Casimir-Esther story and the heroine's name necessarily spark an association with the Book of Esther. Both the Polish and Jewish traditions are full of such associations. In Julian Krzyżanowski's index of Polish tale types (1962), type 951D is designated "Esther." Krzyżanowski relies on a text presented by Zawilinski (1953) and notes that the authority for it sees the legend as about Casimir the Great, when in fact it is a folk reworking of the Biblical story of Esther. Shmeruk mentions the existence of such associations in the earliest Polish chronicles. In one of them, Casimir is explicitly described as "Asswerus nasz polski Każimierz Wielki" (our Polish Ahasuerus, Casimir the Great). At Casimir's first meeting with Esther in Kraszewski's famous *King of the Peasants,* the priest who accompanies the king blurts out, when he hears her name, the Latin "nomen omen" (the name is a sign) (Shmeruk 1981, 210–213). In *Zemah David,* too, David Ganz's Hebrew chronicle that first appeared in Prague in 1595–which, according to Shmeruk, is the earliest Jewish chronicle that deals with the relations between Casimir and Esther (ibid., 222–223)– the text arouses associations with the Biblical Esther. Another indication of the link between the story and the Book of Esther is the fact that Kuzmir Jews used to put on *Purimspielen* (Purim plays) about Estherke and Casimir, as Schneiderman relates. According to him, every year the Kuzmir tailor Leibush Getzels would stage a *Purimspiel* entitled "The Kuzmir Queen Esther." Getzels himself wrote the play and played the part of King Casimir. Adds Schneiderman: "From my early childhood, there stills lives in my memory the scene of the Purimspiel, when the short Leibush Getzels would appear as a giant in platform shoes, and Estherke, who was played by a boy, would show the king the golden ark curtain, which she had made for the Kuzmir synagogue" (Schneiderman 1970b, 105–106).

The play was staged in the packed living room of Vevche Bromberg. During the performance participants would bring the ark curtain, whose embroidery was ascribed to Estherke, out of the large trunk where it was stored throughout the year. According to Schneiderman, Getzels's *Purimspiel* was written down by Chaim Ziskind, the town scholar, who devoted himself to transcribing the annals of Estherke. Schneiderman adds that he himself read it in Ziskind's house after Getzels's death (ibid.).

Purimshpiel as displayed in a diorama in the Ethnographical Museum in St. Petersburg. From Rivka Gonen, ed., *Back to the Shtetl: An-Ski and the Jewish Ethnographic Expedition 1912–1914* (Jerusalem: The Israel Museum, 1994). With kind permission of the editor.

The association between the story and the Book of Esther is also found in the drama *Estherke,* by Heschel Eppelberg, first staged in Warsaw in 1890. According to Shmeruk, this play was an attempt "to contribute a modern–according to Eppelberg's lights–addition to the standard *Purim-spiel* repertoire of the Jews of Poland" (Shmeruk 1981, 255).

In Glatstein's story, as well as in the folktale from IFA cited above, the narrator associates Estherke with the Biblical Queen Esther; in the folk story the narrator refers to "the scroll of the Polish Esther." It is interesting to note that Yehuda Herman actually related the story on Purim (Shushan Purim of 5750, to be precise), noting that in view of the holiday it was appropriate to talk about Casimir's Esther. Thus Jewish tradition linked the two heroines' enterprises for their people, for "writs of favor and freedom," as David Ganz puts it.

"THE HEART AND EYES" LEGEND

As already stated, the folk tradition about Esther and Casimir was reworked in Yiddish and Polish written literature; this topic has been the subject of a comprehensive study (Shmeruk 1981, 206–280). In Hebrew literature, too, the legend received authorial treatment at the hands of Agnon.[7]

Agnon's legend, with its various versions, rarely has been subjected to critical attention.[8] Shmeruk, too, relegates Agnon's stories to a note (ibid., 240–241, n. 62) in which he mentions the existence of several versions of the story.[9]

Agnon's story runs as follows:

The Heart and Eyes

You must certainly know, you have certainly heard the name of Esther, the queen of King Casimir of Poland. Her face was white as snow, like snow that falls on the synagogue on Shabbat Shirah,[10] and her eyes were like the sun in the month of Ziv,[11] and the sweetness of her voice was like the song of the morning, and all her ways were delightful to human beings. There was no lass as beautiful as Esther in all of Poland. Casimir, king of Poland, saw her and was strongly drawn to Esther. He brought her in his golden chariot to his royal city. On her path he strewed gold and sugar. The king came with Esther to his state chamber. The king lived with Esther for many days, never allowing sleep to his eyes nor slumber to his eyelids, so he could look at Esther night and day. For beauty is sweet to the eyes and no man's eye could see all of Esther's charm at once. Her co-wives–Casimir's three wives, Anna of Lithuania, Edelheit of Hesse, and Hedwig of Zagen–were terrified by the king's love for Esther. In their furious jealousy they used their fingernails to scratch evil writs on the walls of Esther's house, all about the Jewish woman the king had taken. For Esther was a Jewish woman, the daughter of a Jewish tailor. But Esther was not afraid and paid no attention, for a kosher mezuza guarded her gates, through which the king used to come to Esther. Esther saw life with her husband the king until she died. With love to her husband the king she died.

Now I will tell you what the king did to his wife Esther when his wife Esther died. When Esther died before the king, the king removed her heart and eyes and placed them in the wall of his house in his state chamber, near his bed, inlaid in gold and precious gems. There was no statue or picture of Esther, because Esther devoted her days to her husband the king and found no time to sit with portrait painters. For Esther devoted her days to her lord, to her husband the king, and her husband the king certainly knew Esther. The king dug a grave for his wife, for Esther, in the vale of flowers opposite his house, and he buried her in the valley of flowers which was the king's.

Esther lay in the valley of flowers in the tomb that the king dug for her. The king looked out of the window of his house at the grave he had dug for Esther. He would look at the wall of his hall, at her eyes and heart, which he had placed in an inlay of gold and precious gems in the wall of his house, in his bed chamber. His eyes never strayed from her eyes and his heart never drifted from her heart.

Esther lay in her grave, the way the dead lie in their graves, but she did not find rest with the dead. For every man and woman whose eyes and heart are not with them cannot find rest in the grave. Esther would rise out of her grave at night, seeking her heart and eyes, which she had given to her husband the king and which the king had taken from her. Esther wandered from her grave to the house of her delights, seeking her heart and eyes, but was helpless to find the door. For Esther had no eyes and could not see, for the king had taken them with her heart. Esther did this every night until her brethren, her people, got up and recited the Shema. When they read these words of the Torah, "you shall not follow your heart and eyes," Esther would return to her grave, to return the next night, seeking her heart and eyes that she followed after.

"The Heart and Eyes" was first published in Hebrew in the daily *Ha'Aretz* on 29 September 1943. Later it was included in the collection *Poland: Legendary Tales,* in the second volume of Agnon's collected works, *Elu Va'Elu.*[12] There are a few differences between the two versions. Except for one change, however, most of them are minor emendations and improvements, not a recasting of the story.

Long before the first Hebrew appearance of the story, however, Agnon had published the story in German, under the title "Estherkas Haus," in Berlin in 1916.[13] The German version includes most of the material that Agnon used in his later recasting of the legend as "The Heart and Eyes" and can be seen as the first version of the story. Nevertheless, a comparison of the Hebrew and German texts indicates a different approach to the problem of composition; the German version is, if we may borrow Shaked's term from another context (1973, 137), a nucleus that the author uses when he comes to write a new story.

Let us examine Agnon's legend, considering his various sources and how he put them together.

RESIDUES OF SOURCES IN THE LANGUAGE OF THE STORY: OVERT PLOT AND UNDERPLOT

Agnon's use of Jewish sources and his selection of the linguistic and cultural code, with its strata and depths, create a secondary plot alongside the overt one; this hidden layer is a key for understanding the story.

The story is divided into two parts, in chronological order. Hence the time related is almost identical to the order in the text, a frequent practice in folk narrative. Each part begins with the narrator addressing the reader. The direct address that opens the second part divides the story into its two sections and emphasizes the passage from the first part, about Esther's life, to the second part, which deals with the period after her death.

In the first part, Casimir's love for Esther is described as an obsession that allows him no rest. As is conventional in folk narrative, here, too, sentiments are described only through action. To this end, Agnon draws in the motif of eyes: first in the description of Esther's eyes, which are "like the sun in the month of Ziv"; later, in the description of Casimir, who follows his eyes–"Casimir, king of Poland, saw her and was strongly drawn to Esther"; and still later–"The king lived with Esther for many days, never allowing sleep to his eyes nor slumber to his eyelids, so he could look at Esther night and day. For beauty is sweet to the eyes." The unavoidable association is with the morning benediction: "Blessed art Thou, O Lord our God, King of the universe, who causes sleep to pass away from my eyes and slumber from my eyelids"; as well as the words of Ecclesiastes: "How sweet is the light, how good it is for the eyes to behold the sun" (Eccles. 11:7). Thus it arises that Casimir acts contrary to the normal world order as envisaged by Judaism, serving Esther as one serves an idol, while Esther, whose eyes are like the sun, becomes his sun and the light of his eyes.

The second part begins with the macabre removal of the heart and eyes from Esther's corpse. To explain this act, the narrator notes that "there was no statue or picture of Esther." The Decalogic prohibition "You shall not make for yourself a statue or any picture" (Ex. 20:4) conflicts with Casimir's need to worship what his eyes see and to create an icon–basic principles of Christianity.

The icon motif returns later: "He would look at the wall of his hall, at her eyes and heart, which he had placed in an inlay of gold and precious gems in the wall of his house, in his bed chamber." Esther, by contrast, finds no rest; every night she goes in search of her heart and eyes but cannot find the door (compare Gen. 19:11), because she has no eyes. The heart and eyes, next to the bed in the royal bed chamber, become an icon worshipped by the king.[14]

A comparison of "Heart and Eyes" with the German "Estherkas Haus" reveals a new element in the Hebrew story not found in its German precursor. In the earlier version we read about the removal of her eyes and the ritual surrounding them; here, however, the heart is added. This addition is a consequence of the key phrase near the end of the story, taken from the morning liturgy.

The verse "you shall not follow your heart and eyes" is cited in "Estherkas Haus," but to explain Estherke's restless wandering–a Jew cannot be buried without eyes. Yet it seems that already in "Estherkas Haus" Agnon was uncomfortable with this explanation; he adds that the phrase must be understood in the abstract. In "The Heart and Eyes," a sophisticated evolution has taken place. Agnon maintains the conventional structure of the folk narrative and understands the verse literally.[15] When the Jews say, "You shall not follow," Esther leaves off her quest and returns to her grave.

But the plain meaning belongs to the overt level of the plot. The very reference to the Shema, from which the verse is taken, directs our attention to the multilayered sources. Examining them permits us to decipher the latent message and lays bare the gulf between Judaism and Christianity, a gap that is expounded through the eye motif.

The Shema comprises three sections, of which Numbers 15:37–41 is the third. The first section contains the imperative, "You shall love the Lord your God with all your heart and with all your soul and with all your might. Take to heart these instructions with which I charge you this day" (Deut. 6:5–6). In Judaism the love of the heart is to be directed to God; appurtenances such as phylacteries, the mezuza on the doorpost, and *tzitzit* (ritual fringes)–the three commandments stated in the Shema– are meant to remind one of the commandments; they are not a goal in and of themselves. A study of the Midrash gives added depth to the meaning of the verse and links it to both idolatry and adultery: "Heart and eyes are panders to the body, for they nourish the body" (*Numbers Rabba* 17, p. 740). Or, at greater length:

> "You shall not follow your heart" refers to heresy, as we learn from the verse, "I find woman more bitter than death; she is all traps, her hands are fetters and her heart is snares" (Eccles. 7:26), whereas "the king shall rejoice in God" (Ps. 63:12). " . . . And your eyes" refers to harlotry, as we read: "But Samson answered his father, 'Get me that one, for she is the one who pleases my eyes' " (Judg. 14:3). "After which you go astray in your lust" (the continuation of the verse in Numbers) refers to idolatry, as we read: "they went astray after the Baalim" (Judg. 8:33). (*Sifre on Numbers,* portion *Shelah* §115, ed. Horowitz, p. 127)

Yalkut Shimoni, too (Numbers, 350a), associates the verse with idolatry and adultery: " 'You shall not follow': let not your heart be your idol.[16] It also says [referring to the spies], 'of those who scouted [the same Hebrew verb rendered as "follow" in the passage from the Shema"] the land' (Num. 14:6); this tells you how many warnings the adulterer transgresses [14 negative prohibitions are enumerated here] . . . 'you shall love' . . ." (see also Rashi on BT Nedarim 50a).

The association between idolatry and adultery is also found in folk narratives, for example, in the story "He Went Out and Came Back," "A story told by the rabbi, the righteous man, the holy one of Israel and its glory, Rabbi Israel of Rizhin, may his memory be a blessing."[17] The hero of the story is a scholar who marries the handicapped daughter of an extremely wealthy man and becomes accustomed to an easy life.

> At first he would take a break from study and rest awhile, after learning for the whole day. After that he had the excellent idea of taking a walk every evening in the cool air, since a walk among the trees or in the fields gives one additional strength and this would enable him to learn more. But because he left the four cubits of halakhah to enjoy the pleasures of the world, he was drawn after the *two panders of sin, the heart and eyes* [emphasis mine]. On his way he encountered attractive women, looked at them and saw their figures, and his soul yearned for them and their delights.

In the end the hero goes after Gentile women and apostasizes.[18]

The two benedictions that precede the Shema in the morning reinforce this meaning. The first is "Creator of light" (associated with the eyes); the second is the blessing of "love" (the heart). In the first blessing we read, inter alia, "enlighten our eyes in Your Torah," which corresponds, antithetically, to "for beauty is sweet to the eyes" in our story; "cause our heart to cleave to Your commandments" in the blessing of love is opposed to "was strongly drawn to Esther"; while "unify our heart to love and fear Your name" contrasts with "his eyes never strayed from her eyes and his heart never drifted from her heart."

The love between the Christian king and Esther the Jewess is necessarily love without surcease, both for the living king, who keeps sleep from his eyes and slumber from his eyelids, and for Esther after her death, when she returns every night to seek her heart and eyes, without which the king cannot manage. The gulf between Judaism, which devotes heart and eyes to the service of the amorphous God, and Christianity, which cannot do without icons, is unbridgeable.

It is the cultural code embedded in the language that creates the special tone of the story and contains its meaning.

THE USE OF EARLIER TRADITIONS ABOUT CASIMIR AND ESTHER

The motifs of this legend are international folk motifs, listed in Thompson's index (1955–58: F81.1.1, obtaining the heart of the dead; D992, magical eyes; S165, removal of eyes; E750.1, a soul that wanders after death). But Agnon relies on more than just folk motifs.

The opening of "Heart and Eyes" is typical of a folk narration: "You must certainly know, you have certainly heard the name of Esther, the queen of King Casimir of Poland." This is a direct address to the audience, a method used by folk narrators to capture the attention. The introduction relies on prior knowledge available to the audience as part of the oral tradition

126

("you have heard"). Folk narrators generally spur audience interest by announcing in advance the theme of the story they are about to tell; sometimes they even propose a list of well-known and familiar stories whose themes they present.[19]

Stating the protagonists' names at the outset also establishes which genre of folk narrative is to follow—the legend. According to its definition, a legend is associated with a particular historical event or historical personage and takes place in the narrator's own geographical space. A legend deals with characters, places, and concrete events.[20]

I have not found the legend "The Heart and Eyes"—that is, the story of Esther's death—in the oral folk versions, but it does appear twice in written literature; in both cases it is attributed to a folk legend told by old men or women of the uneducated classes.

Agnon himself directs his readers to one source, Sholem Asch's *Mashiahs Tsaytn,* in a note to "Estherkas Haus." The second source is mentioned in Shmeruk's article (1981, 238–241, especially n. 62) as part of his discussion of *Mashiahs Tsaytn.* The legend is found in Frischman's story "Memorial Prayer," first published in Yiddish in 1888. In this story, the legend is not associated with Casimir and Esther but deals with the relations between Jewish women and high-ranking Gentiles. The heroine's name is Estherke, all the same. She asks her father: "Tell me, is it true what the old folks tell us about old Count Sczególski? . . . Is it true that that man kidnapped a Hebrew lass and lived with her in the house opposite us, the expropriated house? And that when the girl died the count removed her eyes from their sockets and made himself two gold rings and had the eyes set in the rings the way one sets pearls? And that he never took the rings off his fingers until he died and was buried with them?" (Frischman 1914, 192). Agnon does not mention Frischman, not even in "Estherkas Haus," where he lists other sources.

The second source of the legend, which Agnon does mention, is Sholem Asch's play *Mashiahs Tsaytn,* first published in 1906.[21] In the drama, women servants tell the legend to the heroine, Justina (Yentele). Its core is that Casimir fell in love with Esther because of her beautiful eyes. Those eyes followed him through all of his wars. After her death, Casimir removed them and had them set in gold rings, which he hung on a black-draped pillar in his palace. Every night he would bow down and pray to them. Esther, by contrast, wandered blind in her shroud, a crown on her head, in the underworld. At night she continues to roam in search of her eyes, for without them she cannot find rest, according to the Jewish tradition, since a Jew's body must be buried in its entirety.

We may assume that both Frischman and Asch relied on a folk legend that circulated orally, whose objective was to reinforce the taboo against sexual relations with non-Jews. Support for this hypothesis can be drawn from "Estherkas Haus," which Agnon subtitled, "From an as-yet unpublished volume for Jewish girls," and in which he speaks directly to Jewish girls. Immediately after he cites the macabre legend, he writes, in an ironic tone, that it is not his intention to use the story to frighten Jewish girls and make them forget their dreams about non-Jewish princes, dukes, and counts.[22]

It does not seem to be accidental that Agnon relied on Sholem Asch's play in "Estherkas Haus." The context in which Asch cites the legend and the message of the play are extremely significant for him. Asch's drama is imbued with faith in the possibility of cooperation between the two peoples.[23] Justina, the enlightened heroine of the play, expresses her aspiration to integrate into the life of the Polish people by speaking Polish. When Justina hears that Esther cannot find rest, she leads her to her mother's grave and brings her to her rest: "Arise, dear sister, arise. . . . I will take you by the hand and lead you to your mother's grave" (Asch 1906, 75). In other words, what was impossible in the fourteenth century because of prejudice on both sides is indeed possible in the nineteenth century, thanks to Justina, the model of the new Jewess.

"The Heart and Eyes" is the antithesis of Asch's notion. As we have stated, Agnon rejected Asch's approach already in "Estherkas Haus" through the subtitle "From an as-yet unpublished volume for Jewish girls," and through his ironic address to Jewish girls who dream about non-Jewish princes, dukes, and counts. This attitude is dressed in new garb in "The Heart and Eyes." Here no doubt is cast on the love between the Christian king and the beautiful Jewess; theirs is not a love that depends on material benefits, as both the Jewish and Polish traditions contended. Unlike Asch, however, Agnon sees no possibility of tranquility in such love, because of the existential gulf between Judaism and Christianity. In the legends presented by Frischman and Asch, we read of the removal of the eyes only. This reinforces the hypothesis that the addition of the heart is an allusion to the verse "you shall not follow your heart and eyes" at the story's foundation.

Given that the addition of the heart is Agnon's innovation, not found in his sources, it must be the reason for the only significant change between the 1943 version of the story and the final version. In the earlier version, the second part of the story originally began, "Now I will tell you what you have heard and read in books about what Casimir the Great did to his wife Esther. . . ." The final text reads: "Now I will tell you what the king did to his wife Esther." Unlike the earlier introduction, which directs readers to familiar traditions known from hearing and reading, the later version has only the author's authority, which emphasizes the uniqueness of his account. Agnon avoids drawing any direct analogies with the Biblical Esther story. Such allusions as do appear are not associated with

Esther's action on behalf of her people, since this is not mentioned in the story at all.

At the beginning of "The Heart and Eyes," the heroine is called "Esther, the queen . . . , " which reminds us of the inverse form, "Queen Esther." There is also a textual allusion in the depiction of Esther's appearance. Agnon, like his predecessors, describes her beauty as extraordinary. He chooses to describe this through means that are typical of European fairy tales: "Her face was white as snow"; "her eyes were like the sun." But the expression is distinctly oicotipified: "Her face was white as snow, like snow that falls on the synagogue on Shabbat Shirah, and her eyes were like the sun in the month of Ziv, and the sweetness of her voice was like the song of the morning stars." The last clause associates her with the Biblical Esther, who in later literature was also referred to as the "morning star": (Ginzberg 1913, IV, 293).

We see, then, that there are very few allusions to the Biblical Book of Esther in Agnon's story, and those there are relate to the status of the heroine and chiefly to her beauty. In my opinion, the absence of allusions to Esther's action on behalf of her people is Agnon's declaration that this has nothing to do with the matter: this is not the problem confronted by "The Heart and Eyes."

AGNON'S ESTHER IN THE LIGHT OF EARLIER TRADITIONS

In all three of Agnon's literary versions, Esther is referred to as the "king's wife." This designation indicates that Agnon has adopted the Jewish tradition rather than the Polish tradition. According to the latter, Esther was Casimir's mistress. Shmeruk has discussed this question at length, so I will only mention the main points of the two traditions. According to the Polish tradition, as summarized by Wyrozumski, Casimir had a Jewish mistress named Estherke, the daughter of a Jewish tailor from Opoczno. His affair with her began when he was still unhappily married to Adelaide of Hesse and after he had abandoned his former love, the Czech Rokiczana. The king and Estherke had two sons, Niemierz and Pełka, and several daughters. The sons were raised as Christians, but the king allowed the daughters to remain Jewish (this sparked the ire of the earlier Polish chroniclers). Pełka died in his youth, while Niemierz was killed by accident during the funeral of King Władisław Jagiełło (Wyrozumski 1982, 209–212). According to Shmeruk, this tradition became a permanent feature of Polish antisemitic literatures, going back to the earliest chronicles. The Jews' preferential treatment during Casimir's reign is associated with his favors to Esther. She herself is described in this literature as a beautiful woman with impure motives; the Jews exploited her status to advance their own interests. In written Polish literature, too, Esther is depicted as

Casimir's mistress—even in the novel by Ignacy Kraszewski, first published in 1881 (Kraszewski 1963), which describes Esther as the ideal partner, whose love and devotion are boundless and who is unwilling to exploit her relations with the king in a way that might injure their love.[24]

As already mentioned, Esther is called "the king's wife" in all three of Agnon's versions. Nevertheless, there is a significant difference between the first version, "Estherkas Haus," and the later versions in Hebrew. In "Estherkas Haus" her status is presented in the very first sentence: "Dies ist das Haus der Estherka, der herzensgeliebten *Frau* Kasimirs des grossen, Königs von Polen" [emphasis mine].

The underlying tradition here is that of *Zemaḥ David* (see above, Shmeruk 1981, 222–223). Agnon knew and admired this work, as we learn when he notes at the end of "Estherkas Haus": "This story was also told by the noble, God-fearing, and learned rabbi David Ganz, astronomer and historian, who died in Prague in 1613, in his book *Zemaḥ David.*" In *Zemaḥ David,* David Ganz's Hebrew chronicle, we read: "Casimir, king of Poland, *took as his mistress* a Jewish girl named Esther, a beautiful maiden with no peer in the land. *She became his wife* for many days. For her sake the king showed great favor to the Jews and she obtained writs of favor and freedom from the king for the Jews." Both "mistress" and "wife" appear in this text; in the Yiddish translation of *Zemaḥ David* (1697), however, "mistress" has dropped out and Esther is described as a lawful wife in every respect.

Zemaḥ David is cited explicitly in "Estherkas Haus" but is not mentioned in "The Heart and Eyes," other than in the allusion to older sources in the opening sentence—"You must certainly know, you have certainly heard." Even though the source is not named, Agnon makes use of what it hints at. True, Esther is called "the king's wife," but she is a wife acquired through carnal knowledge,[25] a practice banned by the later Talmudic sages to prevent lewd behavior. At the beginning of the story, it seems as if Agnon is choosing not to avoid this issue, on which the sources are divided, by calling Esther "the queen of King Casimir of Poland." The designations of "her husband" for Casimir and "his wife" for Esther occur only in conjunction with the verbs "come" and "know" (both verbs regularly denote sexual intercourse in classical Hebrew): "for a kosher mezuza guarded her gates, through which the king used to come to Esther"; "her husband the king certainly knew Esther." What we have, then, is a way of expressing ambivalence toward Esther and her actions.

An ironical perspective on Esther is also created by the echoes of Biblical verses embedded in the story. Esther's response to the hostility of the king's other wives is described as follows: "But Esther was not afraid and paid no attention, for a kosher mezuza guarded her gates, through which the king used to come to Esther." The surface plot gives us a heroine of legend who has no fears because of a talisman she possesses (the mezuza on her door). Agnon's echoes of Biblical verses, however, reflect the narrator's ironic attitude toward his character. The mezuza is not supposed to be a talisman; the Biblical injunction, included in the Shema, associates it with remembering the Lord's commandments: "Take to heart these instructions with which I charge you this day. . . . Inscribe them on the doorposts of your house" (Deut. 6:6,9). Here, however, the Gentile king comes to the Jewess Esther through the mezuza-bearing door.

Scrutiny of the first version of the tale, "Estherkas Haus," also tells us something about Agnon's methods of composition. "Estherkas Haus" is an etiological story: the narrator calls attention to the mark on the right side of the door, which, he says, is where Estherke affixed the mezuza. The reference to the mezuza aims to verify the opening line that "this is Estherke's house": the mark left by the mezuza is offered as proof. In "The Heart and Eyes," however, where he abandons the etiological element, the mezuza becomes an ironic element expressing Agnon's attitude toward the heroine.

By way of highlighting the relations between the king and Esther, Agnon describes the reaction of his other wives: "Her co-wives . . . in their furious jealousy . . . used their fingernails to scratch evil writs on the walls of Esther's house, all about *the Jewish woman* the king had married. For Esther was *a Jewish woman,* the daughter of a Jewish tailor" [emphasis mine]. The allusion to Moses' Cushite wife–"Miriam and Aaron spoke against Moses because of the Cushite woman he had married, for he had married a Cushite woman" (Num. 12:1)–brings out Esther's foreignness and infe-riority as perceived by the other royal wives. Agnon's specific reference to their jealousy is historically unfounded, given that Anna of Lithuania died before Casimir married Edelheit. It is a well-known element in the Jewish traditions, however, from which Agnon borrowed. It appears in Herman Sternberg's book of 1860, which, according to Shmeruk, marked the first attempt by a Jewish historian to clarify the relations between Casimir and Esther. Sternberg cites the text of an insulting inscription found on the walls of Estherke's palace: "The palace of a Jewess, queen of Jerusalem, a tailor's daughter." In Yiddish literature, as Shmeruk notes, Shomer-Shaikevitz drew on this element in his *The Jewish Queen,* published in Warsaw in 1884 (Shmeruk 1981, 228).

In "Estherkas Haus," Agnon uses the inscription, like the mezuza, as an etiological element. The narrator draws our attention to the marks on the walls of the house and ascribes them to the inscriptions that Casimir's wives scratched into the wall with their fingernails. In "The Heart and Eyes," the etiological aspects have totally vanished and the narrator does not refer to marks on the wall. When he mentions the graffiti, however, he weaves in the Jewish tradition to serve a new goal–describing the intensity of Casimir's feelings for Esther. The phrasing is compatible with Agnon's

131

"The House of Estherke." Drawing. Published in the anthology by Agnon and Eliasberg (1916).

intention. He uses repetition and tripling, basic elements of folk literature poetics: the repeating element is Esther's Jewishness. This highlights the gap and antithesis between Judaism and Christianity, on which the entire story is built.

Agnon was familiar with the various traditions about Casimir and Esther and incorporated them into an original story that raises a new problem. On the overt level, the theme is the love between Casimir and Esther. The story casts no doubt on the love between the Christian king and the beautiful Jewess. In Agnon's rendering, theirs is not a love that depends on tangible benefits, as was asserted by some of the Jewish as well as Polish traditions. Under the surface, however, lies a fundamental existential theme that yields answers to all the questions that preoccupied the ancient traditions—the gulf between Judaism, which dedicates heart and eyes to the services of the amorphous God, and Christianity, which cannot manage without icons. As we have seen, Agnon uses folk traditions and various aspects of the poetics of folk literature—addressing his audience, repetition and tripling, presenting sentiments through actions, making the abstract tangible, and so on. But all of these are merely the outer garb. The subplot is created by the cultural code inherent in Agnon's language, which produces the special melody of Agnon's legend and embodies its significance. It is this combination of the traditional sources and the poetics of folk legend that create the unique flavor of Agnon's legend.

5

"My Eyes Shed Tears, Because the Enemy has Overcome"

THE TRANSFORMATION OF
LEGENDS OF ORIGIN INTO LEGENDS OF DESTRUCTION

> For these hold back, O Lord, for the destruction of houses of prayer,
> Which, instead of song, have become houses of tears.
>
> *From a* seliḥah *(penitential prayer) by R. Shabbetai ben R. Isaiah Halevi Horowitz*

Thus far we have dealt with legends of origin that are of a general nature, relating to all of Polish Jewry, even though, as we saw, the traditions take on the particular coloration of the place where the story is told. Thus, for example, the Jews of Radom used the legend of Estherke to explain the name of the town, while the Jews of Lublin told it in relation to their own cemetery, where, they believed, Estherke was buried.

In this chapter I will deal exclusively with local legends that grew up around synagogues in various places in Poland. My goal is twofold: first, to scrutinize the many-faceted picture that can be assembled from Polish synagogue legends taken as a whole; second, to examine the transformation of these legends after the annihilation of Polish Jewry in the Holocaust.

The synagogue was the tangible and spatial expression of the existence of a Jewish community.[1] In the cosmic order of legend, some of the sanctity of the Holy Temple of ancient times was deemed to rest in the synagogue of the present, in accordance with the talmudic exegesis of the verse, "Although I have cast them far among the nations and have scattered them among the countries, I have become to them a little sanctuary in the countries where they have gone" (Ezek. 11:16), which reads: " 'I have become to them a little sanctuary': R. Isaac said, 'these are the synagogues and houses of study in Babylonia.' R. Eliezer says, 'it refers to the house of the Patriarch.' R. Shimeon bar Yohai says, 'Look how dear Israel is to the Holy One Blessed Be He–to whatever place they have been exiled, the Divine Presence is with them" (BT Megillah 29a). Thus the synagogue was viewed as the Holy Temple in miniature, without which spiritual and public life was impossible. A Jewish settlement without a synagogue was considered to be temporary; only the erection of a house of prayer was a tangible guarantee for the physical and spiritual survival of the community.

An-Ski describes his encounter with the villages (shtetls) and their synagogues during the ethnographical expedition of 1912–14: "Most of the buildings are low, small, and dilapidated. But in one of the neglected side lanes, between half-ruined alleys and tiny houses, partially sunk into the ground–there suddenly appears a large and magnificent palace, thick-walled and solid, with its own original architecture. A building that, given its dimensions and beauty, could compete with the nobleman's palace. This is the pride and splendor of the town–its old synagogue."[2]

It is only logical that the prominence of synagogues in daily and spiritual life would give them a central place in the communities' folk narratives. What the Jews of Poland relate about their synagogues, what these stories teach us about the collective memory of the community, what ethnographic aspects are revealed in these narratives and, especially, what process these narratives have undergone since the annihilation of Polish Jewry among Jews who left Poland following the tragic destruction of the community are the issues to be addressed in this chapter.

PRE-HOLOCAUST LEGENDS

I have collected pre-Holocaust narratives from documents preserved in community record books and published in various contexts, from sources preserved at YIVO (some of these have been published in journals and books), and especially from the materials of An-Ski's ethnographic expedition of 1912–14. Some of these tales were published in various collections, including An-Ski's article "Old Synagogues and Their Legends" (1925, 244–253).

In regard to genre, these narratives are legends of place; the epic expansion of the spatial description is their most prominent feature. Unlike the norm in folk narrative, which scants description and expands on action, synagogue narratives, like place-related narratives in general, are essentially pictorial. The descriptions of synagogues focus on those elements that constitute the uniqueness, beauty, and sanctity of the place.

The wooden synagogue in Noworola. From Maria Piechotka and Kazimierz
Piechotka, *Bóżnice drewniane, Budownictwo i Architektura*
(Warsaw: Arkady, 1959).

EXTERNAL STRUCTURE

The descriptions are first and foremost of the structure and its external
architecture.[3] These include wooden synagogues, such as the Great Synagogue in Radziwił, described in a narrative transcribed by the An-Ski
expedition: "Even though it was built of wood, it was very tall, with hand-
carved cornices and lattice-work galleries."[4] They also include fortress-
synagogues like the Great Synagogue in Ostra (Ostróg), named for the
Maharsha: "It is built like a fortress, with a tower rising high above the peak
of the roof. A Biblical verse was inlaid in a mosaic of small square stones

135

above the door: 'How awesome is this place! This is none other than the House of God, and that is the gateway to heaven' (Gen. 28:17)."[5] This type of construction resulted from the frequent fires that beset the communities as well as from the fact that the synagogue served as a shelter against robber bands and pogromists:[6] here the community gathered to pray for deliverance; here, too, it was all too frequently slaughtered. Consider, for example, the "Bride and Groom," set in the city of Nemirov during the pogroms of 1648:

> On Tuesday, 19 Sivan, the insurrectionists, like devils out of hell, overran the city and rampaged through it. The groom hastened to the bride's house to save his beloved from harm and catastrophe. He managed to flee with her through a small street as far as the Nemirov stream, on whose banks rose the glorious Great Synagogue, the refuge for the Jewish masses: the building was surrounded by a tall, strong, and fortified wall. But alas! Here, too, there was no respite: the Cossacks, having encircled the wall, had already broken into the building and wreaked havoc there.[7]

The next tale, also set in 1648–49, reflects this experience[8] and also falls under the rubric of the supernatural rescue of a synagogue (to be considered later).

> In 1648, when Chmielnicki's Cossacks murdered thousands of Jews in Ostra, the TaZ,[9] managed to escape with his family to Alik, a small hamlet defended by a strong fortress with ancient cannons emplaced in its walls. Initially, Chmielnicki's men were afraid to approach the fortress of Alik; but later, in 1649, the Cossacks did make an attempt to overrun the fortress. They advanced on Alik and began to shell the town. The Jews of Alik cowered in their synagogue, which was built like a fortress, praying and fasting. Among the Jews of Alik gathered in their synagogue was the TaZ, who was a frail man. As a result of the protracted praying, crying, and fasting he could barely stand on his feet. They say that, almost fainting from exhaustion, he leaned his head against a pillar and immediately fell asleep. He dreamt that a sweet voice was reciting the verse from 2 Kings 19:34: "I will protect and save this city for My sake, and for the sake of My servant David." Waking up, he ordered all of them to keeping praying and crying and wailing, for, he said, salvation was near. And indeed the miracle ensued: Suddenly the old and rusty cannons began to fire, the murderous bands fled to the four winds, and the town of Alik was saved.
>
> In commemoration of the miracle that had occurred, the TaZ composed special penitential prayers. The Jews of Alik had the custom of reciting them every year on the day that the miracle occurred, 26 Sivan.

With regard to its genre, this is a *shevah* (a *saint legend* or *legenda,* to use the common Latin term).[10] The *shevah* celebrates the rabbi who has a revelation in the synagogue and announces the impending miracle and

136

The fortress synagogue in Łuck, 1626. From Majer Bałaban, *Studia Historyczne* (Warsaw, 1927).

salvation of the community. Elsewhere I have considered the fact that, in saints legends, the miracle is a culture-dependent interpretation of an event that another world view might well interpret in a totally different fashion.[11] In the present narrative, a link is constructed between the revelation in a dream, a Biblical verse spoken to the rabbi in "a sweet voice," and the old and rusty cannons that suddenly open fire. The language–the Biblical verse "I will protect and save this city for My sake, and for the sake of My servant David"–bears the cultural code. This Polish diaspora, like other diasporas, continues to live and follow the ancient cultural codes; the charged epoch of the disastrous pogroms of 1648 and 1649 is conflated with the ancient calamity when the Assyrian king Sennacherib besieged Jerusalem and is embedded in that mythical archetype. The Jewish town of Alik is analogous to the holy city of Jerusalem, and just as the Lord saved that city for His own sake and for that of his servant (King) David, so too will the holy community of Alik be rescued through the merit of His servant, Rabbi David Segal (the TaZ). There is also an analogy between the rabbi who hears the voice in the synagogue and the prophet Isaiah, who originally heard the words spoken by the God of Israel.

These synagogue legends register the traumatic events of the pogroms of 1648–1649 in the collective memory. They depict the dread that cast its pall over the period and the role of the synagogue as a place of refuge and prayer, with fortification and even cannons. The TaZ narrative also recounts that the traumatic event affected the community's liturgy: from that time on, special penitential prayers commemorating the miracle were recited each year on 26 Sivan. The community's behavior in the synagogue, as prescribed by its liturgical calendar, helped preserve the incident in the collective memory.

An-Ski notes that the construction of fortress synagogues was encouraged by the Polish government, which found itself powerless to protect the Jews against the frequent assaults on them. In a document of 1626, Sygismund III licensed the community of Luck to build a synagogue, on condition that the Jews outfit it with a cannon at their own expense and employ a trained gunner (An-Ski, 1925, 245). Fortified synagogues are described in many stories, including those about the synagogues in Ostra (built in the fourteenth century), Żółkiew, Tarnopol, and elsewhere.[12]

THE INTERIOR OF THE SYNAGOGUE

Descriptions of the external structure are often accompanied by lengthy attention to the interior of the synagogue, including its dimensions. For example, the synagogue in Ludmir (Włodzimierz, Vladimir-Volynsk) is so large that Count Lubomirski could ride along its foundations in his three-horse carriage.

The Synagogue of Ludmir

The duke, Count Lubomirski, agreed to build a synagogue for the Jews of Ludmir. He dispatched an adequate supply of construction materials as well as his master builder.

When the builder asked the duke: "How thick should the walls be?" the Duke replied, "Build the foundations large enough that I can ride along them in my three-horse carriage. That's how wide the walls should be from bottom to top."

They say, indeed, that when the foundations had been laid, but before they began to build the walls, the duke arrived in his gilded carriage. The Jews of Ludmir, led by their rabbi, came to meet him next to the foundations of the synagogue, carrying the Torah scrolls. The cantor and his choir sang a special prayer for the authorities, which the rabbi had composed for Count Lubomirski. When the cantor and all the congregation who sang along with him began to chant Psalm 118–"Praise the Lord, for He is good, His steadfast love is eternal"–the duke invited the rabbi to sit with him in his carriage, and the two of them rode across the foundations until the people had finished the Psalm.[13]

This narrative tells of harmonious coexistence between Jews and Gentiles, a rather uncommon phenomenon in folk narratives dealing with the relations between the two peoples (Bar-Itzhak, 1991), but one that does occur in synagogue narratives (see below) alongside tales of conflict. Not only does the duke initiate the construction of a synagogue for the Jews, he also takes the trouble to send the materials and master builder. Here the size and features of the synagogue add to the prestige of the nobleman on whose land the Jews live; this finds expression in many other stories as well. The Jews thank the nobleman not only with a reception in which they carry the Torah scrolls in public, but also through a special prayer for the authorities that the rabbi composes especially in his honor. The composition of similar prayers for monarchs and nobles who treated Jews well or rescued them from grave peril is found in many narratives.[14]

The picture–which may well seem surrealistic for contemporary readers–of a Polish nobleman and rabbi, seated in a gilded carriage and circling the foundations of the synagogue under construction to the sound of the thanksgiving Psalms, is one of sublime coexistence. The folk legend preserves this glow in the community's memory, alongside the figure of Count Lubomirski.

The paintings and decorations on the walls and ceiling are also described at length.[15] The synagogue ceilings are painted sky-blue, with gold and silver stars of various sizes or representations of the zodiac. Inscribed on the walls are Biblical verses, paintings of Hannah and her seven sons, the Exodus, Aaron's hands, and scenes from the Holy Land: the Cave of the Patriarchs, Rachel's Tomb, the Western Wall.[16] Also described are ritual objects: the candelabra that hang from the ceiling; the large copper Hanukkah menorahs; the Ark curtain, embroidered with the tablets of the Law and Aaron's hands spread in the priestly benediction, with the donors' names embroidered in gold and silver thread; Torah crowns or finials; the Torah reader's pointer; charity collection boxes; and especially the Holy Ark with its embellishments–carved animals (leopards, lions, gazelles, doves), flowers, and more. Even the *kune,* the pillory where malefactors were punished, is described,[17] as in the following narrative about the Maharsha synagogue:

> It should also be told that in the foyer of the synagogue stood the pillory (the *kune*)–a tall, narrow cabinet in which a malefactor sentenced by the religious court was put on public view. Only one person at a time could fit inside this pillar, standing up, with his arms hanging down. This cabinet had a door, with a sort of visor in its upper half, through which one could see the face of the culprit. Many times, when the culprit had been condemned for a particularly severe transgression, such as theft, slander, adultery or the like, the court ordered that at the end of prayers, when the worshippers were leaving the synagogue, they should pass by the pillory and spit through the visor in the malefactor's face, in order to increase his humiliation.[18]

The interior of the old synagogue in Kazimierz, 1880. From S. Markowski,
Krakowski Kazimierz Dzielnica Żydowska 1870–1988
(Kraków, 1992).

Torah shields (Tas) and Torah pointers collected by the An-Ski expedition. From Rivka Gonen, ed., *Back to the Shtetl: An-Ski and the Jewish Ethnographic Expedition 1912–1914* (Jerusalem: The Israel Museum, 1994). With kind permission of the Israel Museum.

Through their depiction of its exterior and interior, these narratives glorify the synagogue and its ornaments and contents. The sanctity of the synagogue legitimized the Jews' feeling of awe and wonder at the artistry, a feeling reflected in the narratives. But there are also stories that emphasize the antiquity and plainness of the synagogue and associate its sanctity and character with them. Consider the story about the ancient candelabrum of the synagogue in Zabludów:

> In the synagogue of Zabludów, an old lamp burned as the Eternal Light. Because this lamp was very old, one of the leaders of the community contributed 25 rubles to buy a new lamp. After the new lamp had been purchased, the sexton lit it, and the old lamp was placed under a bench. The sexton did his chores and went out. When he returned, he found to his astonishment that the new Eternal Light had gone out, but the old lamp that stood under the bench was still burning. He extinguished the old lamp and relit the new one. After a short while, though, he noticed that the former spectacle had repeated itself. He went and told the rabbi, who instructed him to get rid of the new lamp and restore the old one to its place, where it burns until this very day.[19]

This legend is one of those focusing on synagogue ritual objects. There is a symbolic link between the old lamp and the Eternal Light. Just s the Eternal Light expresses the past and its penetration into the present, so too does the ancient lamp that, in the words of the legend, "burns until this very day," indicate that the sanctity derives from that past.

In a similar vein, the narrative about the prayer house (*kloiz*) of the Braslaw (Wrocław) Hasidim in Dubno reflects an emotional and spiritual attachment to the old structure, expressed through personification. After a wealthy man builds a new house of study, the scholars refuse to relocate there. As they explain: "Our heart won't let us accept your gift! We cannot leave our old place of Torah just like that and go elsewhere! The ancient walls and the ceiling are permeated with the sound of our learning. The walls would pine for us. As long as they stand, we shall remain here with them."[20]

The narratives provide fascinating ethnographic information. For example, a story about the synagogue in Nikolaiev tells about the unusual depiction of the priestly hands on the lectern; blood streams from the right hand, which is missing its thumb. When the members of the An-Ski expedition asked about this unique decoration, they heard the following story:

> This picture goes back to the days of the cantonists, when they used to kidnap young Jewish boys to serve in the army of Tsar Nicholas. Parents who wanted to save their children from the *fonya* [an epithet for the Russians] were willing to cut off the child's thumb, since, according to the law, the deformed and crippled were not subject to conscription. The unknown

The synagogue in Zabludów. From Maria Piechotka and Kazimierz
Piechotka, *Bóżnice drewniane, Budownictwo i Architektura*
(Warsaw: Arkady, 1957).

artist, a member of the priestly caste, let them amputate his only son's right
thumb. But after the operation the child contracted blood poisoning and
died. In memory of his son, the wretched father commemorated the event
in this depiction of the priestly hands on the lectern, above the verse, "I
have kept the Lord before me always."[21]

From this story we learn that synagogue art, in addition to repeating
traditional symbols and aspirations, expressed the horrors of the present
age, when a member of the priestly caste was forced to maim his son—an
act that would disqualify the boy for the sacred service—in order to save
him from being swallowed up by the tsar's army and forever to lost to
Judaism. This use of synagogue art to express personal pain may have
been influenced to some extent by the Christian milieu. In fact, there are
narratives that indicate that the Jewish artists who decorated synagogues
were hired to do similar work in churches.

The following story is an interesting example:

It was ten years after the great fire. By that time, Radziwił had already
been rebuilt with the help of our fellow Jews, who are merciful people and
the descendants of merciful people. Jews once again dealt in commerce and

143

Paper cutout "Mizraḥ" with priestly hands. From Rivka Gonen, ed., *Back to the Shtetl: An-Ski and the Jewish Ethnographic Expedition 1912–1914* (Jerusalem: The Israel Museum, 1994). With kind permission of the Israel Museum.

The Holy Ark (Aron Ha'kodesh) in the High Synagogue in
Cracow. From Majer Bałaban, *Zabytki Historyczene Żydów w Polsce*
(Warsaw, 1929).

prospered. To commemorate the great miracle that the synagogue had been spared by the fire, and also because the Torah scrolls salvaged from other sanctuaries that had not survived the conflagration were stored there, the community decided to construct a new and spacious Holy Ark that would be celebrated and magnificent.

So the heads of the community traveled to Kremenets (Krzemieniec)and hired a renowned master carver, famous throughout the Ukraine for his peerless artistry.

For an entire year the master carver worked on the Holy Ark. The result was a splendid cabinet, a rare and astonishingly beautiful work of art, with carved lions and leopards, gazelles and antelopes, eagles, doves, animals large and small, as well as many species of flowers.

The cognoscenti came from far away just to see the Holy Ark and to wonder at its form and delicate work.

When he completed his task, the carver incised his name into the Holy Ark, at the very bottom: "Ozer son of Yehiel, my handiwork in which I glory. . . ."

Five months after the completion of the Holy Ark, on the first day of the Feast of Weeks, at two o'clock in the afternoon, there was a sudden cloudburst, accompanied by thunder and lightning. A peal of thunder resounded over the synagogue and split open the dome. A tongue of lightning penetrated into the synagogue and seared the bottom of the ark, burning off the name of the carver, along with the words, "my handiwork in which I glory." No other damage was caused, except that the ark curtain was slightly scorched. The people, amazed, asked themselves: Is such a thing possible? Why was the carver denied the privilege of having his name inscribed on this work of art, which he carved with his own hands and with such immense toil and effort? For this Holy Ark was indeed his handiwork in which he could glory.

Not long afterwards it became known that the carver had previously executed similar carvings in a church. The people saw this as a profanation of the sacred and understood why his name had been erased by fire, along with the words, "my handiwork in which I glory."[22]

We learn from this story of the existence of Jewish artists like the woodcarver Ozer, son of Yehiel of Kremenets (Krzemieniec), whose fame had spread throughout the surrounding communities.[23] According to the narrative, he carved the Holy Ark out of deep devotion and dedication, spending a long time on the commission;[24] when he was done, he expressed his pride in his completed work by signing his name to it. We also learn that Jewish artists were employed by and worked in churches.[25] The story rejects this practice, but the very rejection attests to its existence. The legend uses motifs found in sacred legends–the supernatural obliteration of the name, linked to celestial thunder, with all its many connotations. The specific dating of the miracle to a charged time, the Feast of Weeks,

The New Synagogue in Radziwiłłów. From Y. Adini, *Radziwiłłów Memorial Book* (Tel-Aviv, 1966).

the festival of the giving of the Torah, augments the rejection of the artist's action and intensifies its condemnation for contradicting the Torah commandments.

THE SANCTITY OF THE SYNAGOGUE

The sanctity of the synagogue is expressed in both description and plot. In the former vein, there are the frequent tales of an underground passage leading from a synagogue directly to Jerusalem, such as the subterranean stairs in the Maharsha synagogue in Ostra (Ostróg)[26] or the underground passages in the synagogues of Szczebrzeszyn[27] and Sharygród.[28] This association turns the synagogue into a temple in miniature, as an extension in time and space of the Holy Temple in Jerusalem, now destroyed, and as its substitute during exile.[29]

With regard to plot lines, the sanctity of the synagogue is emphasized by supernatural rescue. For wooden synagogues, this is usually deliverance from fire. Many legends associate the deliverance of the synagogue from

The Great Synagogue in Kremenets (Krzemieniec).

fire with birds–typically doves or ravens[30]–that extinguish the blaze with their wings. Consider the following legend about the synagogue of Gorlicz.

How the Doves Saved the House of Study from the Fire

When the first fire broke out in Gorlicz [Gorlice] (45 years ago), the entire city burned down. People ran for their lives to the open country; everything was food for the flames. When the fire got close to the old House of Study, the Jews were seized with a terrible dread and despair. But when the flames came very close indeed, a flock of white doves suddenly appeared in the sky alongside the House of Study, and the beating of their wings kept the fire from reaching the building.[31]

A similar story is told about the synagogue in Radziwił,[32] saved from fire in 1883, and the synagogue in Zabludów,[33] which was saved by ravens.

In the case of stone structures, supernatural deliverance involves vain attempts by robbers or an occupying army to damage the synagogue (see above). A fascinating legend of this sort, associated with the wars between Poland and Russia, concerns the Maharsha synagogue in Ostra.[34] According to this narrative, when the Russians besieged the city in 1792, they thought that the synagogue, then the tallest structure in the town, was a Polish bastion. The Russian guns bombarded the building, but the shells fell on every side without damaging the synagogue itself. Finally, one shell did strike a wall, but stuck there without detonating. Another fell into the synagogue, but it, too, did not explode. To commemorate the miracle, the unexploded shell was suspended from the ceiling of the synagogue, the Ostra *megillah* was written, and a second Purim (7 Tammuz) was instituted to commemorate the miracle.[35] (In post-Holocaust legends dealing with events during the Holocaust, the synagogues' uncanny endurance returns in a slightly different incarnation: the Germans must use an extraordinarily large quantity of explosives to blow up a synagogue.)

THE FOUNDING OF SYNAGOGUES

Most synagogue narratives are legends of origin that recount how a synagogue was erected, why it received the name it did, and so on. A number of paradigms can be traced in these narratives:

1. Synagogues were erected by wealthy and influential Jews. This category includes narratives about the founding of synagogues by legendary Jewish kings of Poland, such as Saul Wahl, who decreed the construction of synagogues during his brief reign; about the Jewess Estherke, wife of King Casimir, who embroidered the fabulous ark curtain in the synagogue of Kazimierz; and about donations by various wealthy and powerful men.

2. Synagogues were established by simple Jews or by an entire community, which collected funds, farthing by farthing, to build a synagogue, an act they considered to be their most sublime achievement.

3. Synagogues were established by non-Jews—Polish kings, dukes, and counts. Sometimes they did so of their free will and initiative, as in the narratives about Casimir the Great, who founded a synagogue for his beloved Estherke in Kazimierz,[36] as well as in stories of Count Lubomirski and Count Potocki. Sometimes they did so in response to an appeal by the Jews or to recompense them for favors they performed for a king or nobleman. And sometimes they did so after the Jews had triumphed in a theological disputation with the priests.

4. Some synagogues are said to have been buried in the ground and uncovered by persons working for the local nobleman, by Jews, or sometimes even by chance. One such narrative deals with the Great Synagogue in Nemirov (Niemirów). This story is particularly interesting because it recounts how the *poritz* wanted to build a church, but whenever the workers tried to start work they would sink into the ground. The count investigates and discovers that a synagogue had stood on the site until it was destroyed

by Chmielnicki in 1648.[37] He summons the Jews and proposes that they unearth the synagogue. When they have done so, he renovates it and builds them a new and splendid synagogue.[38]

Another interesting category comprises narratives about synagogues built by women or named for them. Among the most fascinating of these is the legend about the synagogue established by the maid of Ludmir, which eventually became a house of prayer used by the Zlatopol Hasidim.[39] Another legend in this genre involves the synagogue named for Mirele of Brahilov. The story is part of an entire set of legends, not all of which deal with synagogues, that focus on sexual confrontations between Jews and Gentiles (Bar Itzhak, 1991).

The Mirele Synagogue in Brahilov

In many towns in the Ukraine there are synagogues named for righteous women. Marvelous tales and astonishing events are told about them.

I am going to tell you a tale about the Mirele Synagogue in Brahilov. I heard this tale from the patriarch Yekutiel Segal of Brahilov, the grandson of the great sage and righteous man, Rabbi Abraham Moses Segal, rabbi of Brahilov and author of the book *Mayyim Qedoshim* about saints and martyrs.

For many years the Jews of Brahilov scrimped on their food and collected money, farthing by farthing, until the community coffers contained a sum adequate to build a synagogue.

Everyone in town participated in the holy task. Month after month they worked like bees; they hauled boards, kneaded mortar, sawed planks—and the synagogue building sprouted and grew from day to day. As the building rose, so too were the hearts of the Jews of Brahilov filled with joy. Men, women, and children rejoiced and were glad; all lent a hand and helped with all their might.

When the synagogue building was very close to completion and the Jews of Brahilov gazed at it and were overcome by its majesty and could not get their fill of its ornamental cornices and glittering roof, whose towers rose high above any other building in the town, and even higher than the hill on the outskirts of town—just then the wind blew in the duke from far away, perhaps even from overseas. He came to take a vacation and rest in his lovely castle in Brahilov, in the middle of a thick wood that grew near the town.

The duke was a very wicked person, a fanatical antisemite, who could not bear the presence of a Jew anywhere near him. Toward evening, when the sun had sunk low in the west and its last golden rays were reflected in the large new windows of the synagogue, the furious duke arrived in his carriage in Brahilov. When he saw the new synagogue, he was astounded and overwhelmed by the beautiful building. He decided to expropriate the synagogue from the Jews and turn the lofty structure into a church for the Gentiles.

The next day he sent his servants to summon the town notables, led by the rabbi, to his palace. He ordered them, with no introduction or uncertainty, to make him a gift of the keys to their new synagogue, of their own free will. This was his will, and his will must be done! If not, a bitter end would come to the Jews of Brahilov. He said his say, turned his back, and left the room.

The notables and the rabbi returned to the town like mourners, their heads bowed. The bitter decree broke everyone's heart. For a number of days, day after day, they were sunk in bitter cries and lamentation. The leading householders, the heads of the community, sought to intercede with the duke to get him to cancel his decree, to have pity on his faithful Jews and not to deprive them of their holy house of prayer, their miniature Temple which they had built with such great toil. But the duke hardened his heart. After a few days he sent his servants to padlock the doors of the synagogue.

Now in Brahilov there lived a respected, well-to-do, and truly righteous woman, who was extremely beautiful. Her name was Mirele. Taking all her valuables, Mirele went to the duke's palace and laid before him her gold, silver, and jewels. With tears streaming from her eyes, she begged him to take pity on her and her Jewish congregation and annul his severe decree. At the sight of her beauty, the duke was strongly attracted to her, and his lust was kindled. He told her that he would indeed comply with her petition and immediately annul his decree, but on one condition–that very night she must sleep with him. Only one single night.

Mirele cried and lamented. She fell at his feet and begged him to take all her possessions, so long as he didn't touch her. But the duke remained firm: only in exchange for her body would he annul his decision.

When Mirele realized that the matter was at an end and there was no alternative, she told the duke that she was willing to fulfill his desire. But she, too, had one condition: namely, that he would come to her only after midnight, but must return the key to the padlocked synagogue and issue the permit to complete its construction now, that is, at once.

The duke consented. Without delay he wrote out the permit, sealed it with his signet, and gave it to her, along with the key to the synagogue. Mirele sent the permit and key by special messenger to the townsfolk. The city of Brahilov rejoiced and was merry. Everyone rejoiced at the deliverance.

In the meantime, the duke locked Mirele in a room by herself and stationed a guard outside the door.

When Mirele found herself alone, she raised her eyes to heaven and prayed with all her heart, pleading with the Master of the World: "Master of the World! You have brought me to this trial. Now I ask you, my God, to take my soul and return it to the treasury of pure souls. Take me back to you, so that my body will not be defiled by this wicked man. Help me, my

God, remain pure, as I have been up to now! . . ."

And she sighed until her pure soul left her, in sanctity and purity.

After midnight, when the duke came to her, he found only her corpse. . . .

The Jews of Brahilov quickly completed work on the synagogue. In memory of the holy soul of Mirele, they named it the Mirele Synagogue.[40]

This story contains several of the elements already discussed above. The synagogue is built through the joint efforts of all the Jews of the community. Its majestic height and architecture reflect the community's attitude toward the synagogue and their pride in it. Nevertheless, the story includes an implicit criticism—excessive pride is tantamount to a sin. It is precisely the beauty, height, and design of the synagogue building that instigate the conflict by drawing the attention of the *poritz,* who immediately wants to make the building into a church. Polish Jewry's sinful pride in their synagogues was also developed by Agnon in his story "The Emissary from the Holy Land" (in *Poland: Legendary Tales),* in which the townsfolk say: "Had not the Sages said, 'Anyone who did not see the Holy Temple when it was standing has never seen a magnificent building in his life,' we would say that ours is magnificent" (Agnon 1967, 399).

The brutal conflict brings the figure of Mirele on stage, after all other hopes are lost. The narrator characterizes Mirele directly, through her socioeconomic status (she is a well-to-do woman and truly righteous) and through an external trait (her beauty). As with other heroines who decide, on their own initiative, to confront a Gentile of high status, there is no mention of her family or marital status. Indirectly, through her actions, Mirele is characterized as an independent woman who takes the initiative and makes up her own mind to confront the nobleman and try to persuade him, by entreaties and the offer of her possessions, to release the synagogue building. But doing this unavoidably exposes her to his eyes and lust. The narrative, for all that it honors and glorifies its heroine, bears an implicit message: namely, that an encounter between a Jewish woman and a Polish nobleman is likely to be calamitous and should be avoided unless the spiritual or physical world of an entire community hangs in the balance.

A similar tale is told about *di gildene Roize* (the gilded Rose) of Lemberg (Lwow). The popular name for the synagogue built in Lwow in 1582 by Yitzhak, the son of Nahman, a wholesale merchant and head of the community, was the Gildene Roize Shul (Cahana 1992, 79). This heroine, too, was celebrated for her extraordinary beauty and the golden hair that gave her her name. She, too, is described as a wealthy trader who had contacts with the rich and powerful. Here it is the Jesuits who covet the synagogue and want to turn it into a church. Roize institutes a lawsuit against them. With the help of the archbishop of Lemberg, she wins her case, but the archbishop falls in love with her and demands that she submit to him in return for his assistance in her suit. When she sees that there is no alternative, she throws herself from the roof of his house—unlike Mirele, who dies in response to her prayer. For generations the Jewish women of Lwow visited her grave and entreated her to intercede for them before the Heavenly Throne (Finkelstein, 1947, 229).[41]

Legends that incorporate sexual conflict can be divided into a number of categories, as I have discussed elsewhere.[42] When the protagonist is a woman who confronts a Gentile, a number of subcategories can be distinguished:

1. The heroine surrenders her innocence, but does so for her people. In this case, despite the non-normative nature of her submission, she is viewed favorably and even receives respect and honor. One such figure in the folk narratives of Polish Jews is Estherke, the wife of Casimir the Great, who is associated with other archetypal heroines, especially the biblical Queen Esther.[43]

2. The heroine kills the Gentile (who is always a Jew hater), but must yield to his lust in order to do so. Such characters, too, are associated with archetypes, especially Judith, and tend to be depicted in a positive light.

3. The heroine chooses to die rather than allow her body to be defiled by contact with the non-Jew. In most cases the heroine does this by tricking the man who covets her body. In the seventeenth-century work *Yeven Mezulah,* by Nathan Nata Hannover, which commemorates those slaughtered in the pogroms of 1648 and 1649, we read about the two virgins of Nemirov (Niemirów); one of them tricked the Cossacks into shooting her, while the second threw herself into the river during the bridal procession (Hannover 1968, 39).

The tale of Mirele of Brahilov belongs to the last category. The special regard in which the heroine is held is reflected by the fact that she does not take her own life; instead, her prayer is answered and God takes back her soul. But this story, too, includes the motif of deceiving the non-Jew, in the form of the stipulation she makes. At the same time, Mirele's heroism when she stands before the *poritz* and pleads with him to save the synagogue associates the tale with the second category, despite the fact that the woman does not yield her innocence or physically assault the man.

The synagogue narratives reflect the complex and multifaceted reality of Polish Jewry before the Holocaust, as this was preserved in their collective memory of living in their non-Jewish milieu, of receiving privileges and decrees, joys and persecutions.

By glorifying the architecture and artistry of the synagogue, the legends express the thrill and aesthetic sensation experienced by the Jews at the sight of this work of art. The synagogue is the center of Jewish life. Here the festivals are celebrated, and events both remote and near, which have been incorporated into the cycle of the Jewish year, are marked. Here, too, the various rites of passage are conducted. Even those who have departed this world can be found here, praying in the dead of night; and sometimes, when they lack a tenth man to make up the *minyan*, they call out to a passerby, addressing him by name and inviting him to join them—an act liable to be fraught with catastrophic consequences.[44] The synagogue is a place of refuge in times of peril, where supernatural revelations and deliverance are effected.

By mapping the events and characters, the legends highlight their centrality in the community's social and cultural consciousness. The main characters are the rabbis for whom the synagogues are named or who ministered in them. The events most frequently commemorated are the traumatic massacres and pogroms, especially the Chmielnicki uprising of 1648–49, which the narratives treat as if it were the destruction of the Temple for the Jews of Poland, thereby associating it with the archetypal destructions of Jewish memory. Also preserved is the figure of Bogdan Chmielnicki—Chmiel the Wicked, as he was called by the Jews— who is linked with the archetypal Jew hater, Haman. The impressment of the cantonists into the tsarist army in the time of Nicholas I and incidents during World War I also find their way into the synagogue narratives.

In addition to these traumatic events, the legends preserve the figures of philosemites and joyous and stirring occasions. In the synagogue narratives, these are mainly linked with the construction of the synagogue; the central characters are Casimir the Great, Count Lubomirski, and Count Potocki, seconded by a host of nameless benefactors. Alongside the picture of pogroms and riots, their deeds paint a canvas of sublime coexistence between two peoples, which the legends seek to enshrine in the community's memory.

As we have noted, most legends of origins deal with the erection of a synagogue, its location, its name, and so on. These legends fulfilled a number of functions: (1) They legitimized the synagogue and the community it represented to the outside Gentile world—the synagogue was erected in conformity with the law by rulers or with their consent, following donations by Jews and sometimes as an expression of gratitude to them. (2) Internally, for the Jews themselves, they provided spiritual and theological warrant for their residence in Poland—subterranean passages to Jerusalem, the construction of a synagogue with the assistance of biblical figures like King David and the prophet Elijah, the use of stones from the Holy Temple.[45] (3) They reinforced the link between individuals and their place of residence and community and provided a sense of belonging and continuity.

LEGENDS IN THE POST-HOLOCAUST CONTEXT

My heart's delight and all my good–
Is there an agony like my agony?
From a dirge on the massacres in Poland by R. Jacob, son of R. Moses Halevi

What happened to these legends after the Holocaust, in the wake of the destruction of the community and its physical and spiritual annihilation? Given that their erstwhile functions have lost all significance, should we assume that legends about the origins of the synagogues of Poland would disappear? Anyone close to the world of the survivors of those communities can answer this question with a vigorous "no." The survivors' sense of commitment to their dead and their community produces a sense of obligation to tell their stories and that of the community, which includes the story of its synagogue. Now only the narrative can confirm and sustain the community's existence. Henceforth, the community is a community in memory and of memory, and its continued existence lies in the transmission of the memory to future generations through the telling of the story. This commitment produced the memorial books for communities wiped out in the Holocaust, which frequently note that they stand in place of the grave and tombstone denied the dead. Most of these books were printed in limited editions for survivors and townspeople. The readers knew the writers personally, such that there was a direct and immediate bond among author, narrator, and readers. The roles of narrator and audience keep interchanging within a book, making it an example of the kind of small-group communication that is also typical of folklore communication (Ben Amos 1971; Kugelmass and Boyarin 1983, 14).[46] I have, in fact, found many legends of origin in these memorial volumes.[47]

Legends of origin about Jewish synagogues are still being told, but they have undergone a transformation. Today the origins of Polish synagogues can be recounted only through the lens of the Holocaust. The geography of the narrative is now exclusively a geography of memory; the same place that is sanctified in memory is often considered to be cursed in the present. No longer fulfilling their erstwhile functions, the narratives have become a means for expressing and working through what post-Holocaust Polish Jews see as the true story of the community–the story of its destruction.

We will examine two legends of this type, recorded in Israel.

The ancient synagogue in our town was built more than 900 years ago. They built it over a period of several years but were unable to finish it. Suddenly a Jew appeared from far away. No one knew who he was or where he had come from. He pledged to the community leaders that he would complete the synagogue.

When construction was complete the man abruptly disappeared. The next day the congregation found all the money the community council had paid him for his work in a corner of the synagogue.

People said it was none other than King David, may his merit defend us and all Israel, who built this splendid synagogue, for it was impossible that normal flesh and blood, a *gevaynlikher mentsh,* could build such a glorious holy place.

I myself cannot believe that I ever merited to see with my own eyes this remarkable and magnificent synagogue, which had all the hues and colors of the sun and the moon and the rainbow.

And when I remember and call to mind the Great Synagogue, the ancient synagogue in our town, which was destroyed by the Germans, may their name be blotted out, then my eyes shed tears, because the enemy has overcome; my sighs are many and my heart is sick.[48]

The first part of this narrative is a legend of origins. The synagogue is said to be 900 years old, which gives a stamp of legitimacy to the community's existence in Poland. Its beauty and splendor dignify the town and its congregation, which had the merit of having such a synagogue. The attribution of the completion of the synagogue to King David gives a spiritual and theological seal of approval to the community's presence in Poland, for King David, the greatest king and hero of Israel, is also the ancestor of the Messiah. This part, which was the focus of the legend before the Holocaust, becomes merely the introduction and excuse for what the post-Holocaust narrator wants to tell about himself and his community—destruction, eulogy, and lament.

The following story also exemplifies the new paradigm:

The splendid ancient synagogue in the town of Shebershin was built a thousand years ago, in all its glory and splendor, by the Jewish king of Poland, Saul Wahl. Ever since, a new light shone on the Jewish community of Shebershin.

The Jewish king of Poland reigned for only a brief time, but he took advantage of the royal diadem to benefit his people. He issued a decree that synagogues be built for the Jews, and, *mutatis mutanda,* churches for the Christians.

This great synagogue distinguished the holy congregation of Shebershin. Its ornaments and murals were splendid to behold. The ceremonial objects, too, beautified the Lord's sanctuary. Anyone who visited this synagogue could not stop feasting his eyes on its great beauty and splendor. He was struck with amazement at the colors and hues revealed to his eyes when he entered it. There were all kinds of figures that had been drawn and carved by great artists. The synagogue glinted in the sunlight with all the colors of the rainbow. The ceiling was painted sky-blue and added a charming note.

But now the candles in the synagogue have been extinguished. The Germans burned it, with its worshippers and admirers and hundreds of Torah

156

scrolls. The Jews were gathered in the blazing synagogue, wearing their *kittels* and *tallises,* praying and chanting and praising their God. They hurled themselves into the flames with the Torah scrolls to sanctify God's name.

All the candles in the Great Synagogue of Shebershin have gone out. Only one light burns: the memorial candle, the *yohrzait-likht,* hissing and casting a shadow on the wall. In my heart, too, a small flame burns; whenever I am not working, and during sleepless nights, it recalls to me the past and the destruction.[49]

Thus legends of origin turn into legends of destruction. The paradigm is as follows:

1. First comes the narrative of origins, rooted in the distant past and distinguished by its splendor and glory. This part is generally recounted in the third person and the past tense.

2. The initial narrative is followed by the threnody for the destruction. Here the narrator switches from the past to the present and from the third-person account to a more intimate first-person narrative, concluding with a dirge and lament, always in the elevated style of traditional Jewish dirges.[50]

Sometimes the order is reversed: the narrator begins in the present, describing the destruction, and only then flashes back to the glorious past. But the rhetoric remains the same. Consider this narrative about the synagogue of Kublinek:

> There are no Jews left in the town of Kublinek. With time, even its name has vanished, and today it is know as Narocz. . . . There is no memory of the Jewish community in the town and nothing to recall our presence there. Those who were our neighbors for so many years find it more comfortable this way, since with their own hands they helped the Nazis annihilate us and then obliterate every sign of our existence. The cemetery was "cleaned" of its tombstones. There is no marker on the mass grave that conceals our dear ones who were murdered, located outside the town, and no one visits it. The synagogue, the institution that more than any other symbolized our small community–it, too, no longer exists. . . .
>
> The synagogue was built many years ago. It was older than the town elders. . . . It was the Gentile lord of the local manor, on whose land and with whose permission the Jews of the place built their house of prayer. It was built of wood. Frequent fires afflicted the town. Many brick houses were built to replace the wooden houses that were destroyed, but the old synagogue remained standing, despite all the calamities.[51]

Whatever the sequence, the legends of origin have become a means to tell of the destruction of the community and to mourn for it. It is no coincidence that the narrating society selected legends of origin as a way to deal with the trauma of destruction. The antithetical analogy created by these stories make it possible to probe the trauma without using explicit

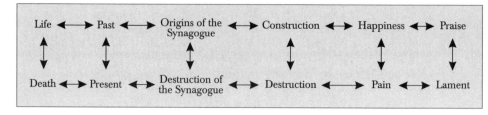

Figure 6

language. The mechanism of analogy leads to the conclusion while heightening the disparity: The full intensity of the calamity is emphasized by the contrasting background of the original grandeur and glory. The narratives generate a chain of opposites that mediate between the fundamental poles of life and death (see Figure 6).

The communal life of Polish Jewry lies forever in the past. There, in the past, are found the origins, the construction of the synagogue, the happiness and glory. The present in which the synagogue legends are recounted is the era after the death and destruction of the community, and an expression of the pain and lament. So much for the verbal level. In the folk text, however, the context is part of the text, and the context generates an inversion that exceeds the power of words. On the one hand, the context makes the destruction tangible, since the narrators are survivors and the narrative is told repeatedly in Israel at Memorial Day gatherings. On the other hand, the very fact that there are survivors who can recount the story to their fellow survivors, along with the families they established in Israel after the Holocaust, is a sign of life. The narrator is alive, in a place felt to be sheltered against the dreads of the past; in particular, the narrator is a man or woman who is remembering. Both the destruction and the glory are preserved in memory, and memory is survival, existence, life. The narrative becomes a ritual that makes it possible to restore and renew the bygone origins and to link the historical time of the present with the mythical time of the beginnings. The human capacity to overcome the destructive force of time lies in the link created between the new start and memory. The narrative is the concrete expression of memory, which, by constructing a myth of creation and destruction, stresses life and resurrection. In Eliade's terms, the terrible chaos experienced by the narrators becomes a cosmos and expresses the desire to give order and meaning (Eliade 1968, 15).

In this way, the legends of the origins of Polish synagogues, having become legends of their destruction, construct the myth of the Jewish people, which includes its origins on Polish soil, its catastrophe, and its rebirth in the Land of Israel.

Afterword

In this book I have examined the various categories of the legends of origin of Polish Jewry: legends telling of the Jews' arrival in Poland and their acceptance in the country; legends about the Jews' ties with the early kings of Poland, including those about the Jew Abraham who was chosen king of Poland but abdicated in favor of Piast, the founder of the glorious dynasty of Polish kings; legends about Esther and King Casimir the Great, who expanded the Jews' right of settlement in Poland; and legends about the founding of synagogues in various communities. What all these legends have in common is their setting in the earliest days of the community. They have an etiological bent and attempt to explain and justify life in the present through the medium of a sanctified past or, alternatively, to use the depiction of an idyllic life in the past in the struggle to change life in the present. There are a few key themes: providing a spiritual and religious stamp of approval to the very act of settlement in and continued residence in Poland; anchoring the beginning of Jewish settlement in Poland in the earliest history of that land and its people; explaining the first settlement as the result of an invitation extended to the Jews by the rulers or the people, in anticipation of their future contribution; the Jews' contribution to the host country by saving it from catastrophe, such as drought; the description of the Jewish past in Poland as a favorable situation that deteriorated later; and finally, adding to the community's prestige by linking it to an ancient and honored Jewish center.

A central objective of this study of legends of origin has been to demonstrate that these legends should not be treated as nothing more than amusing diversions, as was formerly the trend among historians; rather, they constitute an important and fascinating object of scholarly study in and of themselves and provide a window onto the creative genius of the community, its collective memory, and the way in which it created and consolidated its identity during the course of its history.

On the one hand, I made a great effort to locate all the relevant legends in various languages (Hebrew, Yiddish, Polish, and German) that have been transcribed, supplemented by those that I was fortunate enough to record from the oral tradition, and provide a close reading of each legend. On the other hand, had I focused on each story in isolation from the others, I would have missed the goal that I set myself, that of examining how a community creates its own history, how it constructs and consolidates its identity through the application of the narrative medium to its origins and establishment, and how identity thus changes from age to age. To do this I had to study the connection between the various legends and the sociohistorical situation, that is, what Bruner and Gorfain, following Bakhtin (Bakhtin 1981), called "dialogic narration." A story must not be read in isolation, as a static monologic entity, say Bruner and Gorfein, but in a dialogic or interactive context: "All stories are told in voices. . . . A story is told in a dynamic chorus of styles which voice the social and ideological positions they represent" (Bruner and Gorfain 1984).

Indeed, such a study of the corpus of the origin legends of the Jews of Poland shows that they create a complex and polyphonic narrative that expresses the condition, problems, and changing aspirations of Polish Jewry in various periods. It is this narrative that I have attempted to present in this book.

The legends preserve in the collective memory central incidents in the annals of Polish Jewry, as they were interpreted by society in various periods, along with major figures who had a decisive influence upon their destiny. Thus, for example, we have encountered reflections of traumatic events such as the Chmielnicki massacres of 1648–1649, conscription of young Jewish boys into the Russian army in the time of Tsar Nicholas I, and the Holocaust. The origin legends also give prominence to events of joy and spiritual exaltation, as we saw, for example, in the stories about the founding of the synagogues of various communities. Alongside the figures of persecutors, both anonymous and all-too-well known, such as Bogdan Chmielnicki, the legends also perpetuate individuals who treated the Jews well, such as the legendary King Leszek, Casimir the Great, Count Lubomirski, and Count Potocki.

We have seen that the legends were part of the fabric of Jewish life. Thus, for example, in the town of Kuzmir Jewish tour guides spiced their accounts with the story of Esther and Casimir; a Purim-*spil* based on the legend was acted every year; and the ark curtain embroidered by Esther, according to the legend, was put on public display every year.

The legends give symbolic and metaphoric expression to the internal problems that preoccupied the Jewish communities of Poland and the relations that prevailed between them and the surrounding non-Jewish world. The legends teach us about various ways in which a society finds creative solutions to its most pressing existential and spiritual problems. For example, in the legends about the arrival of the Jews in Poland we saw how the Jews adopted a foreign country as their own and Judaized an alien space by using well-known methods of the Jewish classical literature—expounding the signification of names, for instance, and ancient symbols, such as pages of the Talmud. In this way the geography of the non-Jewish world was Judaized and drafted into the service of Jewish history.

We have noted that the central dilemmas of Polish Jewry are expressed in the legends. For example, legends about the first settlement in Poland pose the desire for a long-term and tranquil domicile in Poland, and creation of a substantial Jewish spiritual life there, against the myth of the ultimate redemption, according to which a full spiritual life is possible only in the Land of Israel. The legends find solutions that make it possible to overcome the dilemma by turning the Land of Israel into the eternal sanctified space of the Jews' spiritual longings, from which a degree of sanctity emanates onto the present domicile. Poland is thus associated with repose and the continuation of the ancient Jewish tradition of learning; but it is also associated with night, darkness, and transience. The legend proposes, by way of resolution, that when the messianic redemption comes, this earthly Poland, with its synagogues and houses of study, will be bodily transferred to the Land of Israel. Such solutions to the dilemmas and the dissonance they raise made life in the Polish Diaspora possible, while preserving the ancient Jewish myths.

The question of the relations between the Jews and the people among whom they lived arises in many of the legends, and with particular poignancy in the legends of acceptance. In these, written down in various periods of Jewish life in Poland, we were able to see the dialogic narration between the various legends and the changing sociohistorical reality. As a function of the age from which they date, various legends build different models of relations between Jews and Poles, ranging from total separation and estrangement to a model of cooperation based on compassion and later to cooperation based on equality, in the spirit of liberalism and the Jewish demands for emancipation. These models express the changing cultural consciousness of Polish Jewry and the various ideological currents that flowed within it.

Elements in the legends become metaphors for Jewish life and even key symbols. For example, in the legends of acceptance rain becomes a metaphor for Jewish existence and a key symbol, which by its very nature is complex and has a multiplicity of meanings (Ortner 1973). Rain symbolizes the humiliation of Jewish life in the Polish exile, in that the Jews are forced to prove their utilitarian value to the host country. But it also symbolizes the superiority of the Jews, who are the only ones with the power to bring down rain when needed, through their prayers, and of Judaism, the source of this special power, through the Jews' bond with the formless deity by virtue of their observance of the Torah and precepts. It symbolizes their Christian neighbors' mistaken perception of the Jews as magicians, as well as the Jewish view that the hegemonic people depend on the Jews for their very physical survival, since without rain life is impossible. Thus rain is a symbol that epitomizes the entire web of relations and embodies the full spectrum of meanings that link different worlds of content.

But not only the vicissitudes of Jewish life in Poland express the dialogic narration between legends and history. Zionism, the movement that sought to uproot the Diaspora community and return it to independent political life in the Land of Israel, is also reflected in the origin legends of Polish Jewry. This trend is evident in S. Y. Agnon's retelling of the legends of origin. Agnon uses the origin legends of Polish Jewry and inverts their original intention. Instead of justifying the original settlement and continued domicile in Poland, he rejects any possibility of finding a Jewish modus vivendi in the Diaspora and expresses a clear preference for the Land of Israel as the place for Jewish life, in the spirit of the Zionist world view.

Even the ultimate trauma of Polish Jewry, the Holocaust, is reflected in the legends of origin. We saw how the discourse between legend and historic reality depicts the most dramatic change in the legends of origin. Because the Holocaust represents their utter antithesis, that is, the liquidation of the Jewish communities in Poland, the legends undergo both a formal and a material inversion and are transmuted from legends of origin into legends of destruction, even while the context in which they are related embodies the message of renewal and rebirth in the Land of Israel.

Notes

Preface

1. For a discussion of myth, accompanied by an exposition of various research approaches, see Maranda 1972; Dundes 1984; Puhvel 1987.

2. Ben-Amos points out the problem of using analytical categories in the genre analysis of folk literature and proposes the use of ethnic categories—that is, the terms that the narrating society gives to its stories, a sort of "folkloristic interpretation of folklore genres" (Ben-Amos 1976, 215–242). Goodman refers to the existence and importance of myths in modern industrial cultures and to the link between their exposure as myths and their influence in that culture:

> Myths are as prominent in modern, industrial cultures as they were in ancient cultures, and as powerful as they remain in tribal cultures. If their presence is not evident, that is partly because one's own myths are less noticeable as myth than exotic or archaic myths are. But that is not the only reason. Myths *in situ* are still living. And recognition of a myth as a myth, that is a fiction, can radically diminish its power. When maximally effective, myths remain almost unnoticed. (Goodman 1993, 107)

3. This is said with an awareness of the complexity of seeing myths as true stories and the question of whether people believe in their own myths. For a fascinating discussion of these aspects, see Goodman 1993; Veyne 1988.

4. Gershom Shalom gave some thought to Agnon's penchant for anthologies and to this anthology on Polish Jews. According to Shalom, Agnon's work as an anthologizer was more than a mere sideline: "It is true that Agnon was never a scholar, if we understand this term to mean a man who devotes himself to historical and critical analysis and to the study of phenomena in a particular conceptual framework. Nevertheless, he always had a bent for research that was compatible with his love for studying the basic Jewish texts" (Shalom 1970). During the years he lived in Germany, Agnon produced both the anthology on Polish Jewry and *Ma'oz Tsur* on the Hanukkah festival.

In Jerusalem he devoted much time to three more anthologies. On the anthology on Polish Jews, see also Werses 1989, 112–113, Werses 1994, 16.

5. For Agnon's decision to settle in Palestine and a cultural perspective on his life, see Band 1968 and Laor 1998.

6. For a discussion of Agnon's Zionism, see Laor 1994, 1998.

Chapter 1

1. Or, as he puts it: "All these stories are in the nature of etiological legends explaining existing situations or traditions, and were probably created in the eighteenth and nineteenth centuries for apologetic and political reasons" (Weinryb 1973, 18).

2. It should be noted that in an earlier article, Weinryb took a somewhat different position and argued that it seems to be impossible to discover when the legends were first composed. Even there, however, he adds that some scholars hypothesized that they were created in the nineteenth century, for apologetic reasons (Weinryb 1962, 454).

3. Kirshenblatt-Gimblatt, who studied the folklore of eastern European Jewish emigrés in Canada, noted that it was precisely the first contact that generated folklore. Stories grow up around the emigrants' traumatic points of contact with their new residence. My own fieldwork among immigrants who came to Israel in the 1950s led me to similar conclusions (Bar-Itzhak 1998).

4. Garsiel asserts that there is a substantive difference between biblical name explanations and name-*midrashim*. Name explanations are incorporated in the text and rely on the convention that a name is unique and the invention of its giver, and that the reason and sense of this invention are known and overtly declared, whether by a character or the narrator. A name-*midrash* has nothing to do with why the name was given; rather, it relies on the broad spectrum of latent phonetic potentials, which are exploited by the narrator in various ways during the course of the literary work. At the same time, notes Garsiel, there is an interaction between the explanation and *midrash*, as well as cases in which the distinction between them is not clear-cut (Garsiel 1987, 19–20).

5. Many have noted the multilingual character of Polish-Jewish folklore, but not necessarily with respect to name-*midrashim*. See chiefly An-Ski 1925, 257–262, and Noy 1962, 49–56.

6. YIVO, Inv. C 47,115 (Shebershin Lubliner); published by Cahan 1938.

7. According to Mahler, it is important to publish lexicons of the Jewish geography of countries that had large concentrations of Jews to facilitate the study of both language and history (Mahler 1953, 146). On the Yiddish versions of Polish place names, see Stankiewicz 1965, 158–181; on Yiddish place names in other countries, see, for example, Guggenheim-Grunberg 1965, 147–157.

8. IFA 5220.

9. It is interesting to note that research among Polish immigrants in Israel indicates that the same strategy was used after their *aliya*. Consider the case of the Polish Jews who settled in Upper Nazareth in the late 1950s. At the time, the town was called Kiryat Natzeret, but the *olim* referred to it as *Kiryat Na-tzores*, or "City on Troubles"–combining Hebrew *kiryat* 'city', Polish *na* 'on', and Yiddish *tzores* 'trouble' (Bar-Itzhak 1998).

10. YIVO, Inv. C 57,452 (Ostre, Vohlyner), published by Cahan 1938. Compare Horodetzky 1947, 452.

11. I heard this *midrash* from Dov Noy, to whom I am grateful. I have not found it incorporated into a story.

12. The *midrash* is based on the Yiddish and Hebrew pronunciation *Polin* instead of the Polish *Polska*.

13. Poland has a number of different names in medieval and early modern Jewish literature: Polin; Poloniya, Polania, Polonio, Polenden. Compare Huberband 1969, 325.

14. Written with an asterisk and the explanation "Polonia."

15. Lewin cites the story as told by Professor Berliner from Berlin, who heard it in his youth in Owersitzko (Obrzycko).

16. "Migrate" here represents the Hebrew *alu* 'went up'–the idiom normally used exclusively for immigration to the Land of Israel.

17. The traditional talmudic euphemism for "Israel" in contexts like this.

18. Regarding the stories in German, I accept the assertion of Shmuel Werses, who says: "The [German] versions of these stories should not be considered to be translations of the various versions of the Hebrew original later published in the anthology *Poland,* as many bio-bibliographers of Agnon believe. What we actually have is a translation from a different Hebrew version that does not survive, with many differences in content and emphasis" (Werses 1989, 112–113).

19. In Yiddish "blatt" means both leaf and page.

20. In the first version, Agnon actually uses the variant *Polania,* as in the elegy.

21. Compare Horodetzky 1947, 81–85.

22. The Talmud (JT Berakhot 9,1, 13b) relates the story of a Jewish lad whose prayers rescued a shipload of non-Jews, after the Gentiles' prayers had been in vain. At the end of the story, the Gentiles tell him: "As for you, every place you go, your God goes with you–'[for what great nation is there that has a God so close at hand] as is the Lord our God, whenever we call upon him?' (Deut. 4:7)." Frenkel argues that the Gentiles in the story interpret the failure of their prayers as meaning that their gods are far away, in the royal capitals of their respective countries; because their gods have a house, they are found only there. After the destruction of the Temple in Jerusalem, however, the God of the Jews has no house; hence he travels with every Jew wherever he goes (Frenkel 1981, 151).

23. The name Narol was garbled in *Hatequfah* and printed, erroneously, as "Gral."

24. The poet is referring to the opening words (the traditional mode of identification) of chapters in the following Talmudic tractates:
"These are liable to death by burning": Sanhedrin 9
"How does one roast?": Pesahim 7
"These are liable to death by strangulation": Sanhedrin 10
"They hang": Shabbat 20
"These are liable to be flogged": Makkot 3
"These are liable to be exiled": Makkot 2.
The passages from Sanhedrin and Makkot deal with forms of punishment and thus are relevant in their original sense. On the other hand, the passage in tractate Pesahim is actually inquiring as to the proper method of roasting the paschal lamb, while that from Shabbat, in context, is stating the opinion of R. Eliezer that "one may hang a strainer [to remove the lees from wine] over a container on a festival day."

25. On the legend of Esther and Casimir, see Chapter 4, below.

26. Ps. 90:4.

27. Zeitlin 1980. In 1993 Y. Sheintuch published a different version of Zeitlin's work "Estherke and Casimir the Great Ahashverus in Poland," which was translated into Hebrew by Shlomo Zuker (Zeitlin 1993, 125–185).

28. YIVO, Inv. C 47,115 (Shebereshin, Lubliner), in Cahan 1938. An English version

of the story can be found in Silverman-Weinreich 1988, 347. It is regrettable that in this translation the name Kawenczynek was omitted.

29. IFA 5218. The name of the story was given by the narrator himself, Fischel Rider.

30. Thus, for example, the Saints Legend (Shevaḥ) of the Yemenite Jews speak of a subterranean passage leading to Jerusalem from the tomb of R. Shalem Shabazi in Ta'ez (Bar-Itzhak 1992).

31. On this, see Chapter 5. See also Druyanov 1945; Schwarzbaum 1993a, 137–149. For specific stories from other Diaspora communities, see Sluszec 1957; Vilnai 1959, 521; Bergman 1953, 122; Pascheles 1850, II:14; Sasson 1949.

Chapter 2

1. Lévi-Strauss's structuralist approach emerges dialectically along with Propp's formalistic approach (see note 6 below). The gap between the two approaches is clarified by Lévi-Strauss in his survey of Propp's *Morphology of the Fairy Tale* (Lévi-Strauss 1976, 2:115). There he argues that structuralism, unlike formalism, refuses to contrast the real with the abstract and to recognize the added value of the latter. Myth, according to Lévi-Strauss, is a model of social relations. The scholar's concentration on tangible elements permits an ongoing connection with the cultural milieu, which is why there is a reference to ethnographical details that do not overtly appear in the story. His is a paradigmatic approach; the material undergoes reorganization in the process of a search for structural contrasts that construct the model of the story as a whole. The poetic solution is realized through a process of mediation between the various contraries and is expressed in the plot of the story (Lévi-Strauss 1963, 206–231; see also Hendricks 1991, 368–369; Shishkoff 1976, 271–276; Meletinsky 1974, 73–139).

2. On Yoseph Perl's archives, see Brawer 1956, 200.

3. On the memoirs of Dov of Bolichow, see Zinberg 1959, 5:109–111.

4. Provincial lords.

5. "Interesting, for example, is his [Birkenthal's] perspective on the arrival of the Jews in Poland, which lacks the slightest shadow of the gratitude that the inhabitants overtly demand of the Jews" (Brawer 1956, 203).

6. Propp's studies served as one stage in the development of surface structure in the study of prose fiction. In transformational generative grammar, a surface structure is an abstract representation of the organization of a sentence. Propp borrowed these concepts in an attempt to study the infinite variety of stories created from a limited number of basic structures. He distinguishes content from form and establishes a two-level division of fixed and variable aspects. Any individual story contains characters and actions, which differ from story to story. The analytical stratum is one of formal fixity. Here we find the roles played by the characters and the narrative functions. They are abstract, general, and invariable. Propp lists seven roles in the Russian folktale he analyzes, one of them that of the donor, as defined by the action. If we transfer this role into another genre, of course, its field of action will change in accordance with the genre.

7. We should note what Shmeruk writes in his article on Yiddish literature in Poland before 1648 (Shmeruk 1987): "Conspicuous throughout the period in question is the lack of any evidence in Yiddish literature of contact with Polish literature or any other literature in a Slavic language, not even Polish folk-urban literature. This attests to the spiritual segregation of the Polish Jewish community already in this period and the absence of cultural and literary contacts with the surrounding population beyond necessary business communication and vital areas" (ibid. 312).

8. According to Brawer, Birkenthal's book seeks to provide educated persons with answers to questions that Christians pose about the Jewish religion. He endeavors to strengthen the religious faith of the *maskilim* by demonstrating the superiority of Judaism. According to him, the main foundation of Judaism is the revealed or rational law. Kabbalah, too, is sacred, but he believes it best to steer clear of it, citing the episode of Frank and the Frankists as decisive proof for his stand.

9. The main aim of the periodical was to distribute knowledge about Jewish history and to improve Jews' living conditions by making reforms. The editor, Julius Fürst, was born in Poland and a son of a Darshan. He studied at the University of Berlin with Hegel and at the University of Breslaw. At Leipzig University he taught linguistics, literature, Bible, and more. His main publication is the monumental Bibliotheca Judaica (1849–1863). He was active in many literary activities with P. Delitsch and L. Zunz. The periodical was divided into two sections. One was dedicated to the life of the Jewish community; the other, named "Literaturblatt des Orients," was dedicated to Jewish history and literature. Among the contributors were Just, Letris, Smolenski, Frenkel, Gretz, Jelinek, and Luzato. For more information about the periodical and its editor, see Zinberg 1960, 7:137, 309, 313. See also Weil's book in German (Weil 1840).

10. Leon Weil relied on the anonymous publication (Anonymous 1801). My translation from the German is somewhat free. In addition, Weil's indications of his sources have been relegated to the notes so as not to interrupt the continuity of the text.

11. Here Weil draws on Leon Hollandersky and Anonymous.

12. Here Weil bases himself on Anonymous. According to Lelewel (1851–1856, 3, 417), R. Akiva and R. Nathanel were from Spain, R. Hezekiah and R. Emanuel from the Land of Israel, and R. Levi from India.

13. Here Weil notes that Gniezno was founded long before the rule of Piast and that Czech or Lech, the first duke of Poland, is credited with the founding of Gniezno. The kings of Poland had their seat in Gniezno for about 200 years before the capital was transferred to Cracow.

14. Weil notes that according to Anonymous, Rabbi Levi presented a brief summary of the Jews' misfortunes from the destruction of the First Temple until the persecutions in Germany.

15. According to Weil, the charge that many made against the Jews for having engaged only in commerce and trade throughout Europe, and especially in Germany and Poland, is groundless. They adopted these livelihoods, he asserts, only when all other occupations were closed to them and they were forced to take up trade so as not to die of starvation. Here he is clearly responding to the charges of nonproductivity frequently directed against the Jews.

16. Weil notes that in the matter of the questions and answers he relies on Anonymous, but does not provide a precise text.

17. This is stated in the body of the text with an explanation in a note. The two passages read: "When you reap the harvest in your field and overlook a sheaf in the field, do not turn back to get it; it shall go to the stranger, the fatherless, and the widow. . . ." "You shall enjoy, together with the Levite and the stranger in your midst, all the bounty that the Lord your God has bestowed upon you and your household."

18. Weil notes that, according to the *Poznań Provinzial Bletter* of 1845, synagogues were constructed in Gniezno and Witkowo in the tenth century.

19. Weil notes that the Jews of Poland had the great fortune of not being subject to the nobles. According to him, until the middle of the fourteenth century, there were only

hree classes in Poland: nobles, serfs, and Jews. It was Casimir the Great, who ascended the throne in 1333, who established the bourgeois class.

20. Weil notes: "The Jews' happy state lasted as long as the Poles remained pagans. But immediately upon the advent of Christianity, in the reign Mieczysław I (964–999), the skies grew darker and darker until they became completely black."

21. The motif of emissaries is a central one in legends of acceptance and is present in all the legends cited here. The motif appears also in legends of other Jewish communities. For example, see the legend of acceptance of the Jews of Bohemia, which describes almost an identical picture of the interrogation of the emissaries by the king (Pascheles 1850, 111–119). This motif in legends of acceptance is a poetic expression of the unstable condition of the Jewish communities in the diaspora when they wanted to settle among another people. To do so they needed impressive representatives to deal with the foreign ruler and people. Legends of foundation of new Torah centers in the diaspora also give a poetic expression to this situation, but as these legends are focused on internal Jewish confrontation, the transition of the founder of the new center is by wandering, captivity, and liberation, as in the Ashkenazi "legend of Rabbi Meshulam" or the Sephardi legend about the "Four taken captive" (Zefatman 1993, 81–158).

22. The opening paragraph of the Kaddish.

23. On Daniel Neufeld, see Biderman 1976, 19–20.

24. Ironically, as Shmeruk notes (1978, 287), the *Varshaver Yiddishe Tsaytung,* which first appeared in Warsaw in 1867–68, was founded by some of those involved with *Jutrzenka.*

25. Litinski accepts this as factual and adds a note: "Unfortunately the chronicles of these events were lost during the war between Poland and one of the German emperors in 1049. If only communities that have record books in which such things are sometimes found would make copies of them and place them in archives and safe places so as to preserve the chronicles if, Heaven forbid, they should catch on fire, as happened in a number of communities! Then later generations would know everything that happened to their ancestors in the olden days." This recalls Brawer's remarks about the story cited by Birkenthal to the effect that Birkenthal was uncritical "and did not distinguish between clear reports and chroniclers' legends." From our perspective, this again points to the essence of legend, which the narrating society considers to be true, and to the key role it plays in the legendary events it depicts.

26. Pinḥas Guterman was born in 1906. He related the story in 1961 and said that he had heard it from his grandfather, Yirmiyahu Guterman. Stories about bringing down rain after a request or demand from a foreign ruler are told by other Jewish ethnic groups as well. In IFA there are eight stories of this kind: IFA 3738 (Kaukas); 8718 (Iraqi Kurdistan); 9236 (Syria); 9827 (Yemen); 9955 (Israel–Ashkenazi); 1062 (Israel–Sephardi); 10878 (Yemen); 12069 (Iraqi Kurdistan).

27. On Casimir the Great, see Chapter 4 below.

28. The narrative structure is typical of rainmaking stories. The style is very close to that of the tale of Honi Hame'agal (*BT Ta'anit* 19).

29. My emphasis.

30. *Yad Avi-Shalom* was written by Joseph Shalom ben David, rabbi in Pisanz (Moravia), and was published by his son in 1779 after his death.

31. The poet lived c. 1340–1420 in Saragossa.

32. Compare Shmeruk 1987, 313. *Shevet Yehuda* was published in Yiddish in Krakow in 1591 and in Amsterdam in 1648. *Shevet Yehuda* was first published in Adrianopol (Savionta?) without mentioning the year, probably 1560–67. It is interesting to note

that when Agnon wants to indicate that his hero, who lives in Poland, is well-versed in Jewish history, he notes that one of the books with which he was familiar was *Shevet Yehudah*: "at night our ancestor told Peretz things that had happened to the Jews, for our ancestor was well-versed in *Yossipon* and *Shevet Yehuda* and *Yuhasin* and *Zemah David* and knew all the generations and all the countries, from the birth of the Patriarch Abraham, may he rest in peace, until his own generation (Agnon 1967, *Ha'esh ve'ha'etzim,* 69–70).

33. Various sources and studies indicate that there were Jews in Christian Spain who were fluent in Latin. Yitzhak Ber states unequivocally that Rabbi Shlomo ben Avraham Aderet (the Rashba), active in Barcelona in the second half of the twelfth century, knew Latin (Ber 1959, 168). David Romano mentions that Jews translated from Arabic to "vulgar Latin" and that some of them also knew High Latin (Romano 1992, 95, 104). Ramon Gonzales Ruiz states that educated Jews were fluent in three or four languages, sometimes including Latin (Ruiz 1983, 150). I would like to thank Dr. Aviva Doron for help in this matter.

Chapter 3

1. On the legend of Saul Wahl, see Bałaban 1930, 17–38; Bershadski 1890; Karpeles 1895, 272–292; Tollet 1992.

2. See, for example, Mahler 1946, 18; Dubnov 1916, 40.

3. This motif, which appears in the Bible in connection with Jephthah's daughter, is a well-known motif in international folklore. It is found in Jewish folk narratives in Hebrew and Yiddish and even found its way into a Purimspiel (Schipper 1938, 315–316).

4. "We have learned that Rabbi Yose says: Israel received three commandments when they entered the land: to appoint a king, to destroy the seed of Amaleq, and to build the Temple. But I do not know which of them comes first. When it says: 'Hand upon the throne of the Lord, the Lord will be at war with Amaleq throughout the ages' (Ex. 18:15), it means they should appoint a king first, since there is no throne without a king, as it says: 'Solomon sat on the throne of the Lord as king' (1 Chron. 29:23). I still do not know whether they should build the Temple first or destroy the seed of Amaleq first. But when it says 'He grants you safety from all your enemies around you and you live in security,' followed by 'the site where the Lord your God will choose to establish His name,' (Deut. 12:10–11), it means that they should destroy the seed of Amaleq first. For of David it says, 'when the king was settled in his palace and the Lord had granted him safety from all his enemies around him,' and then we read 'the king said to the prophet Nathan: "Here I am dwelling in a house of cedar, while the Ark of the Lord abides in a tent"' (2 Sam. 7:1–2)." BT Sanhedrin 20b.

5. For the generally negative attitude toward monarchy in Judaism, see below.

6. But not Zamojski, as erroneously in Fruchtman 1976, 39–43; Werses 1989, 119, probably because of a print error in Marek 1957, 168.

7. Zmorski was born in Warsaw to a noble family. Much of his childhood was spent in the countryside. In 1840 he made Warsaw his home and was one of the most prominent representatives of the group of young artists known as *Cyganeria Warszawska.* In addition to his literary endeavors and work as an editor, he was an active folklorist, roamed Poland collecting folk tales, and accompanied an ethnographic mission to Pomorze and Śląsk. For more on his biography and political activities, see Śliwińska and Słupniewicz 1972, 405–411.

8. Or, in Krzyżanowski's words, "Podanie to docierało do słuchaczy polskich, wywołując zrozumiałą uciechę" (Krzyżanowski 1965, 10).

9. In the original, "na tron Lechów"–on the throne of the Lechs. This is a standard designation for the Lech dynasty.

10. Zmorski's text was translated into Yiddish by Schipper and appeared in his article in the Yiddish newspaper *Der Moment* (Schipper 1928).

11. "Propinacja" is a decree that the peasants are allow to buy alcohol only in the tavern that belongs to the nobleman and which was usually leased by a Jew.

12. In Yiddish in the Polish original.

13. A clergy student.

14. Here the Polish original has the Hebrew word *Adonai.*

15. Anyone who knows the style of the Polish *Myszeidy* (Krasicki 1945), with its comic touches, will find it hard to escape the impression of a stylistic influence on the version presented by Zmorski.

16. On the centrality of the context to folk creation, see Ben-Amos 1971.

17. On the legend as a genre that is based on a world of reality, see, for example, Dorson 1972, 159–162. On legend as a story believed by the narrating society, see, for example, Georges 1971; Domötor, 1981.

18. Compare also Dégh and Vazsonyi 1976, 89–96.

19. The legend of Popiel, in the context of similar legends from medieval Europe, is discussed at length by Szajnocha 1881, 167–197; see also Biernacki 1963, 57–67.

20. Piast the wheelwright (*Piast kołodziej*) is a well-known Polish tradition (Maślanka 1984, 268–270).

21. After Num. 16:5.

22. Num. 24:12.

23. Gen. 37:10.

24. After Ps. 142:3.

25. After Isa. 32:15.

26. Judg. 3:25.

27. After Gen. 18:22.

28. After Gen. 18:4.

29. After Gen. 45:1.

30. Inverting Prov. 14:28.

31. After Ex. 32:1.

32. After Num. 27:17.

33. Inverting Eccles. 8:2.

34. From 1861 to 1863, *Hanesher* was a supplement to *Hamevasser*. Starting in 1864, however, both became biweeklies, appearing in alternate weeks for financial reasons: in Austria, weeklies had to pay a newspaper tax, whereas biweeklies were exempt. The contributors to the literary section of *Hanesher* included S. D. Luzzato, Joseph Halevy, Dr. Solomon Rubin, R. Yaacov Reifman, and others (Klausner 1954, 4:125).

35. Mr. Jonathan Ben-Naḥum (Prochownik) told me that the tradition was known in his family. However, the story itself was not told. I would like to thank Mr. Ben-Naḥum for his useful suggestions and assistance in finding Prochownik families in Israel. Before World War II many Prochownik families used to live in Radziwiłow and its surroundings. However, in the memorial book of this community, the story is not mentioned.

36. These legends of origin, as told after the Holocaust, are transformed and become legends of destruction (see below, Chapter 5).

37. The legend is mentioned in a novel by the Russian-Jewish writer Baharav (1878), which was translated into Hebrew in 1900 (Baharav 1900).

38. The story was first published in *Haolam* in 1924. The collection *Poland,* which

includes fourteen legends, was published by Hedim in 1925.

39. For Agnon's recasting of folk legends, see Weinman 1982, Werses 1987; and Shenhar-Alroy 1989.

40. Werses has noted that the motif appears in Agnon's story "Cantors" (Agnon, *Ir U'Melo'ah,* 1973). In this story, the Jews of Buczacz cannot agree on the selection of a cantor, and then one of them suggests: " 'Let us do what the princes of Poland did with regard to choosing a king. . . .' So they agreed that whoever came to the city first the next morning would be their king" (ibid., 120).

41. See also Bałaban 1925, 206–207. Bałaban relates that in Opatow there was a tray belonging to the Shomerim La'boqer Society, made in 1739 by Jonah son of Isaac, and that the society had another tray made in 1748 (Bałaban 1929, 87).

42. The designation "Hebrew" generally appears in the Bible in the context of dangerous confrontations with non-Jews. Thus Genesis 14:13, when Lot's fate is reported, "the fugitive brought the news to Abram the Hebrew, who was dwelling at the terebinths of Mamre the Amorite"; Genesis 39:14, regarding Potiphar's wife's false accusation against Joseph: "she called out to her servants and said to them, 'Look, he had to bring us a Hebrew to dally with us! This one came to lie with me; but I screamed loud' "; Genesis 41:12, regarding the interpretation of Pharaoh's dream: "a Hebrew youth was there with us, a servant of the chief steward; and when we told him our dreams, he interpreted them for us, telling each of us the meaning of his dream"; Exodus 2:11, in connection with the confrontation between Moses and the Egyptian taskmaster: "Some time after that, when Moses had grown up, he went out to his kinsfolk and witnessed their labors. He saw an Egyptian beating a Hebrew, one of his kinsmen"; and Jonah 1:9 when the sailors cast lots to determine who was responsible for the storm: " 'I am a Hebrew,' he replied. 'I worship the Lord, the God of Heaven, who made both sea and land.' "

Chapter 4

1. This is the source of the title of Jozef Ignacy Kraszewski's novel *Król Chłopów, Czasy Kazimierza Wielkiego* (King of the Farmers; Warsaw 1963), first published in 1881.

2. The names of these places are derived from what Casimir said when he ordered a rest stop on his way to Wrocław–"my tu będziem, a tam czeladź"–while those for whom there was not enough room he told to go "za górą" (behind the mountain) (Krzyżanowski 1965, 166).

3. Shmeruk (1981) discusses this at length.

4. I presented a paper on Junosza as a Polish transcriber of Jewish folktales at the Inter-university Conference of Literature Departments held at Haifa University in 1993. See also Bar-Itzhak 1998.

5. I would like to thank Barbara Kirshenblatt-Gimblett, who sent me Mayer Kirshenblatt's story and slide.

6. IFA 17,168.

7. It should be noted that in Hebrew the story is also found in a children's book by I. H. Kronenberg, "In the Castle of the King of Poland"; but it has no connection to Agnon's story.

8. I first discussed this story in Bar-Itzhak 1989. For a study of the story in the context of the relations between Jews and Poles in Agnon's writings, see Werses 1994, 91–94.

9. This is the place to note that even though Shmeruk does not deal with Agnon's

stories, his study made it possible for me to locate many traditions in Polish and Yiddish which I could probably not have found without him.

10. The Sabbath when the Song of the Sea (Exodus 15) is read in the synagogue. It always falls between mid-January and mid-February.

11. The Biblical name for the second month (1 Kings 6:1,37), corresponding to April–May. It was in Ziv that Solomon laid the foundations of the Temple. The Hebrew *ziv* means "brilliance" or "light."

12. References here are according to the ninth edition, 1967, 360–361.

13. In the book Agnon edited with Ahron Eliasberg, *Das Buch von den polnischen Juden,* 17–18.

14. Relics of saints play a key role in Catholic ritual; it is probable that Agnon relied on this tradition here. I have not managed to find a source for the use of a woman's heart and eyes, and this is evidently Agnon's own invention. Nevertheless, it is known that Jacques de Vitry (bishop of Liège 1227, cardinal 1229) recounts in his letters that he used to carry with him a finger of Mary of Oignies. To this relic he attributes his safe arrival in Milan in 1216, despite the danger of crossing the flood-swollen rivers of Lombardy (Bolton 1976, pp. 145 and 156; Huygens 1960, p. 72). I would like to thank Judith Bishop for her help in this matter.

15. Building a story on the plain meaning of a verse is frequent in folk narrative. For example, there are stories based on the verse "Send your bread forth upon the waters" (Eccles. 11:1), in which a man throws bread to the fish, or in which the hero, after hearing the rabbi's sermon that God loves hearts, runs off to the market, buys a heart, and prepares it as a meal for God (Attias 1976, 36–42).

16. The midrash is associating the Hebrew word אליל 'idol' with the Aramaic root אלל, which Targum Onkelos uses to render the noun and verb "spy."

17. Printed in Ben-Yehezkel 1961, 189–193, relying on *Ohel Issachar* (Lublin 1933).

18. The Bible associates adultery and polygamy with idolatry: for example, in the laws of the king in Deuteronomy 17:14–20 and, regarding foreign women, in 1 Kings 11.

19. Agnon uses this folk-narrator technique in several of his works. Werses has written at length about Agnon's astonishing expertise in the process of folk storytelling (Werses 1987, 255–260).

20. Because it has historical pretensions, a legend must arouse associations in the mind of the audience with famous people, known geographical places, or familiar episodes. The criterion for a legend, according to Dorson, is that it is known to a group of people who have some common denominator: they live in the same region, belong to the same ethnic group, or have a shared destiny, etc. Such groups preserve and transmit legends. Written sources that deal with local chronicles or popular literature frequently reinforce these oral traditions. For more on this, see Ranke 1967; Jason 1977; Dégh and Vazsonyi 1976; Jolles 1965; Dundes 1971, 17–31; Georges 1971, 1–13.

21. For a discussion of the play, see Shmeruk 1981, 238–244.

22. It should be remembered that love between a Jewish woman and a non-Jewish man and the accompanying conflict were a widespread theme of Yiddish novels at the end of the nineteenth century and the beginning of the twentieth century. These drew on Yiddish folklore (Shmeruk 1971, 265–285).

23. Shmeruk designates Asch's thesis as the possibility of symbiosis and cites I. L. Peretz's criticism of Asch, which accuses him of "flirting" with the Poles.

24. The theme entered Polish literature during the nineteenth century, evidently through the influence of Walter Scott, especially *Ivanhoe,* which presents a similar situation. Shmeruk commented on this (1981, 215–222). In all works of the period,

Esther is the king's mistress, even though the attitude toward her varies. As against her positive image in Kraszewski's *King of the Farmers,* which is the most distinguished work among those published in the nineteenth century, the lovely Esther is painted in an unfavorable light in Alexander Brunikowski's book of 1828. That book is full of antisemitic digs at her and at the Jews in general. On the other hand, Berntowicz's *Nałącz,* published the same year, depicts Esther positively, although her coreligionists are cast in an extremely negative light.

25. Mishna *Qiddushin* 1,1 enumerates three alternative ways to contract a marriage ("acquire a wife"): by money (i.e., giving the woman a gift with sufficient value), by document (i.e., a marriage contract), and by consensual intercourse.

Chapter 5

1. A comprehensive survey of Polish synagogues can be found in Bałaban 1927, 45–105. It includes: (1) *general information,* including a literature review, a discussion of the rights of the state and church with regard to the construction of the synagogue and the immediate surroundings of the synagogue; (2) *the construction of synagogues,* including style and structure, interior design, later additions to synagogue buildings, and wooden synagogues; (3) *the interior of the synagogues and their layout,* including the sanctuary, decorations, ark, lectern, choir, and benches; (4) *embroidery, silver objects, and candelabra,* including a description of the mantles for the Torah scrolls, embroidery, silver articles, the pointer, Torah crown, finials, goblets, spice boxes, *etrog* cases, candlesticks, candelabra, and the eternal light; (5) miscellaneous.

2. On the An-Ski ethnographic expedition, see, for example, Vanvild 1923; Rechtman 1958; Noy 1982b; Bar-Itzhak 1999.

3. I do not intend to deal here with aspects that have been investigated by students of art and architecture, but only with the reflection of these elements in folk narrative. On synagogue architecture, see, for example, Szyszko-Bohusz 1926; Dawidowicz 1982.

4. Rechtman 1958, 39. On the art of wooden synagogues, see: Zajczyk 1929, Piechotka and Piechotka 1959, Dawidowicz 1982.

5. From a story recorded by the An-Ski expedition: Rechtman 1958, 65.

6. On fortress synagogues, see: Bałaban 1929, Dawidowicz 1982.

7. Printed in 1889 by Gurland, based on the oral tradition: Gurland 1972, 4: 35.

8. Transcribed by the An-Ski expedition: Rechtman 1958, 70–71.

9. Rabbi David ben Samuel Halevi Segal (1586–1667) is known as the TaZ after his most important work, the *Turei Zahav,* a commentary on the *Shulḥan Arukh,* the Code of Jewish Law. He served as rabbi of Ostra after the death of his father-in-law, Rabbi Joel Sirkis, who died in 1641.

10. On this topic, see Bar-Itzhak 1987.

11. Ibid.

12. According to Dawidowicz, similar orders are known to have been issued to the communities of Luck, Lublin, Brody, Rzeszów, Leśniow, Tarnopol, Szarygrod, Szydłowiec, Żółkiew, Lubomir, and Brzeziny; he quotes some of them. See Dawidowicz 1982, 120.

13. From the collection of the An-Ski expedition: Rechtman 1958, 60.

14. Bałaban notes that, until 1918, all synagogues had plaques on the wall with the text of the prayer for the authorities, written in special calligraphy and ornamented with many miniatures. This prayer had a fixed text that did not change over hundreds of years. In the Old Synagogue of Cracow there was preserved a prayer for "Kazimierz

King of Poland." Bałaban held that this meant Jan Kazimierz, because all older documents and objects vanished during the period of Swedish rule (1655–1657) (Bałaban 1929, 97–98).

15. I am not dealing here with folk art, but with how synagogues are depicted in folk narratives. On synagogue art, see, for example, Grunwald 1934, Dawidowicz 1982.

16. See Schneiderman 1970a, 12.

17. On the *kune,* see Elzet 1919, 29; Bałaban 1925, 189. Dawidowicz asserts that *kunes* were found both in stone synagogues in Lwow, Vilna, Pińczów, Lissa, Vishogrod, Piotrków, and Przysucha, as well as in the wooden synagogues in Szedborz, Gąmbin, Warka, Dwart, and elsewhere (Dawidowicz 1982, 84). Our story adds the synagogue in Ostra to the list of stone synagogues with a *kune.* According to Bałaban, legends about the TaZ, who died in 1667, are associated with the *kune* in Lwow (Bałaban 1929, 101).

18. From the collection of the An-Ski expedition: Rechtman 1958, 68.

19. YIVO, inv. C, 35651: Cahan 1938, 143.

20. From the collection of the An-Ski expedition: Rechtman 1958, 83.

21. Ibid., 47.

22. Ibid., 40–41. See also the Memorial Book of Radziwiłłów (Adini 1966, 58–60). An English version of this story was published in Roskies and Roskies 1975, 180.

23. Bałaban mentions other artists who dared write their names on their works in the synagogue, such as on the polychromy in the wooden synagogue in Mohilev (Mohylów). That artist also noted the year, 1740, and his name, Hayyim son of Yitzhak of Słuck (Bałaban 1929, 72).

24. This motif is also found in Agnon's "Agunot."

25. Bałaban also refers to the opposite phenomenon, namely, Christian artists hired to work in synagogues. He associates this with the presence in synagogues of motifs borrowed from church art (Bałaban 1929, 75).

26. Ibid., 77.

27. YIVO collection, inv. C, 47115.

28. Krupnick 1945, 135.

29. Cf. Schwarzbaum 1993b, 137–149.

30. For a similar tale about a synagogue in Prague, see Pascheles 1850, 2: 158.

31. YIVO collection, inv. C, 47224: Cahan 1938, 149.

32. Collection of the An-Ski expedition: Rechtman 1958, 39–40.

33. YIVO collection, inv. 35646: Cahan 1938, 149.

34. From the collection of the An-Ski expedition: Rechtman 1958, 65–66.

35. Rechtman includes the complete text of the Ostra *megillah:* ibid., 66–67.

36. See Schneiderman 1970a, 12.

37. We should recall that Nemirov came to symbolize the destruction of communities during the Chmielnicki pogroms.

38. Collection of the An-Ski expedition: Rechtman 1958, 76–78. The story by S. J. Agnon, "The Great Synagogue" (Agnon 1967, 361–364), recounts a similar tale concerning the synagogue in Jaslowicz. In Agnon's story, it is children who find the synagogue on the eve of the Fast of the Ninth of Av.

39. The complex biographical story of the Maid of Ludmir demands attention in and of itself as an example of Polish Jewish legends about a woman. This is not the place for that. For a historical examination of the story which seeks to investigate the status of women in Hasidism, see Rapoport-Albert 1988, 495–525.

40. From the collection of the An-Ski expedition: Rechtman 1958, 79–81.

41. Cahana cites the text on the tombstone, which indicates that she died a natural

death in 1635. There is no reference to the murder or martyrdom alluded to by the legend (Cahana 1992, 80). For a full-scale historical investigation of the legend, see Bałaban 1906; for a folkloristic-literary approach, see Sadan 1990, 122–143.

42. See my article on relations between Jews and Gentiles in the folk narratives of Polish Jewry (Bar-Itzhak 1991).

43. On the legend of Casimir and Esther, see above, Chapter 4. See also Shmeruk 1981, 206–279; Bar-Itzhak 1989, 65–76.

44. Compare the legends from the YIVO collection: Cahan 1938, 153–154, inv. C, 22100, 10935, 50044, 22103.

45. On the use of stones from the Holy Temple to build synagogues, and the link between synagogues and the prophet Elijah or with sacred objects brought from Jerusalem, see Schwarzbaum 1993a, 137–149. For specific tales of this sort from other communities, see Sluszec 1957, 97; Vilnai 1959, 521; Bergman 1953, 122; Pascheles 1850, 2: 14; Sasson 1949, 165.

46. Written Jewish folk narratives have been considered from various perspectives. See Elstein 1974, 94; Shenhar 1982, 7–12; Bar-Itzhak 1987, 1–2; Yassif 1991, 7–72; Hasan-Rokem 1990, 109–131, and especially p. 127.

47. In addition to the memorial books cited here, I have found synagogue legends in the following: *Zikkaron li'Qehillat Bychawa; Sefer zikkaron li'Qehillat Ganibosz; Sefer qehillat yehudei Dąmbrowa Górnicza ve-hurbana; Sefer zikkaron li'Qehillat Drohiczin; Sefer Łańcut-Hayyeha Ve'Hurbanah shel qehillah yehudit; Sefer yizkor qehillat Kuzmir de'Lublin; Sefer Kublink; Sefer Kock; Qehillat Lublin (dappei hanzahah); Venn de visl hot geredet yidish; Kremenets u-Wiszgorodok un Patishayow yizkor-bukh.* We should also note that the memorial books contain abundant material that was originally published before the Holocaust.

48. The legends have been transcribed and preserved in the Israeli Folktale Archive (IFA), IFA 5219.

49. IFA 5217.

50. On the lament as a Jewish response to disaster, see, for example: Roskies 1993, 9–22; Mintz 1982, 1–7; Roskies 1988, 5–6.

51. Zigelman 1967, 15.

Bibliography

Adini, Yaakov, ed. 1966. *Radziwiłłow Memorial Book*. Tel-Aviv.

Adini, Yaacov, ed. 1969. *Zikkaron li'Qehillat Bychawa* (Bychawa Community Memorial Volume). Tel-Aviv.

Agnon, S. Y., and Ahron Eliasberg. 1916. *Das Buch von den polnischen Juden*. Berlin: Jüdischer Verlagn.

Agnon, S. Y. 1920. "Polin: Aggadot Mini Kedem" (Poland: Legends from Antiquities). *Hatequfa* 5: 23–36.

———. 1925. *Polin: Sippurei Aggadot* (Poland Legendary Tales). Tel-Aviv: Hedim.

———. 1967. *Kol Sippurav shel Shmuel Yoseph Agnon* (All Stories by Shmuel Yoseph Agnon). Jerusalem: Shocken.

———. 1973. *Ir U'Mlo'ah*. Jerusalem: Shocken.

Anonim Gall. 1965. *Kronika Polska*. Wrocław: Bibloteka Narodowa, seria 1, no. 59.

Anonymous. 1801. *Phylacterium oder Argenton und Philo im Schooße der wahren Glückseligkeit*. Berlin.

An-Ski, S. (S. Z. Rapoport). 1920. "Agadot Ha'Am Bidvar Gzerot Tah" ("Folk Legends about 1668 Pogroms"), *Ha'Olam*, April, 12–14.

———. 1925. *Gesammelte shriftn* (Collected Works). 15 vols. Vilna: Ferlag An-Ski.

Asch, Sholem. 1906. *Mashiahs Tsaytn* (The Time of the Mesiah). Vilna.

———. 1919. *Kiddush Ha'shem und Andere Erzelungen* (Kiddush Ha'shem and Other Stories). New York: Porverts.

Attias, Moshe. 1976. *Notsat Ha'Zahav Shel Zipor Ha'pele* (The Golden Feather of the Wonder Bird). Haifa: Israeli Folktale Archives.

Bader, Gershom. 1927. *Draisig Dores Yiddn in Poilen* (Thirty Generations of Jews in Poland). New York.

Baharav, G. 1900. *Ktav Yad Yivri* (Jewish Manuscript). Pietrkiv: Tushiya (trans. Y. Grazovski).

Bakhtin, Mikhail M. 1981. The *Dialogic Imagination*. Austin: University of Texas Press.

177

Bałaban, Majer. 1906. *Żydzi lwowscy na przełomie XVI i XVII wieku.* Lwów.

———. 1925. *Historja i Literatura Żydowska,* 3. Lwów: Wydawnictwo Zakładu Narodowego imienia Ossolińskich.

———. 1927. *Studia Historyczne.* Warsaw: Ksi"garnia M. J. Freid i S-ka.

———. 1929. *Zabytki Historyczne Żydów w Polsce.* Warsaw: Nakładem Towarzystwa Krzewienia Nauk Judaistycznych w Polsce.

———. 1930. *Yidden in Poilen.* Vilna: Vilner Farlag fon B. Kleckin.

———. 1931. *Shalshelet Ha'Yahas shel Mishpahat Orenshtien-Brode* (The Geneology of the Orenstein-Brode Family). Warsaw: Ha'Hevra Le'Hafatsat Madaei Ha'Yahadut Be'Polania.

———. 1948. *Beit Yisrael be'Polin: Mi'yamim Rishonim ve'ad Limot Ha'hurban* (Jewish House in Poland: From the First Days until destruction). Ed. Y. Halperin. Jerusalem: World Zionist Organization.

Band, A. J. 1968. *Nostalgia and Nightmare: A Study in the Fiction of S. Y. Agnon.* Berkeley and Los Angeles: University of California Press.

Bar-Itzhak, Haya. 1978. "Tavnit shel Milui Pearim Be'Sippurei Horadat Geshamim" (A Filling Gap Structure in Stories of Bringing Down Rain). *Yeda Am* 19: 62–68.

———. 1984. "Merhav U'zman Be'Aggadat Qedoshim Shel Yehudei Teiman" (Space and Time in Saints Legends of Yemenite Jews). In *Orhot Teiman,* ed. Sh. Gamliel, M. Masuri-Caspi and Sh. Avizemer. Jerusalem: Mahon Shalom LeShivtei Yeshurun. 311–319.

———. 1987. "Aggadat Qedoshim Ke'zaner Ba'sifrut Ha'Amamit Shel Edot Yisrael" (The Saints Legend as a Genre in the Folk Literature of Jewish Communities). PhD diss., Hebrew University, Jerusalem.

———. 1989. "Li'Meqorotav Shel 'Ha'Lev Ve'Ha'enayyim' Le'Sh.Y. Agnon" (On the Sources of Agnon's "The Heart and Eyes"), *Dappim Le'Mehqar Be'sifrut* 5/6: 64–76.

———. 1991. "Interrelationship between Jews and Gentiles in Folk Narratives Told by Polish Jews," *Jewish Folklore and Ethnology Review* 13.1.

———. 1992. "Ha'Merhav Be'Aggadat Qedoshim Amamit Yehudit" (Space in Jewish Saints Legend). *Tura* 2: 121–133.

———. 1993. "Narration and the Components of Communication in the Jewish Folk Legend", *Fabula* 35: 261–281.

———. 1998a. "Les Juifs polonais face au 'monstre' israélien, Récits d'aliya en Israël," *Cahiers de Littérature Orale* 44, 191–205.

———. 1998b. "Mihutz La'Heksher Ha'Tivi–Sippurey Am Yehudiym Berishumo Shel Sofer Polani: Yiun Ba'Sefer 'Ha'Nes Be'Beit Ha'Kvarot Le'Klemens Junosza" (Outside the Natural Context–Jewish Folk Stories Recorded by a Polish Writer–Analysis of "The Miracle in the Cemetary" by Klemens Junosza). *Mehkarei Yerushalaim Be'Folklor Yehudi* (Jerusalem Studies in Jewish Folklore), 19–20, 211–238.

———. 1999. "Hearot La'Masa 'Ha'Etnopoetica Ha'Yehudit' Le'Sh. An-Ski' " (Comments to the Essay "Jewish Ethnopoetics" by Sh. An-Ski). *Chulyot–Journal of Yiddish Research* 5, 363–368.

Bascom, William. 1965. "The Forms of Folklore: Prose Narratives," *Journal of American Folklore* 78: 3–20.

The Beginning of Polish Kings and Princes. 1855. Lwow.

Ben-Amos, Dan. 1971. "Toward a Definition of Folklore in Context." In *Toward New Perspectives in Folklore,* ed. A. Parades and R. Bauman. Austin: University of Texas Press. 3–15.

————. 1976. "Analytical Categories and Ethnic Genres." In *Folklore Genres*, ed. Dan Ben-Amos. Austin: University of Texas Press. 215–242.

Benet, Shmuel. 1961. "Dappim Historiyim." In *Radom–Sefer Zikkaron* (Radom–Memorial Book), ed. A. S. Stein. Israel. 28–29.

Ben-Yehezkel, Mordekhai. 1961. *Sefer Ma'asiot* (Book of Folk Tales). Tel-Aviv: Dvir.

Ber, Yitshak. 1959. *Toldot Ha'Yehudim Bi'Sfarad Ha'Notsrit* (The History of the Jews in Christian Spain). Tel-Aviv: Am Oved.

Bergman, Yehuda. 1953. *Ha'Folklor Ha'Yehudi* (The Jewish Folklore). Jerusalem: Reuben Mass.

Bernstein, Shimon. 1945–46. "Divan Shirei Ha'Kodesh Shel Shlomo Ben-Meshulam Da Pierra" (Holy Poems Divan by Shlomo Ben-Meshulam Da Pierra). *Hebrew Union College Annual* 19.

Bershadski, S. 1890. *Yevrej Korol Polskij*. St. Petersburg.

Biderman, Israel. 1976. *Mayer Balaban, Historian of Polish Jewry: His Influence on Younger Generation of Jewish Historians*. New York: Dr. I. M. Biderman Book Committee.

Biernacki, A. 1963. "Z dziejów podania o Popielu." *Literatura Ludowa* 2/3: 57–67.

Bolton, Brenda M. 1976. "Mulieres Sanctae." In *Women in Medieval Society*, ed. Susan Mosher Stuard. Philadelphia: University of Pennsylvania Press. 141–158.

Brawer, Avraham Ya'acov. 1956. *Galicia Vi'Yehudeya, Meḥkarim Betoldot Galicia Ba'Mea Ha'Shmone Esre* (Galicia and Its Jews: Studies in the History of Galicia in the 18th Century). Jerusalem: Mosad Bialik.

Bruner, Edward M., and Phyllis Gorfain. 1984. "Dialogic Narration and the Pardoxes of Masada." In *Text Play and Story: The Construction and Reconstruction of Self and Society*, ed. Edward M. Bruner. Washington D.C.: The American Ethnological Society. 56–79.

Brunvand, J. H. 1968. *The Study of American Folklore: An Introduction*. New York: W. W. Norton & Co.

Cahan, Y. L. 1938. *Yiddisher folklor* (Yiddish Folklore). Vilna: YIVO.

Cahana, David. 1992. *Bi'Zevat Ha'Sin'ah: Yahasei Yehudim U'Polanim Le'Orekh Ha'Dorot* (In the Grip of Hatred: Relations between Jews and Poles over the Generations). Israel: Iggud Yoz'ei Levov Ve'Ha'sevivah.

Cygielman, Shmuel Arthur. 1991. *Yehudei Polin Ve'Lita Ad Shnat 1648; Mevo'ot U'Mekorot Mevoarim* (Jews in Poland and Lita until 1648: Introduction and Interpreted Sources). Jerusalem: Merkaz Zalman Shazar.

Czynski, Jan. 1848. *Le réveil d'Israël: histoire, statistique, chronique du jour, variétés littéraires, vignettes et portraits*. Paris: Jules Renouard et ci.

Dawidowicz, David. 1982. *Omanut Ve'Omanim Be'Batei Kneset Shel Polin* (Art and Artists in Synagogues in Poland). Tel-Aviv: Ha'Kibbutz Ha'Meuḥad.

Dégh, Linda, and Andrew Vazsonyi. 1976. "Legend and Belief." In *Folklore Genres*, ed. Dan Ben-Amos. Austin: University of Texas Press. 93–123.

Domötor, Tekla. 1981. "Some Questions Concerning Belief-Legend as Genre." *Studia Fennica* 26: 11–27.

Dorson, Richard M. 1972. "Legends and Tall Tales." In *Folklore: Selected Essays*. Bloomington: Indiana University Press.

Druyanov, A. 1945. "Meal Gag Beit-Ha'Kneset Ha'Gadol" (Above the Roof of the Great Synagogue). In *Ktavim Nivharim*, vol. 2. Tel-Aviv: Brith-Rishonim. 787–802.

Dubnov, S. M. 1916. *History of the Jews in Russia and Poland,* Philadelphia: Jewish Publication Society of America.

Dubs, Marek. 1861. "Pierwsze Poznanie Się." *Jutrzenka* 7: 50–51; 8: 58–60.

Dundes, Alan. 1971. "On the Psychology of Legend." In *American Folk Legend: A Symposium*, ed. Hand W. D. Berkeley and Los Angeles: University of California Press. 1–13.

———, ed. 1984. *Sacred Narrative, Readings in the Theory of Myth*. Berkeley and Los Angeles: University of California Press.

———. 1996. "Madness in Method Plus a Plea for Projective Inversion in Myth." In *Myth and Method*, ed. Laurie L. Patton and Wendy Doniger. Charlottesville: University Press of Virginia. 147–159.

Eisenstein, Aron. 1934. *Die Stellung Der Juden in Polen*. Cieszyń.

Eliade, Mircea. 1968. *Myth and Reality*. New York: Harper and Row.

———. 1991. *The Myth of the Eternal Return or Cosmos and History*. Bollingen Series XLVI. Princeton, N.J.: Princeton University Press.

Elstein, Yoav. 1974. *Structuralism In Literary Criticism: A Method and Its Application to Two Representative Hasidic Tales*. PhD diss., University of California, Los Angeles.

Elzet, Yehuda. 1919. "Unzer Muzeum: Di Kune" (Our Museum: The Kune). *Ilustrirte Velt* 2. Warsaw.

Epstein, Eliezer. 1873. Divrei Ha'Yamim Le'Malkhei Rusia (Chronicles of the Kings of Russia). Vilna.

Feldman, Elazar. 1934. "Di Eltste Yedies Vegen Yiddn Yin Pilishe Shtet Yin XIV–XVI Y." (The Oldest Information Regarding Jews in Polish Cities in XIV–XVI c.). *Bleter Far Geshihte, Yunger Historiker* 3. Warsaw.

Finkelstein, Leo. 1947. *Megillat Polin* (Scroll of Poland). Buenos Aires.

Finnegan, Ruth. 1970. *Oral Literature in Africa*. Oxford: Clarendon Press.

———. 1992. *Oral Traditions and the Verbal Arts*. London: Routledge.

Frenkel, Yitzhak Yedidiah, ed. 1953. *Sefer Linczyc* (Linczyc Book). Israel.

Frenkel, Yona. 1981. *Yiunim Be'Olamo Ha'Ruhani Shel Sippur Ha'Aggadah* (Readings in the Spiritual World of the Aggadah Story). Tel-Aviv: Sifryat Ha'Kibbutz Ha'Meuhad.

———. 1991. *Darkei Ha'Aggada Ve'Hamidrash* (Modes of the Aggadah and Midrash). Tel-Aviv: Yad Le'talmud, Masada.

Frischman, David. 1914. *Kol Kitvei* (All Works), 11. Warsaw: Hotsa'at Merkaz.

Fruchtman, Dov. 1976. "Reshit Ha'Yehudim Be'Polin Be'Sippurei Sh. Y. Agnon" (The Beginning of Jews in Poland in the Stories by S. Y. Agnon). *Turim* 3: 39–43.

Frye, Northrop. 1957. *Anatomy of Criticism*. Princeton N.J.: Princeton University Press.

Ganz, David. 1983. *Sefer Zemah David* (The Book Zemah David). Ed. M. Broyer, Jerusalem: Magnes. (First pub. Prague 1592.)

Garsiel, Moshe. 1987. *Midrashei Shemot Ba'Mikra* (Names Midrashim in the Bible). Ramat-Gan: Revivim.

Georges, Robert A. 1971. "The General Concept of Legend." In *American Folk Legend: A Symposium*, ed. W. D. Hand. Berkeley and Los Angeles: University of California Press. 1–13.

———. 1983. "Folklore." In *Sound Archives: A Guide to their Establishment and Development*, ed. D. Lance. International Association of Sound Archives, Special Publication 4, 135.

Gerber-Talmon, Yonina. 1952. "Ha'zman Ba'mitos Ha'primitivi" (Time in the Primitive Myth). *Yiun* 2.4: 201–214.

Ginzberg, Louis. 1913. *The Legends of the Jews*. Philadelphia: Jewish Publication Society of America.

Glatstein, Ya'acov. 1940. *Ven Yash iz gekomen* (When Yash Arrived). New York: Farlag Shklarski.

Goldberg-Mulkiewicz, Olga. 1989. *Ethnographic Topics Relating to Jews in Polish Studies.* Jerusalem: Magnes.

————. 1991. "Księga Pamięci A Mit Żydowskiego Miasteczka." *Etnografia Polska* 35: 187–199.

Gonen, Rivka. 1994. *Back to the Shtetl: An-Ski and the Jewish Ethnographic Expedition 1912–1914.* Jerusalem, The Israel Museum.

Goodman, Lenn E. 1993. "Mythic Discourse." In *Myth and Fiction*, ed. S. Biderman and B. A. Sharfstein. Leiden: E. J. Brill. 101–203.

Grunwald, M. 1934. *Zur Ikonographie der Malerei in Unsern Holzsynagogen.* Baden.

Guggenheim-Grunberg, Florence. 1965. "Place Names in Swiss Yiddish: Examples of the Assimilatory Power of a Western Yiddish Dialect." In *The Field of Yiddish II*, ed. U. Weinreich. London: Mouton & Co. 147–157.

Gurland, H. I. 1972. *Le'Qorot Ha'Gezerot al Yisrael* (Annals of Jewish Persecutions). Jerusalem: Kedem. (Orig. pub. Cracow, 1890–1891.).

Halevi-Zvik, Yehudit. 1984. *Reshita Shel Bikoret Agnon 1919–1932* (The Beginning of Agnon's Criticism 1919–1932), Haifa: Haifa University Press.

Ha'Mevasser/Ha'Nesher. 1861. 1(14), 109–110.

Hanover, Natan Nata. 1968. *Sefer Yeven Mezulah.* Ed. Yisrael Halperin. Rev. ed. Tel-Aviv: Hakibbutz Ha'Meuḥad.

Hasan-Rokem, Galit. 1990. "Qavvim Le'Ḥeqer Hashva'ati Shel Ha-Sippur Ha'Amami Be'Midrash Ha'Aggadah: Sippurim Ḥidatiyyim Me'Eikhah Rabbah 1" (Comparative Study of Folk Narrative in Homiletical Midrashim: Riddle-stories from Lamentations Rabba 1). *Tarbiz* 109–131.

Hendricks, William O. 1991. "Semiotics and Narrative." In *Recent Development in Theory and History, The Semiotic Web*, ed. Thomas A. Sebeok and Jean Umiker-Sebeok. 1990. Berlin: Mouton de Gruyter. 365–388.

Herder, Johann Gottfried von. 1967. *Auch eine Philosophie der Geschichte zur Bildung der Menscheit.* Frankfurt a. M.: Suhrkamp.

Hill, J. D., ed. 1988. *Rethinking History and Myth: Indigenous South American Perspectives on the Past.* Urbana: University of Illinois Press.

Hirshberg, H. Z. 1945. "Maftehot Shel Geshamim" (The Keys of Rains). *Yediot Ha'Ḥevra Ha'Ivrit Le'Ḥakirat Eretz Yisrael Ve'Atikotea* 11: 46–54.

Horodetzky, S. A. 1947. *Yahadut Ha'Sekhel Ve'Yhadut Ha'Regesh* (Judaism of Reason and Judaism of Emotion). Tel-Aviv: Tverski.

Huberband, Shimon. 1969. "Mekorot Le'Toldot Yisrael Ba'Aratsot Ha'Slaviot Be'Polin, Be'Rusya U'Be'Lita Bifrat" (Sources to the Jewish History in the Slavic Lands–In Poland, Russia and Especially Lithuania). In *Kiddush Ha'Shem–Ketavim Mi'Yemey Ha'Shoa* (Martyrdrom–Works from the time of the Holocaust), ed. N. Blumental and Y. Kermish. Tel-Aviv: Zahor. 315–334.

Huygens, R. B. C., ed. 1960. *Letters de Jacques de Vitry.* Leiden: E. J. Brill.

Jason, Heda. 1975. *Studies in Jewish Ethnopoetry.* Taipei: Chinese Association for Folklore.

————. 1977. *Ethnopoetry: Form, Content, Function.* Bonn: Linguistica Biblica.

Jolles, Andre. 1965. *Einfache Formen: Legende, Sage, Myth, Ratsel, Spruch, Kasus, Märchen, Witz.* Tubingen: Max Niemeyer Verlag (1 Auflage 1930).

Junosza, Klemens. 1905. *Cud na kirkucie.* Warsaw: Skład Główny w Ksiegarni E. Wende i Spółka.

Kadłubek, W., 1974. *Mistrza Wincentego Kronika.* Warsaw.

Karpeles, Gustav. 1895. "A Jewish King in Poland." In *Jewish Literature and other Essays*. Philadelphia: Jewish Publication Society of America. 272–292.

Kirshenblatt-Gimblett, Barbara. 1978. "Culture Shock and Narrative Creativity." In *Handbook of American Folklore*, ed. Richard M. Dorson. Bloomington: Indiana University Press. 39–47.

Klausner, Yoseph. 1954. *Historia Shel Ha'Sifrut Ha'Ivrit Ha'Hadasha* (The History of the Modern Hebrew Literature). Jerusalem: Ahiasaf.

Krasicki, Ignacy. 1954. *Pisma Wybrane*. Warsaw.

Kraszewski, Józef Ignacy. 1963. *Król Chłopów Czasy Kazimierza Wielkiego*. Warsaw. (First pub. in 1881.).

Kraushar, Alexander. 1862. "Przyczynki do Historii Żydow w Polsce." *Jutrzenka* 5: 35–37.

———. 1865. *Historya Żydów w Polsce*. Warsaw.

Kronika Wielkopolska. 1965. (Oprac. B. Kubisuwna). Warsaw.

Krupnick, Hayim Aharon. 1945. "Aggadot Szarygrod" (Legends of Sharygrod). *Reshumot* n.s., 1: 135.

Krzyżanowski, Julian. 1962. *Polska Bajka Ludowa*. Warsaw.

———. 1965. *Słownik Folkoru Polskiego*. Warsaw: Wiedza Powszechna.

Kugelmass, Jack, and Jonathan Boyarin, eds. 1983. *From the Ruined Garden: The Memorial Book of Polish Jewry*. New York: Schocken.

Lahover, P. 1938. "Mesapper Ha'Am" (Folk Narrator). *Ha'Aretz* (8 December 1938). Reprinted in *Rishonim Ve'Ahronim*. Devir, 1966. 384–378.

Lamdan, Yitzhak. 1938. "Ba'al Ha'Aggadah" (The Legend Narrator), *Gilionot* 7: 5–6, 359–360.

Laor, Dan. 1994. "Zioniuto Shel Agnon" (The Zionism of Agnon), *Ha'Zionut* 18: 213–245.

———. 1998. *Hayei Agnon* (The Life of Agnon). Tel-Aviv: Shocken.

Lelewel, Joachim. 1851–56. *Polska wiekow srednich*, Poznań: Nakł. J. K. Żupańskiego.

Lerner, Falik. 1965. *Kremenets, Vizshgorodek un Patiszayow Yizkorbukh* (Kremenets, Vishgorod, and Patiszayow Memorial Volume). Buenos Aires.

Lévi-Strauss, Claude. 1963. "The Structural Study of Myth." In *Structural Anthropology*. New York: Basic Books. 206–231.

———. 1976. "Structure and Form: Reflections on a Work by Vladimir Propp" In *Structural Anthropology II*. Chicago: University of Chicago Press. 115–146.

Lewin, Louis. 1907. "Deutsche Einwarderungen in polnische Ghetti," 2. *Jahrbuch der Judish-Literarischen Gesellschaft* 5: 75–154.

Litinski, Menahem Nahum. 1895. *Sefer Korot Podolia Ve'Kadmoniot Ha'Yehudim Sham* (The Book of the Annals of Podolia and Jewish Antiquities There). Odessa: M. A. Belinson.

Mahler, Rephael. 1946. *Toldot Ha'Yehudim Be'Polin (Ad Ha'Mea Ha-19) Kalkala, Hevra, Ha'Matsav Ha'Mishpati* (Jewish History in Poland until the 19th Century–Economy, Society, Legal Status). Merhavia: Sifriat Poalim.

———. 1953. "Shemot Yehudiyim Shel Mekomot Be'Polin Ha'Yeshana" (Jewish Place Names in Old Poland), *Reshumot* n. s., 5: 146–161.

Maranda, P., ed. 1972. *Mythology*. Harmondsworth: Penguin.

Marek, Berl. 1957. *Di Geschichte Fun Yidn in Poiln biz sof fun XV Y.H.* (The History of Jews in Poland until the 15th Century). Warsaw: Farlag Yiddish Buch.

Markowski, S. 1992. *Krakowski Kazimierz Dzielnica Żydowska 1870–1988*. Kraków: Arka.

Maślanka, Julian. 1984. *Literatura A Dzieje Bajeczne*. Warsaw: Państwowe Wydawnictwo Naukowe.

Meletinsky, E. et al. 1974. "Problems of the Structural Analysis of Fairytales." In *Soviet Structural Folkloristics,* ed. P. Maranda. The Hague: Mouton. 73–139.

Mintz, Alan. 1982. "The Rhetoric of Lamentations and the Representation of Catastrophe." *Prooftexts* 2; 1–7.

Noy, Dov. 1959a. *Gola Ve'Eretz Yisrael* (Diaspora and the Land of Israel). Jerusalem: Sha'ar.

———. 1959b. "Tefilat Ha'Tamim Morida Geshamim" (The Prayer of the Innocent Brings Down Rain). *Mahanayim* 51: 34–45.

———. 1962. "Ha'Qayemet Bedihat Am Yehudit?" (Does a Jewish Folk Joke Exist?). *Mahanayim* 67: 49–56.

———. 1967. "Rabbi Shalem Shabbazi Be'Aggadat Ha'Am Shel Yehudei Teiman" (Rabbi Shalem Shabbazi in the Folk Legend of Yemenite Jews). *Boi Teiman*. Tel-Aviv. 106–131.

———. 1982a. "Mavo," introduction to *Hasippur Ha'Amami Shel Edot Yisrael* (The Folk Narrative of Ethnic Groups in Israel), Aliza Shenhar. Tel-Aviv: Gome Sifrei Mada U'Mehkar, Tsherikover. 7–23.

———. 1982b. "Meqomo shel An-Ski Ba'Folkloristikah Ha'Yehudit" (An-Ski's Place in Jewish folklore Studies). *Mehqarei Yerushalayim Be'Folklor Yehudi* 2: 94–107.

Oring, Elliott. 1992. *Jokes and Their Relations*. Lexington: University Press of Kentucky.

Ortner, Sherry B. 1973. "On Key Symbols." *American Anthropologist* 75: 1338–1346.

Papirna, Abraham Ya'acov. 1952. *Kol Ha'Ktavim* (All Works). Tel-Aviv: Mahbarot Le'Sifrut.

Parry, M., and A. B. Lord. 1953–54. *Serbocroatian Heroic Songs,* 1–2. Cambridge, Mass.: Harvard University Press.

Pascheles, Wolf. 1850. *Sippurim: Sammlung Judischer Volksagen, Erzahlungen, Mythen, Chroniken*. Achtes Bandchen. Prague: Druck und Verlag von Jakob B. Brandeis.

Patai, Raphael. 1939. "The Control of Rain in Ancient Palestine." *HUCA* 14: 251–286.

———. 1979. *The Messiah Texts*. New York: Avon.

Peretz, I. L. 1947. *Ale Verk* (Complete Works), 2. New York: Ziker Biher.

Piechotka, Maria, and Kazimierz Piechotka. 1959. *Bóżnice drewniane, Budownictwo i Architektura*. Warsaw: Arkady.

Pinqas Kremenets (Kremenets Register). 1954. Tel-Aviv.

Pniel, Noah. 1970. *Siah Le'et Erev–Shirim* (Discourse at Night–Poems), Haifa: Pinat Sefer.

Porat, Eliyahu, ed. 1961. *Sefer Kock* (Kock Memorial Volume). Tel-Aviv.

Propp, Vladimir. 1968. *Morphology of the Folktale*. Indiana University Research Center in Anthropology, Folklore and Linguistics. Bloomington: Indiana University Press.

Puhvel, J. 1987. *Comparative Mythology*. Baltimore: John Hopkins University Press.

Qehillat Lublin (Dappei Hanzahah) (The Lublin Community–Memorial Pages). Haifa, 1973.

Ranke, Kurt. 1967. "Einfache Formen." *Journal of Folklore Institute* 4: 17–31.

Rapoport-Albert, Ada. 1988. "On Women in Hassidism. S. A. Horodetzky and the Maid of Ludmir Tradition." In *Jewish History: Essays in Honour of Chimen Abramsky*. London: Peter Halbaum. 495–525.

Rechtman, Avraham. 1958. *Yiddishe etnografie un folklor* (Yiddish Ethnography and Folklore). Buenos Aires: YIVO.

Romano, David. 1992. *La Ciencia Hispanojudia*. Madrid: Mapfri.

Roskies, Diane K., and David G. Roskies. 1975. The *Shtetl Book*. New York: Ktav Publishing House.

Roskies, David G., ed. 1988. *The Literature of Destruction: Jewish Responses to Catastrophe.* Philadelphia: Jewish Publication Society.

Roskies, David. 1993. *El Mul Penei Ha'ra'a. Teguvot La'pur'anut Ba'tarbut Ha'Yehudit Ha'hadashah* (Confronting Evil: Responses to Disaster in Modern Jewish Culture). Tel-Aviv: Hakibbutz Hameuhad.

Rosman, Moshe. 1991. "Ha'Yishuv Ha'Yehudi Be'Polin: Yesodot Geografiyyim, Demografiyyim U'Mishpatiyyim" (The Jews of Poland: Geographic, Demographic, and Legal Bases). In *Polin: Peraqim Be'Toledot Yehudei Mizrah Eiropah Ve'Tarbutam* (Poland: Chapters in the History and Culture of East-European Jewry). Tel-Aviv: Open University. 1–2.

Ruiz, Ramon Gonzales. 1983. "La Sociedad Toledana Bajo Medival," siglos (XII–XIV). *I Congreso Internacional Encuentro de las tres culturas,* Toledo.

Saba, Abraham. 1985. *Zeror Ha'Mor.* Israel: Makhon Zvor Ha'Mor. (Originally printed in 1567 by Msir Zurzo Dikabali.)

Sadan, Dov. 1954. "Alter Terakh: The Byways of Linguistic Fusion." In *The Field of Yiddish*, 3, ed. U. Weinreich. New York: Linguistic Circle of New York. 134–142.

———. 1990. *Shai Olamot–12 Mehkarim Be'Folklore* (Twelve Studies in Folklore). Ed. Dov Noy. Jerusalem: Magnes.

Sasson, David Salomon. 1949. *A History of the Jews of Baghdad.* Letchworth.

Schipper, Yitzhak. 1926. *Di virtshaftsgeshikhte fun di yidn in Poiln be-etan mitelalter* (The Economic History of the Jews of Poland in the Middle Ages). Warsaw.

———. 1928. "Yiddish Poylishe Legendes" ("Jewish-Polish Legends"). *Der-Moment* 156: 4.

———. 1938. "He'arot Zu Di Purimspillen" (Comments to Purimspiellen). In *Yiddisher Folklore* (Yiddish Folklore). ed. Y. L. Cahan. Vilna: YIVO.

Schneiderman, L. 1970a. "Kazimierz, Kuzmir: Mezi'ut Ve'Aggadah" (Kazimierz, Kuzmir: reality and legend). In *Sefer Yizkor Qehillat Kuzmir de-Lublin* (Memorial Volume for the Kuzmir Community), ed. David Stockfish. Tel-Aviv.

———. 1970b. *Ven Di Visel Hot Geredt Yiddish* (When the Visla was Talking Yiddish). Tel-Aviv: Farlag I. L. Peretz.

Schwarzbaum, Haim. 1993a. "Lamed Vav Zaddikim Ba'Folklore Ha'Yehudi" (Thirty-Six Righteous Men in Jewish Folklore). In *Roots and Landscape–Studies in Folklore,* ed. Eli Yassif. Beer-Sheva: Ben-Gurion University. 89–95.

———. 1993b. "Beit Ha'Kneset Be'Aggadot Am" (The Synagogue in Folk Narratives). In *Roots and Landscape–Studies in Folklore,* ed. Eli Yassif. Beer-Sheva: Ben-Gurion University Press. 137–149.

Sefer Łańcut: Hayyeha Ve'Hurbanah Shel Qehillah Yehudit (Book of Łańcut: The Life and Destruction of a Jewish Community). 1964. Israel.

Sefer Qehillat Yehudei Dambrowa Górnicza Ve'Hurbanah (Book of the Jewish Community of Dambrowa Górnicza and Its Destruction). 1971. Tel-Aviv.

Sefer Zikkaron Le'Qehillat Drohiczin (Drohiczin Memorial Volume). 1969. Tel-Aviv.

Sefer Zikkaron Le'Qehillat Gniewszów (Gniewszów Memorial Volume). 1971. Tel-Aviv.

Shaked, Gershon. 1973. *Omanut Ha'Sippur Shel Agnon* (The Art of Agnon's Narration). Tel-Aviv: Hebrew University Press and Sifriat Poalim.

———. 1989. *Panim Aherot Bi'Yetsirat Sh.Y. Agnon* (A Different Interpretation of Agnon's Works). Tel-Aviv: Ha'Kibbutz Ha'Meuhad.

Shalom, Gershom. 1970. "Sh.Y. Agnon–Aharon Ha'Klasikaim Ha'Yivriyim?" (Sh.Y.

Agnon–the Last of the Hebrew Classicists?). *Lamerhav/Masa* 11 (13 March 1976); 12 (20 March 1970).

Shatzmiller, J. 1985. "Politics and the Myth of Origins: The Case of the Medival Jews." In *Les Juifs au regard de l'histoire: Mélanges en l'honneur de B. Blumenkranz,* ed. G. Dahan. Paris: Picard. 49–61.

Shenhar, Aliza. 1982. *Ha-Sippur Ha'Amami Shel Edot Yisrael* (Folk Narratives of Jewish Ethnic Communities). Tel-Aviv: Gome-Cherikover.

Shenhar-Alroy, Aliza. 1984. *Koha Shel Tashtit.* Tel-Aviv: Eked.

———. 1989. Ha'Panim Lifnim–Tashtit Be'Sippurei Agnon (Sh. Y. Agnon–Stories and Sources). Tel-Aviv: Papirus.

Shishkoff, Serge, 1976, "The Structure of Fairytales: Propp vs. Lévi-Strauss." *Dispositio* 1: 271–276.

Shmeruk, Chone. 1971. *Peretzes Yeush Vizie* (Perets's Despairing Vision). New York: YIVO.

———. 1978. *Sifrut Yiddish: Perakim Le'Toldotea* (Yiddish Literature–Historical Chapters). Tel-Aviv: Mifalim Sifrutiyim.

———. 1981. "Ha'Magga'im Bein Ha'Sifrut Ha'Polanit Le'Vein Sifrut Yiddish al Sippur Esterke Ve'Kazimir Ha'Gadol Melekh Polin" (Contacts between Polish and Yiddish Literature Concerning the Tale of Estherke and King Casimir the Great of Poland). In *Sifrut Yiddish Be'Polin* (Yiddish Literature in Poland). Jerusalem: Magnes Press.

———. 1977. "Kavim Li'Demuta Shel Sifrut Yiddish Be'Polin U'be'Lita Ad Gezerot Tah Ve'Tat" (Characteristics of the Yiddish Literature in Poland and Lithuania until 1648–49). *Tarbiz* 46.1/2: 258–314.

Silverman-Weinreich, Beatrice. 1988. *Yiddish Folktales.* Trans. Leonard Wolf. New York: Pantheon Books.

Śliwińska, Irmina, and Stanisław Słupniewicz. 1972. "Zmorski Roman." *Instytut Badań Literackich P.A.N. Romantyzm.* Uzupełnienia, MCMLXXII, P.I W. 405–411.

Sluszec, Nahum. 1957. *Ha'i Pliah* (The Island Pliah). Tel-Aviv: Dvir.

Stankiewicz, Edward. 1965. "Yiddish Place Names in Poland." In *The Field of Yiddish,* 2, ed. U. Weinreich. London: Mouton & Co. 158–181.

Sternberg, Herman, 1860, *Versuch einer Geßchichte der Juden in Polen, seit deren Einwanderung in dieses Land (um das IX Jahrh.) bis zum Jahre 1848.* Wien.

———. 1878. *Geschichte der Juden in Polen unter dem Piasten und Jagellonen.* Leipzig: Dunder & Humblot.

Stockfish, David, ed. 1970. *Sefer Yizkor Qehillat Kuzmir de-Lublin* (Memorial Volume for the Kuzmir Community). Tel- Aviv.

Szajnocha, K. 1881. "O myszach kròla Popiela." *Szkice historyczne,* vol. 2. Warsaw, 167–197.

Szyszko-Bohusz, Adolf. 1926. *Materiały do architektury bóżnic* w Polsce. Cracow: Towarzystwo Opieki nad Zabytkami Przeszłosci.

Thompson, Stith. 1955–58. *Motif-Index of Folk-Literature: A Classification of Narrätive Elements in Folktales, Ballads, Myths, Fables, Medieval Romances, Exempla, Fabliaux, Jest-Books and Local Legends.* Bloomington: Indiana University Press.

Tollet, D. 1992. "La Legende de Saul Wahl." Unpublished manuscript.

Trachtenberg, Joshua. 1939. *Jewish Magic and Superstition: A Study in Folk Religion.* New York: Behrman's Jewish Book House Publishers.

———. 1993. *The Devil and the Jews.* Philadelphia: Jewish Publication Society.

Vanvild, M. 1923. *Bai unz yuden, zamelbuk far folklor un filologie* (With Us Jews, an Anthology for Folklore and Philology). Warsaw: Pinhas Graubard.

Veyne, Paul. 1988. *Did the Greeks Believe in their Myth: An Essay on the Constitutive Imagination*. Chicago: University of Chicago Press.

Vilnai, Zeev. 1959. *Aggadot Eretz Yisrael* (Legends from the Land of Israel). Jerusalem: Kiryat Sefer.

Virga, Shlomo. 1947. Sefer Shevet Yehuda Le'Rabbi Shelomo N. Virga (The Book Shevet Yehuda by Rabbi Selomo N. Virga). Commentary by A. Shoḥat; ed. Y. Ber. Jerusalem: Mosad Bialik.

Weil, L. 1840. *Beitrag zur Geschichte der Juden in Polen*. Orient & Jahrgang.

———. 1849. "Beitrag für Geschichte der Juden in Polen." *Der Orient* 31: 143, 154; 35: 159–160.

Weinman, Arie, 1982, *Aggada Ve'Amanut–Yiunim Be'Yetsirat Agnon* (Legend and Art–Readings in Agnon's Creation). Jerusalem: Reuben Mass.

Weinryb, Bernard D. 1962. "The Beginnings of East-European Jewry in Legend and Historiography." *Studies and Essays in Honor of Abraham A. Newman*. Leiden.

———. 1973. *The Jews of Poland: A Social and Economic History of the Jewish Community in Poland from 1100 to 1800*. Philadelphia: Jewish Publication Society of America.

Werses, Shmuel. 1987. "Tahalikhei Higgud Shel Sippurei Am Be'Yetzirat Agnon" (The Process of Folk Narrative Storytelling in the Writings of Agnon). In *Mi Mendele ad Hazaz-Sugiot Be'hitpatḥut Ha'sifrut Ha'Yivrit* (From Mendele to Hazaz–Topics in the Development of Hebrew Literature). Jerusalem: Magnes. 230–256.

———. 1989. "Bein Metziut Historit Le'Teur Sippuri: Bein Yehudim Le'Polanim Be'Kitvei S. Y. Agnon" (Between Historical Reality and Literary Description: Relations between Jews and Poles in the Writing of S. Y. Agnon). *Galed* 11: 109–160.

———. 1994. *Relations between Jews and Poles in S. Y. Agnon's Work*. Jerusalem: Magnes.

Wiernik, P. 1901. Di Yiddishe Geshichte fun Abraham Avinu Biz Die Yetztige Zait (The Jewish History from Abraham the Patriarch until our time). New York: Hebrew Publishing Company.

Wyrozumski, Jerzy. 1982. *Kazimierz Wielki*. Wrocław: Zakład Narodowy imienia Ossolińskich.

Yassif, Eli. 1991. "Mavo" (Introduction) to Judah Yudel Rosenberg, *Ha'Golem Mi'Prag U'Ma'asim Nifla'im Aḥerim* (The Golem of Prague and Other Wondrous Tales). Jerusalem: Mossad Bialik. 7–72.

Zajczyk, Szymon. 1929. *Bożnice drewniane na terenie województwa białostockiego*. Białystok: Województwo Białostockie, Towarzystwo Opieki nad Sztuką, Kulturą i Pomnikami Przyrody w Województwie Białostockim. 44–47.

Zamarski, Roman. 1854. *Domowe wspomnienia i powiastki*. Warsaw.

Zawilinski, R. 1953. *Powiesci Ludu na Śląsku*. Cracow.

Zefatman, Sara. 1993. *Bein Ashkenaz Li'Sefarad, Le'Toldot Ha'Sipuur Ha'Yehudi Bi'Yemei Ha'Beinaim* (Between Ashkenaz and Sepharad–The History of the Jewish Narrative in the Middle Ages). Jerusalem: Magnes.

Zeitlin, Aharon. 1980. *Drames*. Tel-Aviv: Farlag I. L. Peretz.

———. 1993. *Brener, Estherke, Weitsman the 2nd*. Ed. Y. Sheintuch. Jerusalem: Magnes.

Zigelman, Yitzhak, ed. 1967. *Sefer Kublinek* (Book of Kublinek). Haifa.

Zinberg, Yisrael. 1958–71. *Toldot Sifrut Yisrael* (The History of the Israelite Literature). Merḥavia: Sifriat Poalim & Sheberk.

Zmorski, Roman. 1900. *Pisma orginalne i Tłumaczone*. Warsaw.

Index of Names

Aaron, 131
Abimelech, 85
Abraham, 39, 58, 61, 85, 92, 108–10, 169n. 32
Abraham Moses Segal (Rabbi), 150
Abraham Prochownik. *See* Prochownik, A.
Abraham the tavern keeper, 67
Adini, Y., 174n. 22
Agnon, S. Y., 19, 22, 31–34, 36–38, 43, 44, 68, 75, 76, 81, 82, 84–87, 104, 106–9, 111, 122–32, 152, 162, 163n. 4, 164 n. 5, 165nn. 18, 20, 169n. 32, 171nn. 39, 40, 7–9, 172nn. 14, 19, 174nn. 24, 38
Agnon, S. Y., and Eliasberg, A., 19, 20, 33, 35, 76, 132, 172n. 13
Ahasuerus, 119, 120
Alfonso of Portugal (King), 72
Amaleq, 92, 169n. 4
Anna of Lithuania, 122, 131
Anonim Gall, 92, 98
An-Ski (S. Z. Rapoport), 17, 18, 32, 41, 121, 134, 135, 138, 141, 142, 164n. 5, 173nn. 2, 5, 8, 13, 174nn. 18, 20, 32, 34, 38, 40
Asch, S., 42, 127, 128, 172n. 23

Bader, G., 34, 38
Baharav, G., 170n. 37
Bakhtin, M., 160
Balaam, 83, 84
Bałaban, M., 11, 90, 137, 145, 171n. 41, 173n. 14, 174nn. 17, 23, 25, 175n. 41
Balak, 83, 84
Band, A. J., 164n. 5
Bar-Itzhak, H., 17, 28, 40, 67, 91, 97, 139, 164nn. 3, 9, 166n. 30, 171nn. 4, 8, 173n. 10, 175n. 42
Bascom, W., 14
Ben-Amos, D., 14, 15, 19, 25, 163n. 2, 170n. 16
Benet, S., 115
Ben-Nahum, J., 170n. 35
Ben-Yehezkel, M., 67, 68, 172n. 17
Ber, Y., 169n. 33
Berek, 115
Bergman, Y., 166n. 31, 175n. 45
Berliner, A., 165n. 15
Bernstein, S., 73
Berntowicz, 173n. 24
Bershadski, S., 169n. 1
Biderman, I., 168n. 23
Biernacki, A., 170n. 19
Bishop, J., 172n. 14

187

Index of Places

Temple (in Jerusalem), 59, 92, 108, 133, 134, 147, 152, 154, 165n. 22, 167n. 14, 169n. 4, 172n. 11, 175n. 45
Toledo, 72, 73

Ukraine, 146, 150

Venice, 31
Vilno (Vilna), 70, 174n. 17
Vishogrod, 174n. 17
Visl. *See* Wisła
Vladimir-Volynsk. *See* Włodzimierz

Warka, 174

Warsaw (Warsawa), 64, 67, 93, 119, 131, 168n. 24, 169n. 7, 171n. 1
Wawel, 116
Western Wall, 139
Wisła (Visl), 118, 175n. 47
Witkowo, 138, 167n. 18
Włodzimierz (Vladimir-Volynsk, Ludmir), 138, 174n. 39
Wrocław (Breslaw), 142, 167n. 9, 171n. 2

Zabludów, 142, 143, 148
Zagóże, 114
Zlatopol, 150
Zloczów (Zloczew), 42
Żółkiew, 138, 173n. 12

Books in the Raphael Patai Series in
Jewish Folklore and Anthropology

The Myth of the Jewish Race, revised edition, by Raphael Patai
and Jennifer Patai, 1989

The Hebrew Goddess, third enlarged edition, by Raphael Patai, 1990

Robert Graves and the Hebrew Myths: A Collaboration, by Raphael Patai, 1991

Jewish Musical Traditions, by Amnon Shiloah, 1992

The Jews of Kurdistan, by Erich Brauer, completed and edited
by Raphael Patai, 1993

Jewish Moroccan Folk Narratives from Israel,
by Haya Bar-Itzhak and Aliza Shenhar, 1993

For Our Soul: The Ethiopian Jews in Israel, by Teshome G. Wagaw, 1993

*Book of Fables: The Yiddish Fable Collection of Reb Moshe Wallich,
Frankfurt am Main, 1697,* translated and edited by Eli Katz, 1994

From Sofia to Jaffa: The Jews of Bulgaria and Israel, by Guy H. Haskell, 1994

Jadid al-Islam: The Jewish "New Muslims" of Meshhed, by Raphael Patai, 1998

Saint Veneration among the Jews in Morocco, by Issachar Ben-Ami, 1998

Arab Folktales from Palestine and Israel, introduction, translation, and annotation
by Raphel Patai, 1998

Profiles of a Lost World: Memoirs of East European Jewish Life before World War II,
by Hirsz Abramowicz, translated by Eva Zeitlin Dobkin,
edited by Dina Abramowicz and Jeffrey Shandler, 1999

A Global Community: The Jews from Aleppo, Syria, by Walter Zenner, 2000

Without Bounds: The Life and Death of Rabbi Ya'akov Wazana,
by Yoram Bilu, 2000

Jewish Poland—Legends of Origin: Ethnopoetics and Legendary Chronicles,
by Haya Bar-Itzhak, 2001